Globalisation
and
Dimensions of Management in India

Edited by
Atmanand

SHIPRA

Dedicated to

IMT

GHAZIABAD

ISBN : 81-85402-93-0

First Published, in India, in 1997

Published by :
SHIPRA PUBLICAIONS
115-A, Vikas Marg, Shakarpur,
Delhi-110092 (India)
Phones : 2458662, 2200954
Fax : 91-11-2423078

Laser Typeset by :
Sunshine Graphics, Delhi-32

Printed at :
Nice Printers, Delhi

Foreword

Economic liberalisation is a process of removing barriers, releasing impulses for human enterprise, building connectivity with the world at large and rolling back the presence of government from many unnecessary fields of economic endeavour. To the entrepreneur it means freedom to pursue any field of production unfettered by license and control while facing competition from within and without. To the consumer, liberalisation is choice, the right to demand the best of goods and services produced both locally and globally.

Economic liberalisation in India poses many management challenges in the fields of employment, environment, health, transport, rural development, energy, mass communication and education. Its most important challenge is in terms of social responsibility and market responsiveness. What will be the regulating hand, if any, between responsibility and responsiveness?

The core of economic liberalisation lies in ensuring greater welfare for the greatest number of people; it would make no sense at all otherwise. In a country like India, the process of liberalisation must translate into bread and butter propositions for a vast number of people. For the unemployed and under-employed this means a decent job, providing adequate income and social dignity. Rapid economic growth driven by markets and facilitated by government, must generate expanding opportunities for new employment. Ensuring a quick tempo of investments and accumulation is, therefore, essential. Creation of such possibilities lies at the heart of policy changes in India.

Quality of life being the very objective of development, environmental safeguards and economic development, are no longer seen as conflicting goals. Economic gains cannot be oblivious to avoidable damages to the environment and to any degradation of the quality of life. Strategies for resource allocation which promote non-renewable resource substitution, efficient use of productive resources, eco-friendly technologies are some important initiatives required for sustainable development.

The reform measures under liberalisation and structural adjustments have so far tended to concentrate on the techno-economic policy parameters with a strong urban industrial infrastructural bias. Very little attention has been paid to rural development. For a country with two-thirds of its population still rural, such an orientation cannot lead to an overall improvement in the quality of life. For enabling the vast rural hinterland and two-thirds of India's rural population enter the ambit of liberalisation as active participants, the imminent task is to reinforce rural development and to transform the rural socio-economic environment into a dynamic growth threshold.

Energy is fundamental to economic growth. In order to achieve the objectives of liberalisation, energy sector will have to play a crucial role. Successful and sustainable energy sector development calls for an integrated national energy planning and policy analysis. Improvement of technical and managerial efficiency, restructuring the financing of the energy sector, modernisation of poorly performing thermal power stations, and progress in energy environment analysis are unavoidable.

As India enters global competitiveness, various sectors of its economy will have to assess the impact of globalisation in their own context. Management education, as a service product, must also open out in a competitive situation of the global field. This has major implications for management education. Of crucial importance here is the activity of measuring and meeting consumer expectation in the years to come. There is a need to analyse the competitive implications of being a global participant in management education and the managerial challenges emerging therefrom.

Management schools have, and will increasingly acquire a central place of pride in society under the present climate of rapid change. Unlike the purely academic orientation of the traditional universities which have fallen a long distance away from the scene of action in actual life, the Management Schools are in the heart of it. They are, and should be in intimate relationship with where action is. Yet, they provide and must necessarily do so, a congenial academic environment for the *dramatis personae* of the new society to take a breather away from action, to reflect on the broader questions, drawing lessons from the depths of their experience. The Management Schools will play a crucial role in shaping not only the contours and culture of business organisations, but will also spearhead the growth of what is already forcefully emerging: the Social Sector.

Managers of market economy in liberalised India must function as agents of development. The process should be imbued with a spirit deep rooted in our cultural heritage which at its peak had a dynamic strength and unique creativeness. Western concepts of industrialisation, liberalisation and privatisation should not deter us from looking at the tranditional Indian styles of entrepreneurship and management. Economic change, indeed 'change' *per se*, is an inevitable process. Though the change may be more evident at the macro level of the economic system, the essence of the change is what manifests itself at the micro level. The transforamtion of economic scenario is most spectacular in the corporate sector. There is an imperative need for managers in the corporate sector to uphold human values not only as a successful strategy for profits but also as their essential contribution to society.

It is against this background, that I welcome the present book. This volume makes an attempt to fill the gap in studies on the impact of Globalisation and Liberalisation on management of various sectors of Indian economy. There are papers which cover the impact of economic reforms on areas such as human values, financial sector, marketing, personnel management, information, public sector, management education, employment, faculty development, environmental management, rural development, television etc. based on considerable research undertaken by many experts.

I appreciate the effort of Dr. Atmanand for bringing out this comprehensive volume. The contributors are well known authorities in the field of management and economics. I am sure, the book will be very useful to researchers, policy makers, managers, and research and training institutes.

Sharat Kumar
Director
Institute of Management Technology
Ghaziabad

Acknowledgments

This volume is the outcome of on-going debate on Impact of Globalisation on various sectors of Indian economy. Much has been published on this issue, yet the changes in the domain of management need to be explored further. Here, an initiative has been taken in this direction.

This volume comprises thought-provoking papers by scholars and experts who have provided valuable insights on a theme deserving immediate attention of the cross section of the intelligentsia. I will be failing in my duty if I do not mention and it will not be out of place to express my gratitude, appreciation and most sincere thanks to all the contributors, the great management experts of India, for their response within record time and also their thought-provoking research papers.

In course of preparation of this work, I have acquired many obligations from revered Shri Sharat Kumar, Director, Institute of Management Technology, Rajnagar, Ghaziabad, who is a moving spirit with me and source of inspiration and encouragement for editing the present volume. I would like to place on record my heartfelt thanks to Mr. D. Biswas, Dean, CMDE; P.K. Goel, secretary and all faculty members of IMT, Ghaziabad for their useful suggestions, encouragement and time to time generous academic support in connection with the preparation of this work. Well wishes, encouragement and motivation extended by my father late R.S. Mishra is a significant part of this work. I therefore, extend my deep gratitude to my late father from whom I have imbibed the traits that have made me what I am today. I am also thankful to my wife, Dr. (Mrs) Sarita Sinha for her loving understanding, encouragement and all sorts of cooperation in production of this work. My son, Master Rishabh Raman, student of Standard-III is part and parcel of this work.

For shortcomings, if remain, the responsibility is entirely of mine. Constructive and viable suggestions and criticisms, if any, are most coordially welcome.

ATMANAND

Contents

Introduction

The set of new economic policies initiated by the Government of India stated in July, 1991, has been a major breakthrough in the policy initiatives in the country. The policies have been designed to meet the precarious financial position of the country and have come as a crisis management technique. There are various aspects of the new economic policies. Among them ihe issue of globalisation is an important one. Globalisation, as the name suggests, means making the Indian economy responsive to the developments taking place at the global level and also moving the direction of India in trying to play greater role in the world economic environment.

The subject of economic reforms has figured much in many conferences and under many forums for quite sometime now. It is good to find out what in fact has been achieved in recent years on the reform front and what needs to be done. We must, in particular, separate the sheep from the goats, as the saying goes. Economic reforms itself cannot be achieved without reform in other areas and sectors of the country—political, judicial, social, educational and cultural. Any economic reform process must achieve (i) economic efficiency, (ii) economic growth, (iii) economic stability, internally (nor or little inflation) and externally (equilibrium of balance of payments over relatively short periods), social justice and self-reliance, not merely in terms of financial resources garnered through adequate saving, by all the sectors of the economy, including in particular the government sector, but also by the rapid development of indigenous technology and management.

Globalisation essentially means a free flow of factors of production—goods and services, labour and capital—across the globe without any government restrictions. It is manifested in the following ways:

- MARKETS : It means free access to all the markets in the world without any physical (quota) or fiscal (tariff) or any other government restriction. As a result, global consumers emerge demanding high quality products and more value for their money without any parochial, regional or national considerations.

- PRODUCTS: Globally standardised products would be marketed all over the world. There are already many such examples of "global" products. This would also imply marketing of "lead" products in a region taking care of dominant needs of that region.
- RESOURCES: These are raw materials, finance and technology. Free access to quality raw materials, latest technology and cheap finance are important characteristics of this process.
- MANAGEMENT/ENTREPRENEURSHIP: Free mobility of managerial personnel and entrepreneurs would result into mergers, takeovers and structural regroupings in countries across the globe.

During the remainder of the 1990s and well into the next decade, we will witness a change in the way management conducts its business. Some of these developments will be a direct result of changing management values, attitudes, interests and approaches. Methods, techniques and approaches have undergone refinement through increasing research within the profession and from the contribution of related professions. A true administrative science approach is emerging especially in the case of the strategic decision making used by the top management.

The changing management approach will have two sets of implications on the future of HRM. One, the management will respond in greater measure to the genuine demands of workers, which were formerly dominated by the proprietory interests and two, it will initiate increasing participation of labour at different levels of management. The decisions in future would be joint decisions of workers and management, in participative style of working, rather than decisions taken as a result of negotiations and compromise.

One key strategy for future HR function is to become more service-oriented than the present practice of being company-oriented. To ensure service-orientation, the organisations may have to decentralise the HR departments. Line management's ability to handle such vital activities as hiring, career counselling and compensation administration needs to be developed. According to Peter Drucker, in future, the organisations will be less concerned with management development (adapting individuals to organisational demand), but more with organisational development (adapting organisations to the needs, potentialities and aspirations of individuals).

To be a successful player in competitive market and more so in a global market, the basic thrust is on quality. Gone are the days when organisations could survive and succeed purely through strategies of pricing which were often referred to as 'price wars' in markets. The media explosion might make the industry and business feel somewhat complacent, that they can reach the customers in the global markets through high flying publicity and advertisement, but, interestingly, this media explosion is increasing consumer awareness in terms of quality, cost and alternatives, with the result that consumers' expectations are increasing, particularly in terms of quality. Today, in markets, the consumers are demanding quality for the price they pay. This is true not only in the case of goods from the manufacturing sector but more so in the case of services and the services sector.

This is definitely a positive development although it poses several challenges to Indian industry and business which are in transition phase.

There are no two opinions that, in the changing scenario, the organisation needs to commit itself to Total Quality Management in precept and practice not only for growth but also for survival. The Total Quality Management requires a holistic vision encompassing various aspects and functions of the organisation. Quality Management should no longer be restricted to quality control or quality assurance with a limited perspective, but should provide a vision which may be labeiled as "quality vision". Quality vision should provide a broad canvas on which one can clearly identify the various linkages of the functions and activities not only within the organisation but also covering the customers, vendors and other stock holders. It should help the organisations and managers to tackle the short-term as well as the long-term issues and to facilitate optimal decisions.

India's share in world trade has gradually declined from 2.23 per cent at the time of Independence to well below half percent now. At the macro level the major challenge facing the Indian exporters is of improving the country's share in world trade and its share in world market for many products.

At the micro level, the Indian exporting company faces the following well-known challenges :

- QUALITY: It is to be recognised that guaranteed quality is neither a statistical exercise nor a one time affair. It is no use saying that defective material is only one per cent of total supplies. In the case of refractories used as insulating material in kilns in cement and steel industries, even one defective brick will result in loss of production. What is required is consistently zero-defect supplies.
- DELIVERY: The delivery of goods has to be prompt; prompt in relation to supplies from competitors. In southern African markets, the delivery of products has to be competitive in relation to deliv-

ery schedules from South Africa.

- AFTER SALES-SERVICE: In the case of certain products, they can be exported only with a strong backup of after Sales-Service infrastructure. Their products are consumer durables like refrigerators, air conditioners, office equipment such as fax machines, photocopiers and electronic entertainment products like TV, VCR etc.
- PRICE: Price has to be competitive. But, in practice, it is possible to obtain higher prices if the exporter is able to create a niche in the market for his products.

Indian exports will register a quantum jump on a sustained basis only if Indian companies are internationally competitive. Increasing exports is a short-term phenomenon. A desired level of growth in exports can be achieved in the short run by making exports profitable through a series of measures such as devaluation, grant of special import licenses and exempting export profit from tax. However, sustained quantum jump in exports can be achieved only by improving international competitiveness which is a long-term phenomenon.

The key to success is to add value, to create new values. This is being done at the stage of manufacturing but should be done at market places. More value is added at the market place—in trading and marketing.

Traditionally, trading meant "bringing selling and buyer together" or "buy low and sell high". This concept is changing fast. Globally the link between manufacturer (supplier) and consumer (buyer) is being shortened.

A typical distribution chain between manufactures and consumers is Manufacturer—Exporter—Importer—Wholesaler—Retailer and Consumer.

The length of the chain would depend on the type of product and the way it is marketed. Secondly, manufacturers may not be in the same country as exporter.

Marketing has to add value at every stage in this chain. Value can be added or created, amongst others by:

1. Creating up-to-date data base and information.
2. Providing logistics.
3. Warehousing and stocking.
4. Branding.
5. Assuming risks and weighing relative values.

In today's complex and highly competitive environment, the main role of a manager is to build an organisation which is lean, agile and innovative in responding to changes. The organisation has to be innovative not once or a couple of times but continuously. It is the manager's job to create an environment within the organisation which is open to ideas and suggestions, no matter where these originate from. He must be a good listener and must respect others and their views. Secondly, the organisation has to promote team work and cohesiveness and it has to discourage loners. The manager has to create an atmosphere which is conducive to team work. Such an organisation alone will see the company through the present turbulent period and put it on a pedestal. Today's Indian manager has a critical and crucial role to play in such organisation building.

The manager's relationship with his superior is being put under severe strain. Today, the owner or chief executive of a company cannot sub-serve on his own personal interests at the cost of the organisation he serves. This is because the business has grown into a conglomerate of multi-products, multi-makers, multi-locations and multi-functions. He has to take into confidence a few managers and trust them. The manager has to differentiate between his obligations to his boss and the interests of the organisation, if they are in conflict. He has to discern matters of principles and draw a line between "sleep" mentality and insubordination. At the other end, even if such ethical and obvious choices may not be present, there could be serious differences in perception of the organisation's objectives, polices and game plans. The intensity of such conflicts and pressures is directly related to the hierarchial position a manager enjoys in the organisation—the higher the position, the higher the intensity and *vice-versa*. How a manager responds to such conflicts depends upon his attitude, his level of commitment to the organisation, his financial position and above all his personal value system.

As India makes its foray on to the play field of global competitiveness the various sectors of its economy try to assess the impact of globalisation in their own context looking at management education as a service product, it is possible to draw out a competitive situation scenario as this particular sector opens up to global players, and analyse the implications for management of management education. Till late eighties, health and education were considered as "non-profit" organisation. Till recently, both central and state government and few social service organisations were the major players in the light of liberalisation but many business houses and private organisations are entering into education field. It is interesting to note that some educational institutions have already entered the capital market to raise the money for expansion and modernisation.

The management institutes are best suited to train manpower. They can do it only with the collaboration of business or industry. This cooperation between business and management institutes should encompass the following areas:

- ❒ Research into international business areas (such as government policy framework, international competitiveness of individual industries and firms, their competitive strategies) which would assist the practising managers in decision-making.
- ❒ Building up case studies based on Indian experiences in the areas of international marketing, finance, procurement and manufacturing.
- ❒ On-going executive training to bring them up-to-date with current thinking and developments in international business and to sharpen their thinking, and
- ❒ Running post-graduate specialised programmes in international business which would ease the pressure at entry level.

All these activities are interconnected and are expected to reinforce each other's effectiveness. For example, applied research and preparation of case studies would make executive training and post-graduate teaching effective. Executive training may throw up further areas for research and case studies. Post-graduate level project work will, in turn assist future teaching and training exercises. The final product of such cooperative efforts (students in management institutes as new entrants in business) will be far superior in terms of their theoretical background and practical orientation.

The Indian companies will have to play an aggressive role in such cooperative efforts with management institutes. They will have to actively identify and support such institutes. They will have to be more liberal in financing such education and research activities. They will have to recognise that they are not doing any "favours" to institutes but are really helping themselves. Additionally, the companies will have to:

- ❒ Give access to data/information for research and case studies.
- ❒ Make available executive time.
- ❒ Be mentors to students from the beginning.

The management institutes will also be required to play an innovative role in research, training and teaching activities. Specifically, they will be required to organise:

(a) Meaningingful research in the areas of relevance to Indian industry and as an input for decision-making.

(b) Post-graduate programmes with innovative contents and teaching.

(c) Training of their teachers and executive training.

Every discipline reaches the acceptable level of sophistication. Management is no exception. With recession and formation of new huge trade zones without national boundaries, the hardest thing for management is to know which bridges to cross and which to burn. If management is on trial, so are its experts and gurus and it was veteran Peter Drucker who said recently that the word "guru" had become popular, only because for most headlines, the word "charlatan" was too long. Economic journals report that in Sweden, France, Italy and Germany the new buzz-word in management is "business process re-engineering" or BPR and old theories are in limbo. Not long ago, every corporate executive was talking of "total quality management" (TQM) as the magic formula for success. This was superseded by the Tokyo-inspired just-in-time (JIT) scheduling and by lean, flexible managements. Now we hear the talisman is (BPR)—where you—"re-engineer" the old practice of dividing your hierarchic bureaucracy into specific functions like production, marketing and accounts. The new need of the hour is to delegate responsibility to multi-disciplinary workers and see business as a continuous process aimed at getting the products to the consumer. Briefly, this means starting from scratch and re-designing companies from the bottom up. In management it was Shaw's law that those who do, and those who can't teach. We hear the Martin extension of this is:

"Those who can't teach, administer".

This too has been enlarged :

"Those who cannot even administer, become consultants".

Wisdom has thus come full circle.

1

Intent and Implications of the New Economic Policy : Need for Introspection

K.S. Narayana

A Synoptic Picture in Retrospection

Before India attained her independence, there was a National Planning Committee of the Congress Party and a few alternative plans such as Peoples' Plan, Bombay Plan, the Gandhian Plan etc. The Advisory Planning Board was constituted under the chairmanship of K.C. Neogy in October 1946. The Board suggested the constitution of a Central Planning Commission comprising experts which could centrally plan for the country's balanced development. Nehru was instrumental in the setting up of the National Planning Commission in March 1950 and nurtured its growth in the formative stages.[1]

India had a leaning towards a Welfare State in the early 50's. Later, it oriented more towards socialistic pattern since Nehru was very much impressed and influenced by the Soviet Russia's fantastic achievements in socio-economic fields in a short period of time.

It was also thought that private sector cannot undertake big projects and hence Government should also step into these areas so that large number of employment opportunity could be created. Again, it was Nehru who had high hopes in the role of Public Sector. Under his patronage the Public Sector received a boost, thereby a mixed economy took birth in India. Both the Industrial Policy Resolution of 1948 and 1956 shifted a number of industries to the exclusive domain of the Public Sector. By 1989, the Public Sector provided nearly 70 per cent of the 26 million jobs in the country.[2] Due to various reasons, many outside its control, the Public Sector could however not compete with the private sector.

Over the years, losses accumulated to a gigantic proportion,[3] droughts and famines (1965-68, 1974 in several states, 1972 in Gujarat). Oil crisis in 1973, 1979 and the Gulf war in 1991 shot-up the prices of essential commodities steeply.[4] The Gulf remittances almost dried-up due to large scale re-migration into India from Gulf regions. The fiscal deficit grew unabatedly since the Seventh Five Year Plan. Inflation also has since been growing, alarmingly. Due to all these causes, there was disequilibrium in the aggregate demand and supply (Macro), between savings and investments and between the exports and imports (Current Account). Under these situations the Government of India resorted to heavy external as well as internal borrowings, coupled with inefficient fiscal management. The debt burden thus assumed very serious and alarming proportion. The Mandal Commission Report and the Ayodhya controversy evoked widespread social violence which had its impact on the economy. The Government of India took a loan from IMF in 1981 when it was really not needed. This was to set the stage for the entry of Multinational companies into India.

The cumulative effect of all these resulted in the drying-out of India's foreign exchange reserves to 1.2 billion dollars in 1991.[5] Instead of facing the situation by internal austerity measures, the Union Government found it convenient to approach the International Monetary Fund and the World Bank to bail her out of the economic crises. These world financial bodies imposed several conditionalities as pre-requisites to which India meekly agreed to, thereby losing her economic freedom. Radha Sinha says[6] that the Bretton Woods Twins are set out to help the debt ridden developing countries of the 1980s in solving their budget and trade deficits by stabilisation (the responsibility of IMF) and structural adjustment (the responsibility of the World Bank). These two policies together are known as economic reform. The stabilisation aims at controlling inflation and improving balance of payments while the structural adjustment stresses the opening of a country to foreign trade by reducing trade barriers and enlarging the domain of private sector (including foreign enterprises). Under these circumstances India opted for the New Economic Policy in 1991, more out of external pressure.[7]

Policy Change Initiatives Since 1991

As a consequence of India agreeing to the conditionalities of IMF/World Bank which are used by USA as its mouth-piece,[8] it (India) had no option but to accept the 'Blue-Print' of this trinity. This model has not stood the test of time. This model has succeeded in a few countries while it has created more economic chaos in several other countries.[9] There are more than 65 policy changes effected after the adoption of NEP in India. Broadly, these changes fall in line with: (1) Stabilisation Programme which is intended to balance disequilibria at the macro level between the aggregate demand and supply, between savings and investments and between exports and imports; (2) Liberalisation Programme, intended to facilitate opening-up of Indian economy to the world at large, removing hurdles of licence-raj, allowing the market forces to decide prices, reducing the government's role on the Public Sectors, allowing foreign investors to do business; and (3) Globalisation Programme to orient Indian economy to the world Economic Grid which is popularised as Globalisation; two and three together are the Structural Adjustment Programme.

To effectualise these policy objectives, several experts, known for their leanings in favour of NEP, were identified and appointed as Chairman of various committees to perform the task of suggesting reforms such as the Tax Reforms Committee, Committee of Financial System, Reforms in the Insurance Sector, Drug Policy reforms, Housing Policy reforms, Agricultural Policy reforms, etc. These policy changes cover almost the entire gamut of socio-economic fields.

The Intent of New Economic Policy

All the aforementioned changes have been introduced with the hope of achieving sustained economic growth, self-reliance, modernisation, equity and raising of the living standards of the poor, increased export and earning of foreign exchange, creation of more employment opportunity, control of fiscal deficits, inflation and achieving of better growth rate, to recall only a few.[10]

New Economic Policy and the Constitution of India

The NEP is oriented to economic and social development through the effort of the Indian private sector and the foreign investors. However, from experience of these past four years of reforms it is becoming clearer that the private sector as well as the foreign investors are evincing interest only in the profit-maximising ventures than in social and infrastructure development, to the desired extent. That is the reason why the Union Finance Minister had to announce recently a five year tax holiday to those who invest in infrastructure. Our Constitution makes it obligatory on the part of the Government (both Union and States) to work for the socio-economic betterment of the people.[11] These social sectors cannot be totally left to the whims of market forces. Under Privatisation Programme, no society can ever think of building an equitable and socially justifiable society. Rather, it would be a rat race where every private investor is interested in fast-bucks and not concerned with social implications.[12] This would lead to not only iniquitous, inegalitarian regional disparity but also results in the violation of the Constitutional intent.

The private investors are welcome to invest in social sectors. However, the Government cannot depend entirely on the mercy of private sector, and hence, cannot withdraw from its social responsibility to the people. These private sector entrepreneurs may, at the most, play a supplementary role while Government should continue its major role. Hence, the Government should allocate more and more funds into this vital sector so that constitutional obligation could be realised in a distant future, at least.

The NEP is an attempt against the mercantilism and incorporates *'Laissez-faire'* concept. The classical economists believe that the market mechanism in a free-enterprise competitive economy coordinates production and distributes income in a self-adjusting manner that tends towards full employment without Government intervention. *Laissez-faire* in the form believed by economists and policy makers does not operate today.[13] The free-market is not totally determined by the demand and supply principle. Various other factors like artificial scarcity, under or over estimation of stocks, inflated forecasts etc. play dangerous and major role in the market which is largely advantageous to the trader, occasionally advantageous to the producer and rarely advantageous to the poor consumer. It is therefore not justifiable at this stage to deviate from the constitutional goal to *laissez-faire* economy since it is not compatible to the Constitutional objectives.

New Economic Policy and the Planning Commission

The role of Planning Commission after the introduction of NEP is becoming almost redundant in importance and scope. Therefore, there is no justification for maintaining the present size of the secretariat attached to the Commission. It should also be examined whether the Government is ignoring the Commission's intent with regard to preservation of national economic sovereignty since India now is dependent solely on external borrowings and aid which together have imposed a very heavy debt burden.

It is time to examine whether the Planning Commission needs to be activated as a 'Priorities Board' and all the investment proposals (both external and internal) are sent for its clearance. If this responsibility is entrusted with, it not only could play a more useful role in promoting proper investment but could also prevent entry of investment-ventures detexmental to the health of the nation. Instead of effectively and usefully utilising the Planning Commission, the Government of India has set-up the Foreign Investment Promotion Board headed by the Union Finance Minister. This amply makes it clear that the Government has scant respect for really effectualising and reinvigorating the Planning Commission.

Despite the completion of seven Five Year Plans (the Eighth Plan is nearing completion) the planned targets are not fulfilled so far. However, some credit must go to the planning efforts of the Commission which enabled India's self-sufficiency in agriculture (food, oil, pulses etc.), milk production and to a limited extent industrial and infrastructure development. Though the results are not very satisfactory, the country's planning cannot be left to the market-forces. Hence there is need to reorient and activate the Planning Commission. Otherwise the Commission, which has lost the importance with the globalisation process set in motion, would undoubtedly become an appendage of the Government at the cost of scarce public funds.

New Economic Policy and the Role of Union/State and Local Self Governments

Since 1991, several economic reforms have been introduced in the country to facilitate the privatisation and globalisation of Indian economy. In view of these reforms, the size of both the Union and State Governments should also have been drastically reduced. On the contrary, it is being observed at all levels that the size of the Ministries is swelling. Similarly, the number of departments, bureaucracy and other government employees is also on the increase. While on the one side the responsibilities of the Governments are reduced through reforms so as to encourage private sector, it is a mystery that the policy makers have virtually done nothing to reduce the size of the Government.

It took 45 years to amend the Constitution to compel the State Governments to constitute Panchayati Raj Institutions (PRIs), compulsorily. According to the 73rd Amendment, every State has to have PRIs with elected representatives. Several rural development programme have been entrusted to PRIs for effective implementation. But in reality, the State and the Union Governments have retained most of the decision-making, administrative and political powers in their own hands, thereby defeating the very purpose of local self-governing institutions.

The populist schemes of keeping one crore rupees at the disposal of the members of Parliament is quite distressing while the PRIs are suffering from shortage of funds. The appeasing policies do more harm to society since these measures would cut into the allocation of funds for rural development programmes. In addition, there are several Area Development Boards, independent of the PRIs which are not required when the PRIs are brought into being. Even after the introduction of NEP the attitude of the policy makers is yet to change for the better. Most of the decisions are taken either at the Union or State Government levels involving inordinate delays.

It is suggested that under the liberalisation programme, the Union Government must not add new departments as proposed in 1995-96 budget. Also, it should seriously prune the size of the Union Ministry and also the size of the Government as most of the departments are over-staffed. The State Governments also should take positive measures in this direction. Now that the development programmes are transferred to PRIs, there is no justification for keeping the Governments at existing large size. In addition, the Union Government should make all the states to comply with the 73rd amendment and stringent measures should be taken to prevent violation of this Act. Both Union and State Governments should decentralise financial and political powers to local governments, including clearing private/foreign investment proposals in social sectors. Otherwise, the NEP provides more decision-making power to the Centre which is against the spirit of privatisation and liberalisation.

New Economic Policy and the Public Sector

The Public Sectors became sick due to excessive political interference, bureaucratic control, corruption, over-staffing, very low productivity of labour and unionisation.[15] Every unit has several unions and inter-union revalries has eroded the work culture. Workers are unduly exploiting the management through bargaining power.

Modernisation and technology upgradation involves heavy capital investment which these loss-making units cannot afford. The large army of workers cannot be retrenched mercilessly. To worsen the situation, these units have not stopped recruiting workers through cliques by taking heavy bribes. These recruitees are against some reserved quotas which the cliques manage clandestinely, without public advertisement.

The NEP is not favourable to the existing Public Sector units.[16] If the situation continues, lakhs of workers have to lose their job. Though NEP promised creation of more jobs it has failed in translating this promise to reality. Instead, the job market is shrinking after the economic reforms.[17] The Government cannot expose these units to the international competition suddenly. Modernisation of these units in phased manner is the need of the hour. Foreign investors could be invited to invest in these units so that they can be revitalised by utilising the idle capacity and the precious human resource. These Units should be given autonomy to administer their affairs. Through inculcation of positive work culture most of these units could be made viable. Hence the NEP should not expose these units to stiff global competition but create conducive atmosphere to make them more dynamic, viable and modern.

New Economic Policy Implications on Banking and Insurance Sectors

The banking sector was doing quite well in the 1960s when this industry was not nationalised and was managing the affairs purely on commercial terms. However, 14 banks were nationalised in 1969, and a few more subsequently. By this, the banking industry lost its autonomy and they had to orient their lending philosophy to the Union Government's political ideology. Primarily, these banks were nationalised to promote social lending.[18] Due to this, the goals and objectives of the banks were oriented towards social lending than commercial lending. To further compound the problem, various political parties had 'Loan Waiving' as a major programme of their political manifesto. Accordingly, not only the Union Government but also a few State Governments waived the loans and the interest accrued on them, on more than one occasion. All these political aberrations crippled the banking sector beyond easy redemption. Of course, several bank officials also joined hands with politicians for perpetuating self-interest. Their inertia in rendering service and unending demands for more and more remunerative package, over-staffing, go-slow attitude etc. also contributed to banking industry going sick. Reckless opening of branches has further aggravated the problem. Having nursed the problem for almost two decades, the Government is suddenly changing the policy under NEP to enable entry of foreign companies into banking in India. One should not forget that these foreign banks are not interested in social banking but want to concentrate only in areas of commercial viability. The profit earned by them goes out of the country. Instead of yielding to the US/IMF/World Bank pressure to open the banking industry to the foreign companies, it is possible to reactivate the indigenous banks by restoring total autonomy. Political non-interference in regard to lending and recovery policies is the crucial factor to make the banking sector flourish. Surplus staff may be properly identified and posted to new branches. Along side, computerisation in a phased manner, could further improve the operational efficiency. The policy should not have power to "waive the loans" nor interfere with their management. In addition, there is need to reorient and inculcate positive work culture among the employees to enable the banking sector grow from strength to strength.

It is worth noting here Godbole's[19] address to the press. He says that the liberalisation has pushed the nationalised banks away from social objectives since lending to the priority sector has dropped by nearly 7 per cent (from 43% to 36% in the last 2 years). These banks prefer to lend the Small Industries Development Bank of India thereby nullifying the very purpose of bank nationalisation. It is also revealed that the banks had to write off debts worth rupees 33,000 crores, the defaulters generally being industrialists with political backing. Since 1986 there has been no recruitment to banks which has hampered efficient management of banks. The NEP is overshadowing the development programme since the policy objective is profit-maximising. The NEP should address to these realities.

In the Insurance Sector too the problems are growing due to Governments' interference. Despite several odds, the Insurance Sector is contributing to the national exchequer largely through net-earnings. In addition, the customer service has been improving day-by-day. As compared to what it was a decade ago, one cannot fail to notice a marked difference in the service and efficiency. At this stage, due to external pressure or political exigency. Indian Government is yielding to open the Insurance Sector to the foreign multinational companies. There is so much potential to exploit in this sector to the advantage of India by providing total autonomy to the Indian insurance companies in regard to expansion, recruitment, declaration of bonus, introducing new and attractive policies etc. Alongside, modernisation in a phased manner is going to help the sector grow further. By doing so, the country's economic wealth can be retained within the country. Foreign entry into this sector is deterimental to the existing companies as well as to the nation's long term interests.

Short or hind-sighted policy approaches are not viable from India's long-term perspectives and the Constitutional intent. These two sectors are providing large-scale employment opportunities. There is therefore a danger in inviting the foreign companies into these vital sectors due to external pressure. The time, therefore, is to instil dynamism into these two crucial sectors by providing autonomy and political non-interference in their management. The NEP aimed at inviting foreign companies into these vital organs of Indian economy is not a viable option.

New Economic Policy and the Education Sector

While the constitutional obligation has remained unfulfilled, the higher education is receiving more attention than the universalisation of elementary education.[20] Alongside, we have seen mushrooming of private institutions catering to urban areas from play-home to professional (engineer/medical/dental/technical/managerial) level which are affordable only by a few rich.

When India is in critical juncture as far as educational achievement is concerned, the NEP has its implications on this vital social sector. Most of the research institutions/universities, schools and colleges are facing financial crunch. The allocation is just sufficient to take care of salary of staff, leaving very little for school infrastructure and betterment facilities. Due to this, the basic research is suffering. The industry on the other hand is not forthcoming to support basic research. Without heavy investment technology cannot be developed merely by wishing, says the world renowned scientist Prof. C.N.R. Rao.[23] Due to this India would have to depend on borrowed technology by paying heavy royalty.

On the other side, the private education institutions are exploiting the society by exorbitant charges of capitation and other fees due to which several meritorious aspirants belonging to poorer/middle income groups are put to severe hardship. Since job-market is holding very bleak prospects after the economic reforms, several students cannot venture to take educational loans.

Even in 1990s many small villages do not have primary schools. If schools are available teachers and other infrastructure facilities are lacking.

Under the NEP, the private educational institutions are becoming pro-rich as others are unable to afford payment of high fees and donations. In view of this 'equality of opportunity' and 'social justice' are not being met. Hence the NEP is becoming violative of the spirit and intent of the Constitution. Though literacy campaigns, non-formal education, adult education etc. are supplementing the government effort in eradicating the mass illiteracy, the task is very formidable. Therefore the Governments (Union and State) should play more significant role particularly in the universalisation of informal primary education. School enrolment and retention should improve markedly. The drop out rate which is very high should be contained by educating the parents about the usefulness of children's education. In 1988-89 in classes I-V 46.74% boys and 49.69% girls, 49.62% SCs and 64.53% STs dropped out of the schools. In the same period only 50.5% rural boys and 31.3% rural girls in the age group 6-11 were attending schools.[24] The TV network should be properly utilised to earmark 30 minutes every morning and evening for teaching elementary education through community TVs and the Gram Panchayats and NGOs (wherever available) should be involved in effectualising this programme. Without improvement in education level, the success of the NEP is very much doubtful.

New Economic Policy and the Public Distribution System

It is too a well known fact that the Public Distribution System (PDS) through fair price depots is not satisfactory. The supplies through PDS are of inferior quality. Everyone desires that the system needs ravamping. The quotas of supplies in rural areas are meagre while in cities per unit quota is higher.

The NEP is against providing any sort of subsidy. The external funding agencies have been pressurising India to cut all types of subsidies (food subsidy, fertiliser subsidy, subsidy on fuel etc.). Though the foodgrains supplied through PDS comprises of a subsidy component, the issue prices are quite high. In view of this, many poor families cannot afford to buy them. Instead, they prefer to buy jowar/ragi/bajra in some parts of the country which are either cheaper as compared to rice or they are habituated to eating only these. Due to this reason the stocks in the godowns are pilingup. Hence the Government is planning to export a part of these stocks. Since these grains cannot be exported at the procurement price in the international market, the Government is contemplating to export these at a subsidised rate. Due to the grinding poverty and child labour, the nutritional standard as well as the literacy level of Indians are much below the expected norm. Both these cumulatively affect the health of the vast majority.[25]

The Government has a constitutional obligation to the people and therefore, campaigning against the component of subsidy is not short of hypocrisy. The NEP is violative of this obligation, when viewed from this angle. Hence, it is suggested that the Government should take necessary immediate steps to revamp the PDS. Regionally preferred food-grains such as ragi in Karnataka/Tamil Nadu/Andhra Pradesh, Jowar in parts of Karnataka/Andhra Pradesh/Maharashtra, Bajra wherever it is used as the main food should also be brought under PDS. In several states the domestic oil which was supplied for a few years has since been suspended for various administrative problems. Hence sincere efforts should be made to supply domestic oil, cotton, textile and *'tur-dal'* through PDS. Since large quantities of foodgrains are lying in the godowns they could be supplied at subsidised rate through 'Food for Work' Scheme. The rich should be made ineligible to draw ration from PDS. The surplus stock position is not due to very high production but because many cannot afford to buy them. It is worth recalling Professor C.N.R. Rao's address wherein he mentioned that if the poor Indians start eating one more food everyday, India will have to resort to importing of foodgrains. This is the stark reality.[26] It is time to seriously ponder over the fact that the prices of all the essential goods have gone up by 60 per cent during the reforms period which has reduced the purchasing power of the people. The rupee value is estimated to be between 14 to 17 paise in the market. Due to all these harsh realities the consumption level of the people has come down. The Government should therefore, reorient the New Economic Policy objectives than remain satisfied with the increase in the foreign exchange reserve which is about 20 billion dollars.[27] The Government should assert its sovereign right to resist pressures from the IMF/World Bank authorities with regard to foodsubsidy. Otherwise, the NEP would do more harm to the poor.

New Economic Policy and Agriculture

We are self-sufficient on food front which could be achieved only due to the protection and encouragement given by the Government. Without the supply of fertiliser and other inputs at subsidised rate, and fixing of procurement prices, from time to time, Indian agriculture would not have reached self-sufficiency.

The external pressure to remove subsidy is becoming unbearable on the part of the small and marginal and middle level farmers. Once the input costs go up, the farmers tend to pass the burden on to the consumers. Ultimately, the poor will suffer greater hardship.

Though HYV seeds have been developed elsewhere in the world they have been patented as per Dunkel Proposal. Reproduction of these seeds is not permissible/possible as per this agreement. India's agricultural yield potential is not realised fully. That is the reason why the production level of foodgrains in the country is almost stagnant for over last 7 years. Under these circumstances, the policy makers are contemplating to slash the subsidy, import these patented seeds by paying the prices fixed by the multinationals so as to increase production level of crops. Though it appeals to a few largefarmers, its sounds as a death-knell to small and marginal farmers. Since the seeds are patented, India may have to eternally depend on the mercy of developed countries for seeds.

There are many who preferred to call "Dunkel Proposal" as 'Indecent proposal'[28] while few others called it a `Design for Disaster'[29]. The Patents Act amendment evoked widespread and hostile criticism from various quarters of intelligentsia.[30] Despite these protests, the ruling Congress-I Government at the Centre committed India to join the World

Trade Organisation and amended the Patents Act through a Presidential Ordinance and thereby by-passed the Parliament, willfully.

At this juncture it is more feasible to strengthen indigenous research and development so as to enable development of better varieties suitable to local conditions. India's food production depends largely on dry farm development which is occupying an area of 70 per cent while the irrigated area has reached stagnation in crop yield. There is urgent need therefore to develop micro-watersheds in every Taluk.[31] Otherwise, regional imbalance would be too much in favour of the irrigated regions and to the disadvantage of the dry regions. Even in regions where irrigation facility is available there is need to conserve water for better use. Over-watering and sowing unsuitable crops are also reducing crop yield. Water management (*warabandi*) scheme should be implemented so that the tail-end farms could get sufficient water and wastage of water in traditional flow-irrigation method reduced.[32]

Several multi-purpose irrigation projects across the country are half-way through, due to shortage of funds. The State Governments are not able to mobilise the required funds. The on going projects are therefore progressing far behind the schedule. Till the existing ones are completed, no new projects should be taken up either by the Union or State Governments. If foreign investors are willing to enter into this area, the NEP proponents may examine involving them without jeopardising the country's economic sovereignty. There is no cement-lining in the canal beds and hence there is lot of leakage. Similarly, the dams, canals, field channels have accumulated silt-deposits. The situation is almost identical with regard to several tanks in the country. Desilting and maintaining of these involve very large allocation which is not available in the country. The Government may seek foreign aid into these areas either through the voluntary agencies or through the non-governmental agencies. If all these problems are tackled on priority, the agricultural production of the country could be stepped up largely even without importing the patented HYV seeds. The World Bank is aiding through the NGOs the programme of desilting of few tanks in South India. This is a very good project intending to help the rural society. Similar projects could be worked out with the help of international financial institutions for the desilting of dams and maintenance and up-keep of canals and field channels. The NEP should orient its priorities properly and reconsider acceding to the draconian patenting or slashing of subsidy to agriculture.

New Economic Policy and Fiscal Management

India has failed to bring down the fiscal deficit to promised level of 3-4 per cent during 1994-95; it was actually 6.7% and that too after taking into account over Rs. 2,000 crores realised by the disinvestment of its holdings in the Public Sectors[33]. The inflation has been around double digit (it had crossed 13 per cent in May this year).

The World Bank has warned India that unless there is improvement in infrastructure and adequate investment in human capital development, it will not be able to achieve its medium and long-term objectives of growth and reducing poverty.[34] It has further stated that while India's private savings performance is strikingly comparable to that of Malaysia and other successful East Asian economies, the public savings performance has been much worse which was around 3 per cent in the 1980s but declined to zero by 1995. The debt burden of the Government was up to its ears by March 1995, the figure reaching Rs. 533,054 crores of which Rs. 277,561 crores were internal debt which formed 30.5 per cent of the GDP. The external debt stood at 14.5% of GDP. The Government's total liabilities are of the order of Rs. 483,546 crores (53.2% of GDP) exceeding its total assets which are only Rs. 355,536 crores which are less than its liabilities by Rs. 177,218 crores. Due to heavy debt burden and higher interest rates, a significant part of revenue expenditure goes towards interest payment, reaching 32%. Total revenues used to make interest payments have increased from 40.9% in 1991-92 to 49.2% in 1993-94. The debt servicing consisting of both interest payment and debt repayment was 112.8% of total revenue receipts in 1993-94 which means that debt servicing now costs the government more than its total income.[35] The growth rate achieved this year was around 6% which should have been around 10%. These figures would explain that the financial management of the Government of India is not efficient even after the introduction of the New Economic Policy. Despite consistent increase in the foreign exchange reserves (from 1.2 billion dollars in 1991 to 20 billion dollars in March, 1995) there is no economic stability. The forex has started declining during the past few weeks. The direct foreign investors are yet to view the atmosphere as investor-friendly and therefore direct investment is not forthcoming to the desired magnitude. The share-markets collapse and the political uncertainty are causing concern to these investors. The imports are growing at a much faster pace than the exports, causing greater concern to the policy makers.

At the same time, the Indian policy makers are unable to manage the accumulated reserves to the maximum advantage. Moreover, holding this reserve is uneconomical. There is urgent need therefore to bring all the experts to a common forum and allow them to discuss all the issues and evolve ways and means to effectualise the fiscal and monetary management of the country which is bad at the moment. Otherwise, the NEP would plunge the country in debt-trap, thereby losing her sovereign economic independence and surrendering to the IMF/World Bank/US combine.

New Economic Policy and the Health Sector

The country has over 350 million poor who cannot afford three simple meals a day.[37] The life expectancy is not comparable to the levels reached in the developed countries (life expectancy of male is 61 years, and of female 62 years in India) while the infant mortality in 1994 was 84 per thousand.[38] Under the new policy these social sectors are opened to the foreign companies. The new Drug Policy is an attempt in this direction. It is apprehended that while life saving drugs would become costlier, there will be very few to manufacture and supply bulk drugs. As it is, the medical and nursing facilities in private clinics/nursing homes are beyond the reach of many poor and middle class fixed income groups. India is becoming a large human organs workshop where previous parts are bartered for money. The kidney racket revealed to the public recently is only a tip of the ice-berg. If the health/hygiene are left to the private sphere, very few rich only could afford to buy these facilities. Epidemics which were supposed to have been eradicated re-emerged taking very heavy toll of life. Due to the recent Plague over 1 billion dollars were lost to the economy.[39] Almost all segments of the economy were affected because of this dreaded disease. The Government should improve its public health/hygience/nutrition standards with seriousness. As per Articles 42 and 47 of the Constitution it is the Government's obligation to secure to everyone maternity relief, raise the level of nutrition, standard of living and improvement in public health. Supply of potable water and improving sanitary condition of rural India also goes a long way in improving the health of the society.

In addition to the Governments' efforts, the voluntary agencies, NGOs and international financial institutions should involve in a significant manner and make these essential social sectors reach the people.

New Economic Policy and Rural Development

Most of the villages in India are lacking in infrastructure like roads, water supply, electricity, postal and telephone services. Sanitary condition is pathetically poor. India has over 5 lakh roofless households.[40] Out of the 350 million living below the poverty line, 270 million are in rural India. This is enough to prove how grim the situation is in the 'other India' even after 46 years of independence.

The Panchayati Raj Institutions (PRIs) should play a very crucial role in eradicating these social inequities. With the 73rd Constitutional amendment and the consequential transfer of rural development programmes to the PRIs it is hoped that something better may result in in near future. The NGOs and other voluntary agencies could play supplementary role in effectualising the Government's effort. The Government machinery should be geared to the situation with empathy to the pulse of the poor.

New Economic Policy and the Market Forces

Under the economic liberalisation programme several investor friendly policy reforms have been initiated. This is in line with the Classical Economists' belief in *'Laissez-faire'* economy. It should be reiterated that no system of market is perfect. It is more true with regard to free-market economic system. The market is volatile in nature. The causes for price escalation in several goods are being noticed not because of demand-supply principle. The market forces are unscrupulous and exploiters of society. The sky-high increase in the prices of sugar, coffee, cotton and an unprecedented hike in almost all the consumption goods, fruits and vegetables have wrecked havoc to millions of poor, middle and the fixed income salaried group during the 4 year period of reforms. The prices of essential goods have gone up by over 60 per cent and there is an atmosphere of gloom and hopelessness everywhere. This is particularly distressing that inspite of excess foodgrains stocks in the country the authorities are unable to contain the price level. Under this NEP regime the rich are racing to become more richer as fast as possible while the poor are helplessly being victimised. Over-estimation of shortfall or under estimation of surplus production of commodities, hoarding, creating artificial demand and the nexus between the traders and the policy makers are contributing to this pathetic social order. Frank Andre Gunder writes about the present day economic crisis as : "The economically and politically strongest have obliged the weaker and poorer countries to bear the brunt of the world economic crisis and to pay its greatest cost in the attempt to protect the rich from the same."[41]

Lessons for the Reforming Economics from the Reformed Countries

After the economic reforms through 'perestroika' and 'glasnost' initiatives by the then undivided Soviet Union, Gorbachev could not realise the policy promises. Rather, it created severrest hardship to people which resulted in the disintegration of the country into 14 independent entities. Even after throwing out of the economic policy, for years, these countries are yet to recover from the socio-economic and political crises.

After the economic reforms Mexico was glorified and presented as a model to the whole world by the Brettonwoods Twins and the American authorities. But this glory did not last too long. Suddenly the economic model failed and the economy suffered sudden death-knell. Thereafter a lull prevailed among the proponents of this economic model. Now nobody mentions Mexico even by mistake. Its economy fell like nine pins from high altitude causing large-scale unemployment, hyper-inflation, corruption, etc. The rich-poor gap widened and ultimately the poor suffered the worst part of the problem.[42] Bill Clinton sanctioned 50 billion US dollars to redeem the economy regain its past glory.[43]

The market-led economic reforms have failed to restore sustainable growth in most of the Third World countries. The picture is not very different in several Latin American and African countries either. In Mongolia, Romania, Czechoslovakia, Hungary, Bulgaria and Poland the poverty has increased to alarming levels after the reforms. Due to these, the crude death rate and the crime rate have increased, school enrolment rate has dropped, school drop-out rate has increased, social services are suffering for want of sufficient allocation, black marketers, currency racketeers, drug trafficking, and criminals have maximised their profits during the reforms at the cost of majority. It is also noticed that the living standard has decreased, income inequality is widened, regional disparity and economic stagnation are unbridgeable, posing formidable problems to these economies.[44]

In China though real estate has picked up, Gaungdong and other regions are developing faster, few have been able to amass wealth, the economy experienced very good growth rate, export increased by several fold and became it could attract heavy foreign investments the economy has thrown out several problems too which are almost out-shadowing the development of the economy. During the reforms period of about 12 years, unemployment has increased, regional disparity is predominant, farming section is showing downward trend, the agriculture is losing its importance, village communes and Danwei system are weakened, workers have lost security, child labour is increasing, gender bias has increased, school drop-out has increased, more and more women are feeding the growing prostitution and pornography trades, rural firms are withering away unable to compete with big entrepreneurs, bare-foot doctors are no more available to serve the society, smuggling, corruption, fraud, tax-evasion etc. are increasing. Government revenue dropped from 57% to 39% between 1981 to 1993, deficit increased from 2.6 billion yuan in 1981 to 23.8 billion yuan in 1992, debt was of the order of 90.5 billion yuan (3.8% of GDP), inflation reached 21.7% last year, highest in the last 45 years. Due to all these the prices of several commodities have risen sharply.[45] During the market-socialism people of China are facing hardship. So we can say that the NEP is mixed bag of both success and failure. Social costs of the failure of market reforms is not computable. Hence the NEP needs to be subjected to an objective and detailed examination.

Need for Introspection

Alfred Marshall, a leading neo-classical economist was "the first theorist to prove theoretically that *laissez-faire,* even with perfect competition and independently of these evils of inequality, did not assure a maximum of welfare to the society as a whole".[46] Unequal income distribution, the existence of monopolies undermining the workings of the free market, competitive advertising and the existence of externalities are the main barriers to the maximisation of a society's welfare, accordingly to Pigou.[47]

Radha Sinha shows that the outcome of stabilisation and structural adjustment policies was justifiable neither in terms of analytical nor the historical literature. He says that the very ideological nature and the inherent contradictions of policies inhibited successful implementation and accentuated poverty and inequity in developing countries. He quotes several studies to show that the policy intent to restore growth and long-term development have not been realised. Impact of structural adjustment programmes, in most cases, has been positive on the exports and external account but negative to investment and hard-core poverty worsened significantly even in countries implementing structural adjùstment successfully.[48]

Frequent macro-level policy changes are dangerous to embark upon in a country of this size teaming with 100 crores. In this context it is worth recalling the perception of the following three experts :

(1) *Hanumantha Rao*: "Given the inequities in our system, releasing market forces without simultaneously enlarging the freedoms for the poor, widening opportunities for gainful employment and improving their capabilities to avail themselves of such opportunities can lead to lopsided development and social tensions".[49]

(2) *Valdimir Radyuhin*: "10 years ago Soviet leader Mr. Mikhails. Gorbachev set the world's second most powerful nation on the path

of reforms which were designed to make it still more powerful but in the end destroyed it. Polls show that Russians have not kind feelings either for Perestroika or its architect. A majority does not think it was worth even beginning Perestroika".[50]

(3) *Prem Shankar Jha*: "The market place does not care who wins and who loses. It rewards only the winners. If the world does not find a way to look after the losers, and to give them status and self-respect, they will find it in crime, violence and insurgency".[51]

The common salt (not table or micro salt) is sold at over Rs. 3 a kilo which is enough to realise the rulers' concern for the poor. Gandhiji who led the famous 'Dandi March' protesting of a token (nominal) tax on salt by the British is more felt today to wage a war against the internal anti-poor policy makers.

It is reported in the press that the Planning Commission in its mid-term appraisal, has sharply indicted the Centre for the negative effects of the economic reforms, criticised the policy pursued by it and expressed serious concern over the adverse impact of the reforms. Since 1991 the poverty levels and unemployment have increased since the achievements are far below the targets. The balance of payments position has worsened, imports have become excessive, fiscal deficit has widened, domestic as well as public sector savings have fallen drastically, the foreign exchange liability has increased, the interest payment liability is alarmingly high, allocation to social sectors has decreased, and the fiscal management is causing serious concern to the future of the economy. The Commission, therefore, has warned that the policy makers should initiate far-reaching steps to avert the situation going out of control and consequently creating social-economic havoc in the country.[52] The genuine concern expressed by the highest planning body of the country should be viewed by all right thinking persons very seriously. It is distressing to note that the Prime Minister has indefinitely postponed the meeting of the Planning Commission scheduled for 20th July 1995, to discuss the mid-term appraisal. This attitude is sufficient to show the callousness of the policy makers towards the grave situation affecting 100 crores.

In conclusion, the policy makers should not take hasty steps and examine all the pros and cons of the New Economic Policy, particularly in the light of the experiences of other countries. Sincere efforts to cut government expenditure, pruning the size of governments at all levels, improve fiscal management both at the Centre and in the States, avoid populist schemes, control the price-line, prioritise social sector, create employment opportunity, strengthen the village and cottage industries and instil among all honesty, commitment, dedication and hard work.

Only these efforts could save the country. Without these social inputs (social foundations) no policy can succeed. If the society is inculcated with these positive values even when the policy is faulty, the country is bound to succeed. Hence every effort should be towards improving and strengthening the rural India. Merely orienting the economy to the world grid at the cost of agriculture and social sectors cannot save the country. Industry alone cannot promise economic prosperity. Only when all-round improvement, including human resources, takes place will the country's economy progress. Hence all concerned, including the pepole at large, should strive towards making the Constitutional goal a reality.

REFERENCES

1. Report of the Advisory Planning Board Chairman : K. C. Neogy, 18.12.1946, pp. 1-26.

2-3 Jagdish Bhagwati, *India in Transition :Freeing the Economy,* Clarendon Press, Oxford, 1993.

4. Tapeshwar Singh, *Droughtprone Areas in India,* Peoples' Publishing House, New Delhi, 1978.

5. Sudheer Kumar, *Impact of Liberalisation on Housing and Infrastructure Development in Urban Areas.* Paper presented at the Round Table on Economic Liberalisation, held at ISEC, Bangalore 10-12 September, 1994.

6. Radha Sinha, Economic Reform in Developing Countries : Some Conceptual Issues, *World Development* Vol. 23, No. 4 pp. 557-575, April 1995.

7. K.S. Narayana, New Economic Policy-who Bears the Brunt?, Southern Economist, Vol. 33, No. 18, January 15, 1995, pp. 9-13.

8. S.L.N. Sinha, Mexican Financial Crisis : Implications and Lessons, Southern Economist, Vol. 33, No. 20, February 15, 1995, p. 1.

9. Rehman Sobhan, *Down and Out in Outer Mongalia—Lessons for Economic Reformers for 1995,* Economic and Political Weekly, Vol. 30 No. 10, March 11, 1995, pp. 499-501.

10. K.S. Narayana, see ref. No. 7.

11. Constitution of India.

12. Prem Shankar Jha, *Where is the World Heading?*. The Hindu (Bangalore), May 6, 1995.

13. Encyclopaedia of Sociology, Dushkin Publishing Group Inc., Guilford, Connecticut, 1974.

14. Report of the Advisorty Planning Board, 1946.

15. Jagdish Bhagwati, *see ref. No. 2.*

16. Based on personal Interview with few middle level officers of two public sector undertakings in Bangalore.

17. S.L. Rao, *Industry and Economic Reforms,* Paper presented at the Round Table on Economic Liberalisation, held at ISEC, Bangalore 10-12 September 1994.

18. Address to the Press by R.N. Godbole, Secretary, All India Bank Officers Confederation, *The Deccan Herald* (Bangalore), June 25, 1995.

19. *Ibid.*

20. M.B. Buch (ed.) *Fourth Survey of Research in Education 1983-88, Vol. I and II,* NCERT, New Delhi 1991.
21. Compiled from various Indian Census Reports.
22. *Ibid.*
23. C.N.R. Rao, Keynote Address to the Symposium on *Science and Technology Policy and Economic Reforms,* to commemorate Dr. P.S. Lokanathan's Centenary Celebrations held at ISEC, Bangalore, 5.3.1995.
24. Centre for Monitoring Indian Economy, *Economic Intelligence Service,* Bombay, August 1993.
25. N.J. Nanporia, *Child Labour : Genuine Concern or Bargaining Point? An Aspect Worth Pondering,* The Deccan Herald (Bangalore), June 22, 1995.
26. C.N.R Rao, *see ref. no. 23.*
27. Centre for Monitoring Indian Economy, *Economic Intelligence Service,* Bombay, May 1995.
28. T. Krishna Kumar, *An Indecent Proposal* (unpublished paper), Quantitative Analysis Unit, ISEC, Bangalore.
29. B.K. Chandrashekar and S. Chatterjee (eds.), *Dunkel Draft : Design for Disaster,* Navakarnataka, Bangalore, 1993.
30. National Working Group on Patent Laws (Chairman: Dr. Nitya Nand), New Delhi. The Group comprising of 25 very eminent patrons gave an appeal to Members of Parliament not to amend the Indian Patents Act of 1970.
31. S. Lakshmikanthamma, *Economics of Watershed Development Approach to Dryland Agriculture,* Ph D Thesis (unpublished), Bangalore University, Bangalore, 1994.
32. T. Govindaiah, *Irrigation Development in India,* Chugh Publishers, Ahmedabad, 1986.
33. Centre for Monitoring Indian Economics, *Economic Intelligence Service,* March 1995.
34. *World Bank Warns India to Speed Up Reforms or Suffer Poor Growth,* The Deccan Herald (Bangalore), 17.6.1995.
35. *Government Steeped in Debt,* The Deccan Herald (Bangalore), 18.6.1995.
36. Ashok Mitra, *Prospects Before Aspirants for the Primeministership—A Lark of time*? Deccan Herald (Bangalore), 28.6.1995.
37. Centre for Monitoring Indian Economy, *Economic Intelligence Service,* Bombay, August, 1994.
38. Economic and Social Commission in Asia Pacific, *Demographic Estimates for Asian and Pacific Countries and Areas, 1994* Bangkok, 1994.
39. K.S. Narayana, *Social Sectors Impeding the Success of the New Economic Policy,* Southern Economist, Vol. 34, No. 1, 1.5.1995.
40. Census of India, 1991. Housing and Amenities Tables and the NSS 40th Round 1990.
41. Frank, Andre Gunder, *World Economic Crisis Once Again,* Economic and Political Weekly, February 29, 1992, pp. 457-458.
42. Rehman Sobhan, *see* ref. No. 9.
43. S.L.N. Sinha *see,* ref. No. 8.
44. Rehman Sobhan, *see,* ref. No. 9.
45. Manfred Romich, *Decentralisation and the Danwell System; Economic Reform and Its Impact on Social Development in Chinese Cities,* China Report, Vol. 30, No. 4, October-December 1994, pp. 447-456. And Robert Weil, "China at the Brink : Class Contradictions of Market Socialism", Monthly Review, Vol. 46, Nos. 7-8, December 1994 and January 1995.
46. Schumpeter, Joseph A. Quoted in Radha Sinha's *Economic Reform and Developing Countries, Some Conceptual Issues*, World Development, Vol. 23, No. 4, April 1995, pp. 559-560.

47. Pigou, Quoted in Radha Sinha's, *Economic Reform and Developing Countries : Some Conceptual Issues,* World Development, Vol. 23, No. 4, April 1995, p. 560.
48. Radha Sinha, *Economic Reform and Developing Countries: Some Conceptual Issues,* World Development Vol. 23, No. 4 April 1995.
49. C.H. Hanumantha Rao, *The Burden of Reforms,* The Hindu (Bangalore), May 1, 1995.
50. Valdimir Radyuhin, *Ten Years of Perestroika.* The Hindu (Bangalore), May 4, 1995.
51. Prem Shankar Jha, *Where is the World Heading?,* The Hindu (Bangalore), May 6, 1995.
52. *Poverty Rises,* Jobs Shrink Under Reforms, Deccan Herald (Bangalore), July 20, 1995.

2

Globalisation: Imperatives, Challenges and the Strategies

Rakesh Khurana

The Emerging Dimensions of Global Economy

Over the next quarter century, world will see major shifts in economic strength of nations. Soon the so-called industrial economies which have dominated globally (as they have for the past one and a half centuries) would be dwarfed by newly emerging economic entities. Before the advent of steam engine and power loom, the so-called 'Third World' countries, dominated the manufacturing output. In 1750, China and India accounted for 70% of the world manufacturing output.[1] In 1830, their share was still over 60%. By 1857 or so the share had started reversing and by 1913, the share of China and India in manufacturing output was about 8%. India and China were left behind by Europe's technological revolution. However, the figures are likely to go through a change once again. The projections of World Bank on the basis of purchasing power parity suggest that by 1995, the share of output of developing countries would cross that of all the rich industrialised countries. By year 2000, the ratios are likely to be 52 : 48; by 2010, 58 : 42; and by 2020, 62 : 38. The ranking of 15 largest economies would also go through a major change by 2020. Five largest economies are likely to be China, US, Japan, India and Indonesia. Britain would possibly tie-up with Mexico as 15th largest economy.[2] After a two centuries eclipse, Asia is re-emerging as the economic leader of the world.

The ordinary notion of developing countries as exporters of raw materials from which they earn foreign exchange to pay for manufactured goods is also no more supported by reality. Manufactured goods now account for almost 60% of the developing countries exports up from 5%

in 1955. The Third World's share of world exports of manufactures jumped from 5% in 1970 to 22% in 1993 (Exhibit).

This reversal of roles will of course cause major resentment in the West and would be perceived as threat to their own development. The fact that people in rich countries now fret about developing countries' success, not their poverty, is itself a remarkable tribute to these countries' economic reforms.[3]

If in tomorrow's economy, the share of Asia, and India is likely to be huge, then whether it is consciously thought or strategised or not, global parameters would influence the functioning of business in Asian countries, and so also the politics and governance of the economies, and India would be no exception.

The issue of current levels of technology, low productivity, low wage etc. are not explored here, and their impact on GATT or GATS negotiations are not touched upon.

Globalisation — The Buzzword

Globalisation has become the favourite buzzword for the 90s. Despite its topicality in the business monthlies and corporate Boardrooms, there is no single accepted definition of the word Globalisation.[4] Consultants do push corporations to get on the global bandwagon. Business schools throughout the world talk about global corporations that one may think that such a thing really exists, and that global strategies can be defined and explained according to some well established principles. Like the theory of firm which economists used to talk about, business professors have started talking about the theory of global corporation, but without much success so far. Some even feel that the Global Corporation is really a myth. It cannot be defined because it simply does not exist. No single company has really achieved the "Global" distinction.

About Global Strategies

Regarding the strategies for getting on the global path, certainly no one-size-fits-all strategy for competition on a global scale can be propounded. But then who cares. What matters is what is happening on the ground, or in the Cyberspace, and in-between. Debate on competitiveness has been more fruitful though. Michael Porter's Seminal works on Competitive Strategy followed by the Competitive advantage of Nations[5] have led to debate about what is appropriate at corporate as well as National level. Gary Hamel and C.K. Prahlad's[6] work on core competences and competing for the future have led to better understanding about strategies to be followed at corporate level.

The discipline of strategic management has also taken note of intense competition which countries, industries and firms on a global level face owing to confluence of several major trends. Some of these trends are:

- Decline of tariff and other trade barriers under GATT and consequent rising confidence in the gains from free trade.
- Enormous increase in Direct Foreign Investment.
- Growth of organisation and administrative structures to permit management of resources and risks across sovereign borders and over great distances.
- Gains in technology and their transfer from one another, and perhaps more important.
- Interdependence of complex technologies and economies on one another throughout the value chain.

The field of strategic management has come to realise that often and increasingly competitive advantage can be gained only from a global view of competition. To address such issues, special issue of *Strategic Management Journal* invited various strands of thought to discuss global strategy. While work on competitiveness of Indian Industry in global context is meagre, the debate on American Competitiveness in the world has recently being thrown into some disarray. Rober Reich[7] in his seminal essay "Who is US?" states that in a "borderless" world characterised by "stateless" corporations, it makes little sense to talk of American Competitiveness in terms of American-owned corporations, but rather that American Competitiveness should be defined in terms of the skills and experience of the America work force.

The historical example of Germany and Japanese rising from the ashes of World War II is instructive. It was on the basis of skills, hard work, and strategy of the respective peoples that both economies grew again in a short period of time.

We, in India should also examine our competitiveness *vis-a-vis* international competition from the viewpoint of skills and experience of Indian people.

Kenichi Ohmae in his book "*The Borderless World*"[8] states that "it does not matter who builds the factory or who owns the office building or whose money lies behind the shopping mall or whose equity makes the local operation possible. What matters is that the global corporations —act as responsible corporate citizens."

During the last quarter century, a string of synonyms as international, inter-territorial, multinational, transnational, and worldwide have been used for "Global Corporation". The concept has evolved to the point where it connotes something that has gone beyond nations and has left them behind. The economists of earlier genre talked of "direct foreign investment" which implied the existence of a home nation and "host" countries. Kindleberger defined international corporation in 1969 as "The international corporation has no country to which it owes more loyalty than any other, nor any country where it feels completely at home. What differs between the 1960s and the 1990s is the context of the assertions : in the 1960s, it was the Europeans who worried about US multinationals, now it is the Americans who worry about Japanese and Europeans and also the Third World multinationals. In a recent articles in *Harvard Business Review,* Krugman discusses the notion of "Does Third World Growth Hurt First World Prosperity" and comes to the conclusion that contrary to popular opinion in First World, the economic development of Third World does not hurt the First World. Global economy is a system—a complex web of feedback relationships, not a simple chain of one-way effect. The argument that MNCs have become stateless entities[9] stems from the observation that their business operations cross national borders, *e.g.* General Motors makes the Pontiac LeMans in Korea to sell in the US. Honda makes cars in Ohio that it exports to Japan, and Boeing makes sections of its planes in China, Italy, and Canada for assembly in Seattle. However, while there are increasing examples of this kind of production and marketing operations, the argument that corporations have become "Stateless" is questionable.

Some schools of thought label a firm as "global" or "transnational" because it adopts a "global" or "transnational strategy".[10] Earlier it was the adoption of a global habit of mind that distinguished the "geocentric" company from the "ethnocentric" and the "polycentric" firm. Global Strategy means different things to different people, the main problem is that a strategy or habit of mind cannot be defined or quantified easily. Nor is it easy to measure it accurately through its results. Since the actual outcome depends not only on the strategy but also on the interplay of several internal and external forces, there are different ways of going global. Developing a global strategy is complicated by the fact that there are at least five major dimensions of Globalisation.[11] These are :

- Playing big in major markets.
- Standardising the core product.
- Concentrating value adding activities in a few countries.
- Adopting a uniform market positioning and marketing mix.
- Integrating competitive strategy across countries.

There are indeed number of companies which on the basis of these criteria may be termed as MNCs, *e.g.* IBM, General Motors, Du Pont, Sony, Nestle, Toyota, ICI. However, their ownership and control is increasingly becoming diffused and so are the people who manage such organisations. Hardly any Indian company would qualify as global, based on these parameters.

The Global Paradox

John Naisbitt, the author of Megatrends and a famous futurologist has recently published another book full of powerful ideas, *i.e.* Global Paradox.[12] I cannot resist the temptation of recounting one of his major arguments which has direct relevance to thinking about globalisation in India.

Following paragraphs based on this book are related to one of his major statements, *i.e.* the bigger the world economy, the more powerful its smallest players. A paradox, as generally understood is a statement or formulation that seems contradictory or absurd but is actually valid or true. One purpose of a paradox is that it can provoke fresh thinking, *e.g.* a famous paradox in architecture is "less is more", and in physics "the late twentieth century may be remembered in the history of science as the time when particle physics, the study of the smallest structures in nature, joined forces with the cosmology, the study of the universe as a whole."

A similar phenomenon occurs in the world of politics and economics : The Global Paradox which states that, the study of the smallest economic player, the entrepreneur, will merge with the study of how the big bang global economy works.

Thus, according to this statement the entrepreneur is also the most important player in the building of the global economy. Moreover, the big companies world over are decentralising and reconstituting themselves as network of entrepreneurs. Let us analyse some statistics and cite some examples.

1. In USA, more than 50% of exports are created by companies with 19 or less employees : the same is true of Germany.
2. Only 7% of US exports are created by companies with 500 or more employees.

   Interestingly, though Indian export statistics are not available according to firms with employees less than 19, or more than 500, it is common knowledge that in major Indian export sectors like Handicrafts, Gems Jewellery, Leather, Tea, Hosiery, it is the small companies or firms which contribute the most for exports.

3. The US Fortune 500 now account only for 10% of the economy, down from 20% in 1970. 90% of US economy is elsewhere : Small and medium sized companies.

Thus entrepreneurs-individuals are creating the huge global economy. This is also supported by statistics of Taiwanese, Hong Kong and Thailand exporters.

Towards a Network of Entrepreneurs

To survive, big companies in international exports, *e.g.* ABB, AT & T, GE, Coca-Cola, Bentton, Johnson and Johnson, British Petroleum, Honda, Zerox are reconstructing themselves and creating new structures, as networks of autonomous units. What is going on in American Corporations today is the ODD effect-outsourcing, Delayering and Deconstruction. The result is down sizing, re-engineering and networking. Companies have to dismantle bureaucracies to survive. Economies of scale are giving way to economies of scope, finding the right size for synergy, market flexibility and speed. The example of ABB, the world's largest power engineering company is instructive. Its annual turn over is $ 30 billion from 1,200 companies. Each company averages only 200 people. CEO of ABB says "We grow all the time but we shrink all the time". In the process of deconstructing, the headquarters staff was reduced from 4,000 to 200. More than 90% of the sales of this Swiss Swedish company are from outside the host countries. CEO of ABB says: "We are not a global business but a collection of local businesses with intense global coordination." Jack Welech of GE in his corporate message for 90s says: "What we are trying relentlessly to do is to get that small company soul—and small company speed inside our big company today". There are many such corporate statements from Chief Executives of companies throughout the world. What it implies is that what is required is not the size but ability to organise, and coordinate across boundaries and at great distances—a purely managerial function, which can be mastered as well by Americans, Japanese, Taiwanese, or Indians, and that engines of growth everywhere are small, entrepreneurial companies or Intrepreneurs within large corporations.

Globalisation and the Indian Context

A number of arguments have been raised for and against globalisation in the Indian context. There is one school of thought at the level of PMO and FM which supports liberalisation, deregulation, privatisation and concomitant globalisation. There is another school of political thought which implies that liberalisation means abandonment of social justice and thus protection of Indian industry. Final judgment regarding the impact of liberalisation policies is still awaited, and in fact it is too soon to look at the impact of liberalisation policies. The debate has also been coloured by discussion on GATT and social clauses of GATT Agreement.

24 July 1991 will be considered a watershed date in India's industrial history since this marks the end of colonial and inward looking policies which have for a long time being "followed in the name of social justice and protection of our industries", says Saxena.[13] He analyses the growth of the export from 1970 to 1989 and concludes that while Indian exports grew from Rs. 1500 crores to 20,000 crores, our share in World Trade declined from 1.05% in 1961, 0.64% in 1971 to 0.45% in 1988 and is about 0.4% now. The maximum contribution was made by handicrafts including Gems and Jewellery. The decline in India's share in World Trade cuts across all product categories and there is no product line where we can claim to have a leading market share. There are hardly any Indian brand names recognised outside India. On the other hand, regarding foreign investment in India, Swaminathan S. Ankleshwar Aiyar[14] concludes that foreign investors do not make huge monopoly profits in India and many of the big firms in India like Philips, Metal Box, Guest Keen Williams Ltd., and ICIM have gone into red because of increase in domestic competition. Many of the multinationals left India because of insufficient profitability, *e.g.* AMOCO, Philips Petroleum, Kaiser, Merck and General Foods. India's businesses have also come of age and offer far better competition than they have done sometime back. Rasna has beaten several foreign brands including Tang and J.V.C, Videocon and Onida gave sufficient competition to Philips' TV sets, Nirma gave more than their run for money to Levers, so the entry of the multinationals as such will not kill Indian industries. He also argues that multinationals at some point of history may have been connected with imperialism, but no more. The countries that have attracted maximum investment during last decade (Taiwan, Singapore, Thailand, China) are today far stronger and better able to resist international competition (and in fact offer better competition internationally) than African countries that have failed to attract multinational investments.

It will also not be so easy to attract foreign investors to India unless there are reasonable returns for them. Foreign equity can also bring in specialised skills in technology, and managerial skills.

Many Indian companies have started becoming respectable players on international scene. Lupin laboratories started as a small business just a decade back is now leading producer of TB drugs in the world.

Core Healthcare Ltd. (starting as core paramatals) just a decade ago and started on PF savings by Handas is today world's fifth largest manufacturer of TV fluids, and would perhaps be the leader by the end of decade.

United Phosphorus Ltd. is leading manufacturer for phosphorus based products in India and the world. Dr. Reddy's Laboratories Ltd. started by a professional doctor just a decade back has also grown tremendously and has serious international ambitions. Ranbaxy Laboratories have started plants in different continents and with its strategic alliances is on verge of becoming a serious global player.

Hero Honda Ltd. recently celebrated 1 millionth motor cycle production — shortest time taken from 1 to 1 million motorbikes anywhere in the world. In many consumer durable and light engineering product categories, Indian companies can become global players, if only they can work out their strategies well. Indian investment abroad, especially by Birlas is quite successful. If we would like to expand our foreign exchange earnings, after the stage exports, (just like we expect MNCs to start setting of plants in India), Indian companies would also be expected to open plants abroad. If we would not like to hamper that movement, we cannot expect to put undue constraints on foreign investment in India.

We thus need to look at foreign investment in India and foreign investment from India with a new perspective. Sindwani[15] on the basis of survey of large number of decision makers suggests that there is an urgent need to see the world afresh abandoning our historical biases and ideological prejudices. He argues that India has to reconsider its international and national priorities. He says it is time to critically review our assumptions and identify the areas in the new emerging global scenario where we will have scope. S. Shiva Ramu[16] in his recent book *Globalisations and Indian Liberalisation* argues for re-examination of role of governments and corporations in modern economic context and suggests that it is evolving into mutual dependence, instead of being an independent regime.

The Social Side

There has been major talk about India having about 300 million persons in the middle class category. Without going through the logic or definition of middle class, the fact remains that fairly substantial number of Indian citizens now have incomes and purchasing power equivalent to middle classes in European countries. The darker side of the social scene also cannot be overlooked. India still has the largest number of illiterates, and provision of public health and education is rather poor. One cannot develop a self-sustaining economy, much less a globalised economy unless needs of deprived classes are looked into. Public investment would continue to be required in the areas of health and education, in fact even more than in the past and without a healthy and skilled manpower, we cannot go to the next stage of development change. On the Management side, the estimate suggests that more than a quarter of million applicants try for various management institutions every year while the number of seats is approximately 20,000. This would require massive expansion of management education. State-of-the art programmes for Continuing Education (CE) in Management in massive numbers are required. It is estimated that the number of managers/supervisors from a current figure of about 1/4 million would go upto about one million by year 2,000. If CE is taken at the level of one week/year/person, it will require provision of 5 million man-days of training per year.

Substantial effort will be required, especially for following Sectors

- Government Employees
- Employees in utilities and other infrastructure industries and services
- Self-employed persons
- Small scale businessmen/industrialists
- Voluntary sector organisations/employees. Besides supervisors/managers, there is an acute need for training, orientation and HRD for workers in above organisations.

The current supply of CE in Management and its quality is a small fraction of the emerging requirement, which possibly cannot be met through traditional class-room methods.

Since high quality faculty is limited, it would be appropriate to utilise mass communication media (DD, Satellite based Interactive Network) and other technologies like voice mail, E-mail, EDI, Audio conferencing, Video teleconferencing, etc. to extend limited faculty/ learning resources to institutions and students spread throughout the country.

Fortunately, because of large numbers, these technologies become quite cost effective in our context. Development of innovative strategies for education, especially for management, including change management, would be a major factor, if not the decisive factor, for globalisation and increasing the competitiveness of Indian economy.

Conclusion

The world is becoming more borderless, the role of the State is declining while the roles of individual and entrepreneurial companies are likely to grow. Powerful technologies like computers and telecommunications are helping individuals to connect to each other with or without the approval of State. The role reversal of the so-called developed and developing countries is going through a watershed change. In the increasingly globalised economy, India cannot afford to be left behind. Rather than worrying about its consequences, it would be better to prepare for globalisation and become a major player rather than a side line watcher and complainer.

REFERENCES

1. Paul Bairoch, *International Industrialisation levels from 1750 to 1980,* Journal of European Economic History, 11, 1982.
2. War of the Worlds, *A Survey of Global Economy,* The Economist, 1-7 Oct. 1994.
3. Paul Krugman, *Does Third World Growth Hurt First World Prosperity?* Harvard Business Review, July-August, 1994.
4. Debra Fleenood, *The Coming and Going of the Global Corporation,* Columbia Journal of World Business, Winter 1993, Vol. XXVII, No. IV.
5. Michal E. Porter, *The Competitive Advantage of Nations,* 1992, The McMillan Press Ltd., London.
6. Gary Hamel and C.K. Prahlad, *Competing for the Future,* Harvard Business Review, July-August 1994.
7. R. Reich, *"Who is US",* Harvard Business Review. (Jan.-Feb. 1990)
8. K. Ohmae, The Borderless World (London : Collins, 1990), p. 194.
9. Yao-Su Hu, *Global or Stateless Corporations are National firms with International Operations,* California Management Review, Winter 1992.
10. Christopher A.Bartlett and Sumantra Ghosal. Editiors (Strategic Management Journal) *Special Issue on Global Strategy,* Vol. 12, Summer 91.
    Regina Fazio Maruca, *The Rightway to go Global,* Harvard Business Review, March-April 1994.
    Louis Emmevig, *Globalisation, Regionalisation, and the World Trade,* The Columbia Journal of World Business, Summer 1992.
11. George S. Yip, Pieve M. Loewe, Michael Y. Yoshino, *How to Take Your Company to the Global Market,* Columbia Journal of World Business, Winter 1988.
12. John Naisbitt, *The Global Paradox,* 1994, William Morron and Company Inc, New York.
13. Rajan Saxena, *Globalisation of Indian Industry* in Innovations in Management for Development, 1992, Tata McGraw Hill Co. Ltd., New Delhi.
14. Swaminathan S. Ankleswar Aiyar, *Towards Globalisation : The Case for Foreign Investment,* 1992, Radiant Publishers, New Delhi .
15. T.N. Sindhwani, *India's Role in Globalisation,* 1992, Capital Foundation Society, New Delhi.
16. S. Shiva Ramu, *Globalisation and Indian Liberalisation,* 1994, South Asia Publications, Delhi.
17. Harry G. Broadman and Carol, *Liberalising International Trade in Telecommunications,* Columbia Journal of World Business, Winter 1993.

3

Economic Liberalisation, Social Transformation and Human Values : Role of Management Schools

Sharat Kumar

Historically, the Brahmanical tradition in India treated material wealth in a perspective significantly different from the value that has come to be attached to it in the present day consumerist societies of the Western world. While the Indian view recognised the importance of material wealth, it was only one of the constituents of a comprehensive life-view. The *Arthashastra* lists four *Purusharthas* namely, *Dharma, Artha, Kama* and *Moksha*. The word *Artha* itself signifies a double intent: 'Meaning' and 'Wealth'.

The inefficiencies of the system, both at the economic and ethical levels (the corruption that the command economy model bred at levels of public life), gradually became obvious even to the ruling elite in the eighties.

The reports emerging out of the erstwhile USSR in the 'Glasnost' and 'Perestroika' years accelerated the process, pointing to the inefficiency and corruption perpetuated by the centrally controlled model. Admittedly our system operated at a far lesser ruthless level than the Soviet model. The Indian inefficiency had atleast this beneficial aspect.

The gathering momentum of change, triggered by an acute foreign exchange crisis, led to the current policy of liberalisation, advocating minimum role for state intervention in economic affairs. The word liberalisation comes from liberty which relates to dignity and consequently to human values. But this is only one side of the story. The new policy, now in its fourth year, is seemingly gaining public approval notwithstanding vehement opposition from certain sections of society. Many aspects of the criticism, however bring to focus some critical pitfalls which can have far-reaching dangerous consequences for the society.

Today, Market Economy is seen in almost mystic haze by many governments, especially in the developing world, as the quick and certain way which can resolve all problems facing their countries. But when economics is regarded as the key to every lock of every door, it is only natural that the worth of man should come to be decided largely, even wholly by his effectiveness as an economic tool. This is at variance with the vision of a world where economic, political and social institutions serve man instead of the other way round. We have to consider questions of "I want-it-all" consumer culture, gross individualism and cut throat morality which are encouraged by making material success the measure of prestige and progress. The result is an undesirable society where cultural and human values are set aside and money value reigns supreme. It is easy to see that if material betterment, which is but a means to human happiness, is sought in ways that wound the human spirit, in the long run it can only lead to greater human suffering; the market should serve people instead of people serving the market.

The issues raised above on some aspects of market economy are attracting serious attention world wide. The selection of Professors Robert Fogel and Douglass North for the Nobel prize in economics two years ago reflects the urgent need of our time not only for understanding of the market mechanism *per se,* but for a market economy that will work positively in different settings. These economists emphasised that political, legal and moral institutions, and the changing historical environment of the market are the major determinants of markets' outcomes and of the economic performance generally. Professor North defends the view that institutions—political, legal, cultural—are as important as market activity itself in generating economic growth and in determining the growth paths of particular economics. According to him a socio-economic order comprises not only of universally valid permanent economic elements (*e.g.* laws of supply and demand) but of the institutions peculiar to a particular culture or society. It would perhaps not be wrong to say that the ultimate determinants of the economic performance of a nation (assuming that market processes guide the use of its productive resources) are its history, its religion(s), its laws and the character and culture of its people. The real economy is comparable to the heart of a living organism. It does not exist apart from that organism. It incorporates and is itself wholly a product of the extra-economic mores and values of the societal matrix in which it is embedded. The word 'capitalism' when applied to different socio-economic systems does not have the same meaning. Capitalism operating an unparalleled expansion of its power and prosperity, is equated with a system of dog-eat-dog in which the weaker members of the society were abused and exploited by the powerful. In contrast to this, the post-war West Germany also achieved extraordinary economic revival under free market capitalism but the government assumed, and continues to assume, major responsibility for addressing an array of social problems under a system which has travelled a long distance from historic capitalism and which has been baptized as "social market economy".

The present day capitalism cf the USA also operates with a complex fabric of institutions that undergrid the economy and determine its special character. Many of its institutional frameworks like the anti-trust laws, the laws regulating the securities market and the food and drug industries are the product of decades of patient evolution. This system can not be equated to the capitalist free market of El Salvador with its egregious disparities between poor and rich, and its primitive institutional framework. The Japanese free market system has its own cultural patterns embracing what many would see as a pervasive uniformity, a lock-step mentality that penalises individuality, and an obsession with work that leaves little time for the pursuit of things that lie beyond supply and demand.

Let's be quite sure that a free market economic system needs to surround itself with an appropriate institutional framework. The key factor of market economy is competition. It is the device that transforms the pursuit of self-interest (spelled out with such clarity by Adam Smith two hundred years ago) into an increase in general welfare. Competition ensures reciprocity in exchange. It also keeps prices close to the costs of production and, by that pressure, minimises such costs. It is the goad riggers invention and innovation. It also leads to disaggregation on economic power and promotes democratic forms of government. The classical *laissez-faire* was always an illusion because in absence of establishment and enforcement of rules to prevent monopolisation, competition decays. The continued success of free market capitalism in the U.S.A., when in the 1930s and 1940s it was increasingly seen as the 'enemy' by intellectuals in Europe, resulted in no small measure by the fundamental changes in the market's institutional framework accomplished during and after the Great Depression. These included social security legislation, a panoply of regulations in banking, securities, labour markets, and in increasingly sophisticated employment of macro-economic tools of monetary and fiscal policy in pursuit of growth and stability.

The principal institution affecting the market economic activity on a daily basis is government. It is government which lays down the rules of the game under which market economy must operate. It is the quality of such institutional rules and their stability and predictability which determines the economic efficiency. Government exerts its influence in three major ways: (1) as being responsible for public services and goods and for essential infrastructures which the market cannot or will not supply, (2) as a stabiliser of economic activity through unforeseeable future uncertainties by using monetary and fiscal policies, (3) as a rule maker and enforcer.

It is the third of the above activities, the regulatory function, which is the chief source of contention between modern day champions of *laissez-faire* who are convinced of the self-sufficient and self-policing attributes of the market mechanism, and those who support an active interventionist role for government. It is principally this area which needs to be debated by sociologists, politicians, economists and all responsible public spirited citizens to evolve a practicable congruence between societal objective and their achievement.

The desirable institutional framework will differ from society to society and from time to time. It is necessary to avoid the two extremes of, on the one hand, an economically ignorant moralism or do-goodism or politically expedient populism which in denying the laws of supply and demand produces economic dis-order leading to impoverishment of the people and, the other, a morally obtuse economism which, oblivious to the most important concerns of man, those that lie beyond supply and demand, ends by fomenting a tide of resentment that is capable of sweeping the market economy away.

Institutions are human artifacts. They evolve in relationship to the dynamism of a society, in proportion to the concern and vigilance exercised by its alert citizens who, by virtue of the circumstances of birth or opportunity or inborn talent, have the capability to think imaginatively of such matters in depth. It is necessary to be flexible in such thinking, as indeed one must be in the conduct of one's own individual life. If we get caught in rigid attitudes, the process will cease to be creative and productive. This was what happened in the erstwhile U.S.S.R.

The economic system under which a society functions—be it command economy or the market—is not conterminous with the society. The life of the society extends far beyond things economic which are a subordinate part of a larger social whole. "Not be bread alone" is not an empty statement. Religion, philosophy, art, literature and music lie beyond economic arrangements, but nevertheless infuse them and are reflective of them. It is, however, important to note in defence of the market that whether a life-style is materialistic or ascetic, to a considerable degree it is the outcome of the freedom of choice that a market makes possible. Though the market is ethically neutral the choices of things or actions—good or bad—which it makes possible involve it in a moral debate. Do people determine the character of markets, or markets character of people? Let's also be aware that in the affluent West there is an increasingly sharp awareness of the moral lacunae in market based societies, that many serious social ills are not ameliorable by giving a free rein to the laws of supply and demand.

At another level, a recently published book "*Victims of Development*" points to the hidden weaknesses of affluent societies where the empowering possibilities of monéy have failed to prevent (if not actually caused them) the creative human powers decay and fall into disuse. For instance, the need for creative and imaginative play, as basic as any, has been turned into a craving for ceaseless entertainment and functionless mobility. The need to tell stories, to invent and amuse, to celebrate and sing our lives, has been superseded by an economic system whose superior need is to make money out of keeping us amused. The real subverters, according to the author, are the systems which reduce all the living richness, abundance and diversity of the world to the sterile monoculture of money.

While we have examined many ills inherent in the market, perhaps it may not be improper to look at the problems of the alternatives especially those which necessarily operate through huge bureaucracies such as the erstwhile Soviet 'Nomenclatura' as also many large corporations in the capitalist system itself. It would perhaps be useful to look at a specific case : G.E. of U.S.A.

In this 14 years of brilliantly steering the General Electric to become No. 1 or No. 2 worldwise in all its business (aircraft engines, electric motors, engineering plastics, industrial power systems, medical systems, circuit breakers, transportation lighting, major appliances, defence electronics) Jack Welch determinedly created a new culture in his vast organisation. He systematically rooted out bureaucracies everywhere. This is what Jack Welch had to say on the subject : "the unvarying agendas of bureaucracy is the defeat of change, the muffling of communication, the waste of minds and energies. Bureaucracy keeps business balkanised and focussed on themselves rather than on their customers. It distracts and disengages good minds from productive activity. It favours those who control over those who contribute. It throttles productive growth". Since every government sponsored institution must have a bureaucracy, above views of an eminently successful corporate leader, who led his organisation through persuasion rather than domination, must be kept in mind while developing the cultural contours of new institutional structures.

I can not resist quoting Jack Welch again on another aspect reflecting the bureaucratic attitude, both at an individual and at the organisational level, namely, arrogance:

> ". . . Prosperity and a high comfort level grew an awful arrogance in our corporate culture. . . Arrogant companies, be they arrogant with customers or with employees, are doomed".

Our lives have been witnesses to the greatest and most radical social transformations in the history of mankind. Increasingly it is clear (especially if we judge the quality and quantity of changes in the nature of work and workforce, society and policy of the affluent countries which have hitherto set the model for change for the rest of the world) that organisation of human life, in all its aspects, would henceforth be vastly different from what it has ever been since the beginning of human civilisation.

In all developed countries today, farmers are no more than 5% of the population and work force. At the turn of the century the figure was 50%. The second largest group in the population and work force of every developed country around 1900 was composed of domestic servants. For all practical purposes this group does not exist at all in developed countries now.

By 1900 a new class, the blue-collar worker in manufacturing industry—Marx's "Proletarian"—had arisen. The rise and fall of blue-collar workers in industrialised world has been astonishing. At the turn of the century these workers had miserable working conditions, poor pay and not job security. They lived in squalor and poverty and were exploited. Nevertheless, their lot was much better than that of farmers and domestic servants. There can be no better proof of this than the exponential drop in infant mortality, and consequent explosive growth in population (as is happening in India and other developing countries today) as farmers and domestic servants moved into industrial work. It was a great opportunity, in fact the first opportunity that social history had given them to better themselves substantially without having to emigrate.

The lot of the industrial workers improved dramatically. Within fifty years unionised industrial workers in developed countries had attained upper-middle class income levels with extensive job security, pension paid vacations and comprehensive unemployment insurance. Industrialisation and technology revolution had led to a fifty-fold increase in output per worker over a period of little over hundred years. This is the heart of the economic and social gains of the past century. A major part of this gain accrued to the industrial workers, half in the form of sharply reduced working hours, and half in the form of a twenty-strong force in politics.

By 1990, however, blue-collar workers' power was in retreat everywhere. While they accounted for 40% of the American work force in 1960, the percentage fell to 20% in early 1990s. The union power also fell sharply. It is now clear that the world is rapidly moving into a socio-economic order in which knowledge, and information not labour or even raw materials and capital are the key resources. Increasingly, in today's world the new elite possesses rarefied skills. It has addresses on the Internet rather than on the Fifth Avenue. An unfortunate logical consequence of this for developing countries is that increasingly they will not be able to base their development on their comparative labour advantage, *i.e.* on cheap industrial labour.

The very speed of change has, however, created dangerous social consequences. While the elite thrives on change, the mass fears it since it holds the threat of making them redundant. Increasingly, the mass is needed less and less as producers and workers than as consumers. Today, even in the USA, only 20% of the young Americans have the training and skills to cope with the change. The other 80% have no such abilities and hence no personal bargaining power. A snob in today's world is not someone who flings money about. Instead, unlike the ordinary person, he has knowledge and special skills, he is confident that the future belongs to him. In such a situation, the dangers to social stability are all too obvious. A far-reaching concern for human values which must lead to major policy decisions is inevitable.

Concern for human values is all the more relevant for the 80% of the above noted population of the world which has access to only 20% of the natural resources and which has no possibility (by sheer ecological mathematics) of ever reaching the present levels of material prosperity of the affluent. They must also contend with the fact that at present most of their existing industrial-economic growth patterns, willy-nilly copy the western models. At the current consumption levels of the United States, earth can sustain a population of only 2.5 billion. But at the Indian consumption levels, the earth can support 10 billion people. Clearly our way of living is the basis of our problems and the solutions to these problems also lie therein.

It is all too clear that the western model is not the Utopia that everyone else should long for. Viewing the scene in the affluent societies, Peter Drucker wrote in 1994:66 In every developed country, society is becoming sicker rather than healthier and social problems are multiplying". The need clearly is to reflect creatively on the human situation everywhere. In today's world the concepts of education have moved a long distance away from the nineteenth century Anglo-American model of classical liberal education which took pride in proclaiming that it had no utility whatsoever, that it had nothing to do with what work you did subsequently, that it only focussed (rather romantically in today's context) on the person and personal development. Education is no longer a matter of something you went through in the initial years of life. It is now a question of life-long growth and training to pick up new skills, to keep up with a world which is changing all the time.

In the fiercely competitive knowledge society of the present times, knowledge for the most part exists in application. The core, the central workforce of the knowledge society, consists of highly specialised informed and knowledgeable people. However in the light of the end results pointed out by Peter Drucker, it is necessary to think out new models for growth and development. Perhaps we need better judgment and wisdom than analytical intellectual brilliance. The essence of management today is to make knowledge productive. Management as it is relevant in the present day world, serves a great social purpose. And at this level, in the words of Peter Drucker again, it relates closely to the spirit of the Arts, as indeed do all creative endeavours of mankind in any field. The guiding spirit of the Arts has always been 'ethics' no matter how subtle, unseen or complicated the interconnection may sometimes appear. Practice of management can hardly remain unconcerned with ethical concepts, with human values.

Business schools will increasingly acquire a central place of pride in society which is undergoing unprecedented rapid transformation. Unlike the purely academic orientation of the traditional universities which have moved a long distance away from the scene of action in actual life, business schools are in the heart of it. They are, and should be in intimate relationship with where action is. Yet, they provide and must necessarily do so, a congenial academic environment for the dramatis personae of the new society to take a breather away from action to reflect on the broader questions, drawing lessons from the depths of their experience. This is concrete contribution to society.

The business school, as a social sector institution, will unquestionably play a crucial role in shaping not only the contours and culture of business organisations, but also in spearheading the growth of what is already forcefully emerging: the social sector, a unique value based third power centre challenging the hegemony of public (government) and private sectors in shaping society. A social sector institution aims at changing the human being. The product of a school is the student who has learned something. The product of a hospital is a cured patient. The knowledge society needs a social sector. Modern society and modern polity have become so big and complex that meaningful participation by an individual citizen has become difficult. All we seem to be able to do as citizens is to vote every few years and to pay taxes all the time. Participation in social sector organisations makes it possible for us to make a difference to the functioning of the society once again.

Social sector organisations are beginning to compete with government, though our social and political theories still assume that there are no power centres except government. In modern times, one of the first power centres to arise, almost 120 years ago, was the joint stock business enterprise. Since then many other such centres have come into being. While such organisations—the labour union, the business school, a university, a hospital complex— do not compete for public power or interfere in the work of government, they demand and indeed need autonomy with respect to their functions. They are a power centre because unlike an individual they have economic and organisational strength. Even at the most centralised stage of Soviet power, the managers of major industrial plants enjoyed virtual autonomy within their enterprises. Such autonomy is indeed the necessary condition of health and growth of such units in the emerging society of organisations which the modern world is—Such organisations are what the community was in the past. Their freedom of operation and structural health is analogous to that of the individual in relationship to the world of today.

The business school is, and must be an important pillar of the social sector, and must contribute to the organisational health and functioning of this new sector whose emerging responsibilities and obligations to society are yet at a nascent stage of development. We need to enquire as to what constitutes the performance capacity of an organisation and of an individual, and what can the business school do to enhance this vital capacity. It is necessary to re-evaluate constantly the purpose, values, content and quality of education. We can thus see the vast boundaries of the arena under which a business school can operate. Its inherent advantage of having one leg in the academic world of thoughts and ideas while the other is immersed in the theatre of action, places it in a unique position to shape the emerging society of the twenty-first century.

4

New Economic Policy Strategies for Effectiveness

B.N.P. Singh and Ratan K. Singh

The New Economic Policy is an outcome of widespread changes which have taken place in the international social and economic order as well as a direct offshoot of the management of an 'equilibrium trap crisis', which knocked the door of Indian economy in the beginning of the nineties. For the first time in its history, India was faced with the unbearable pain of defaulting on its international commitments on account of adverse balance of payments having foreign exchange reserves barely enough for two weeks of our imports, withdrawal of NRI deposits at a faster pace, closure of international commercial lending and erosion in international confidence due to drastic fall in foreign remittances. The crisis became more grievous in the wake of joint consequences of the occurrence of Gulf War which brought about the third oil price hike and dwindling down of foreign exchange reserves due to heavy payments for oil imports. All these developments in the margin of crisis forced the Government to think of a major departure from the trade policy followed till then and to make a serious move towards further integration of the Indian economy with the rest of the world by announcing the agenda of economic reforms with a view to combat the several maladjustments prevailing in the different layers of the economy. All the programmes of policy package of economic reforms are known as the New Economic Policies of India.

We always cite the example of other developing countries which have also tried similar policy packages. Some such as South Korea have succeeded dramatically, others, such as Brazil and Mexico had virtually zero growth during the eighties. There may be many reasons for the highly variable results of policies associated with liberalisation. The secrecy of their successfulness is the effective management of policy package as introduced in the countries. Thus, effective policy management may be an important reason for national success or failure.

We will, therefore, need to conceptualise the kind of management decision structures and processes needed in the Government to implement the new policies. Intellectual effort invested in raising and pursuing the question of its effectiveness may greatly increase the probability of success of chosen policies. Here are some specific suggestions to streamline government administration for effective policy management.

In the first place, it may be argued that there is an urgent need to develop an information system for the Government *vis-a-vis* implementation of the new economic policies. Apart from providing it with general statistics relating to monthly or quarterly foreign trade/ foreign exchange flow and figures of major industries, sectors, product groups, trade regions etc., for other prominent Third World nations, such an information system should highlight information on reduction of imports and export controls and results that can be attributed to changes in these controls. Similarly, the information can be given to the Government or cabinet on industrial production and consequences of changes in industrial policy, inflation, etc. By having such informations it would be easier for the Government to react in accordance with the changing character of the economy.

At present, in the various departments of the Government there is an army of surplus staff and in such a case services of surplus personnel should be utilised by rotation for the programmes of mass literacy, rural uplift, agricultural productivity development, consciousness to population, control in all parts of the country. Such measures would save the surplus personnel to be retrenched from the job.

To modernise the heavy paper work load system for quick decision making it is imperative that a major systems-oriented drive should be started in all departments and agencies of the Government to simplify and rationalise the various procedures.

The successfulness of this reform package rests on the scheme of restructuring of the power sector of the country. There is a legitimate fear that the poor performance of power sector might slow down drastically the agricultural and industrial production. In such a situation, the Government should amend the Indian Electricity Act and the intentions for the policy changes being talked about so far are important pre-requisites for involvement of private companies in this sector. However, there is a legitimate apprehension about large investments taking place until modalities are evolved to ensure timely payment of dues by State Electricity Boards to the new generating companies. One alternative can be "tripartite agreements" involving the lead banks of SEBs who should be obliged to honour the bills within two weeks as first charge. For disputes private companies can also be given distribution rights. In addition SEBs should not object to using their grids on payment of wheeling charges to transmit power to identified industrial consumers particularly those who have made matching contribution to equity. Further, the burden of uneconomic tariff should be removed from SEBs. And, the management of funds for new projects should be provided to SEBs through the Power Finance Corporation linked to conditionalities for targeted improvements in their performance. Thus, without stregthening the power sector the whole policy package would be fruitless.

The Government should try to vacate some areas for private investment like the sector of tourism, road transport and power without any delay in the larger interest of the economy.

Reduction in fiscal deficit must be achieved through development-oriented efforts by raising revenue and not by a reduction in development expenditure. If not, the rate of growth of the economy will suffer in the long run and the efforts under the NEP for creating a dent in poverty will receive a set-back. The Indian financial sector has been witness to series of changes in the past three years and now the reforms have entered into a critical phase. Thus, the Government should take proper attention in the field of financial sector reform of the country so as to avoid the inherent contradictions.

The administrative machinery should be restructured in terms of their functions, coverage of responsibilities and mode of coordination. Better to say, number of economic ministries should be minimised and their functions and scope of responsibilities regrouped on proper lines for smooth coordination. For instance, one ministry should be entrusted for evolving integrated policies of industry, trade and technology as well as policy issues concerning SSIs. Promotion and development should be looked after by two more ministries. One for engineering industry including steel and electronics and its role regarding administration of PSEs should also include manufacturing units presently under the control of Defence and Railways and the other cover all the chemical and process industries including fertilisers, food processing, bio-technology, cement, rubber, paper, etc. Some require changes in orientation such as Ministry of HRD which must lay special emphasis on training and retraining for skill improvement and better quality of technical and vocational education. Thus, such reduction in a large number of divisions or sections in the economic ministries would curtail the establishment cost of the different departments of the Government.

It is indispensable to suggest that the entire strength of manpower of the the different layers of Government should be reduced to a substantial level. Recruitment at all levels including that in central services should be reduced to say one-third of the present level for the next five or ten years. Such a measure will reduce unemployed and the disguisedly unemployed Government officials without creating a total gap in the flow of senior personnel in the future. The Government should also consider the option of a 'golden handshake' to reduce the pressure of creating unnecessary employment.

The above illustration is only an indicative and not an exhaustive package of concrete steps to complement the policies. Many vital areas have not been touched even.

There has hardly been any difference of opinion among most of the social scientists regarding the objectives of economic policy. The package of objectives comprises high rates of growth of real national income, full employment, price stability, external stability through stable exchange rates and a balanced current account of external payments, on the average, and finally social justice, on pragmatic, economic as well as ethical considerations. It has also been the experience everywhere that the simultaneous pursuit of all these objectives of this package of reform is extremely difficult to accomplish. Nevertheless, it is a bold step of the present Government to globalise the Indian economy. We must wait and watch for the reactions of the economy to make further comments.

5

A Perspective on Financial Restructuring in India

L.M. Bhole

The policy of financial sector reforms or restructuring as a part of the current phase of New Economic Policy in India has had a run of about five years by now. The key words which express the major plank of these policies are privatisation, marketisation, liberalisation, deregulation, competition, and globalisation. Following the launching of reforms, the Indian financial markets have undergone many significant changes and many more changes are looming large on the financial horizon. The current policy has quickened the pace of structural transformation of the Indian Financial System (IFS), and has laid the basis for the emergence of a structure of certain character in future. However, all is not well with the IFS: there is a dark side to its development. The "state of credit" or the "state of confidence" happens to be quite low in our financial sector.

Financial restructuring essentially involves a normative approach, a vision about how the financial system should look rather then how it will look a few years hence. Restructuring cannot be confined merely to a legislative or regulatory re-design. From this point of view, recent financial reforms, notwithstanding reports of some committees, have been rather starchy, ad hoc, with ideological overload, and without normative perspective. There has been a tendency to treat complex restructuring issues rather simplistically, naively. It is in this context that the present paper examines critically various limitations, drawbacks, inconsistencies and dangers of the deregulation policy, and suggests the foundation for building a viable, stable, sustainable, safe, sound economically and socially efficient (desirable), and people-oriented financial system in India.

Major Features of the Indian Financial System

As historical and evolutionary knowledge enables one to develop a correct and proper perspective on current policies and further development, we present below a brief retrospect of the major structural and other features of the IFS on the eve of financial reforms (*see* Bhole, 1992).

1. The IFS has grown enormously since 1950 in terms of size, innovations, diversity, complexity and sophistication. All the indicators of financial development, namely the Finance Ratio, Financial Interrelation Ratio, New Issue Ratio, and Intermediation Ratio have increased significantly. A considerable widening, deepening and geographical spread of the financial institutions and markets have been taking place over the period of time. The access to finance, financial services, financial instruments, etc. by an increasing number of people in all areas including rural areas has been achieved.
2. The IFS has amply fulfilled the function of promotion of saving and investment. The rates of saving and investment have increased from about 10 per cent to about 24 per cent during 1951-1994. However, the growth in this respect appears to have reached a plateau over the past 10-15 years.
3. Unlike in many other countries, in India, the household sector accounts for the major part (75 to 80 per cent) of aggregate savings. The place of the public sector and private corporate sector in this respect follows in that order, the contribution of the latter being particularly negligible.
4. There has been a substantial increase in the financialisation and institutionalisation of savings in India. Disintermediation and securitisation can't be said to have taken place significantly so far.
5. The most preferred assert of the investors is (bank and other) deposits. Inspite of the attention it has received in media, the "equity culture" has not developed much.
6. Although the banking system remains the largest part of the IFS even now, other financial institutions also have grown over a period of time, and now they account for 50 to 55 per cent of the size of operations of the banking system in terms of outstanding credit or the annual increase in outstanding credit or the aggregate financial assets.
7. The secondary markets in different financial instruments have remained underdeveloped so far. The markets for many financial instruments are narrow, and the institutional ownership of even the corporate securities has increased over the period of time.

8. The financial markets in India are marked by centralisation, concentration and oligopolistic or monopolistic imperfections. They are almost entirely owned and closely controlled, regulated, and monitored by the Government.
9. Almost all the interest rates have been administered by the authorities.
10. Financial development has often taken place in spurts and as a result of fiscal concessions. The investors feel cheated in respect of risk, return and liquidity from an increase in non-performing assets, bad debts, defaults, low profitability and sickness. The enormous financial development has failed to reduce creditable economic development in terms of quantity and quality.

Financial Reforms: Objectives and Measures

The major objectives of financial sector reforms are said to be as follows (Rangarajan, 1994) : (a) To promote a diversified, viable, efficient, transparent and competitive financial system; (b) To increase the allocative efficiency of available savings; (c) To increase return on investment; (d) To promote competition by creating a level playing field and allowing free entry and exit particularly to private sector institutions; (e) To ensure that flexible and market interest rates along with some concessional rates prevail in the markets; (f) To get the IFS integrated with the global financial system; (g) To modernise the instruments of monetary control so as to make them more suitable for the conduct of monetary policy in a market economy; *i.e.* to replace physical controls on monetary variable by instruments based on market incentives; (h) To promote accelerated growth of the real sector. Specifically, reforms are directed to improve the financial health and conditions of banks, and to develop stock markets and equity culture in the country.

A large number of measures have been visualised/introduced to achieve these objectives. Some of them are listed below (GDI, 1994):

(i) Reduction in Cash Reserve Ratio (CRR) and Statutory Liquidity Ratio (SLR); (ii) Reduction in the number of interest rates slabs on bank advances and introduction of the policy of deregulation of various interest rates, *viz.* debenture and bond rates; (iii) Introduction of prudential norms for income recognition, classification of assets, and provisioning of bad debts in case of commercial banks; (iv) Introduction of capital adequacy norms for banks, other financial institutions, brokers, etc.; (v) Private sector allowed to set up various types of financial institutions, *viz.,* banks, mutual funds, insurance companies; (vi) Banks lending norms liberalised; the system of direct allocation of credit to be dismantled; and banks are to be restructured; (vii) Convertibility clause not to be obligatory for assistance sanctioned by term lending institutions; (viii) Indian companies permitted to access international capital markets through equity, bonds, commercial loans; (ix) Investment norms for NRIs and overseas corporate bodies liberalised; (x) Foreign Institutional Investors (FIIs) permitted to invest in Indian capital market, (xi) Capital flows liberalised; flexible exchange rate system introduced, rupee made convertible on current account, exchange controls to be dismantled, (xii) Over the Counter Exchange (OTCE) and National Stock Exchange (NSE) made operational; (xiii) Capital Issues Control Act, 1947 and the officer of Controller of Capital Issues (CCI) abolished; instead, Securities Exchange Board of India (SEBI) set up and empowered with the authority of registration, regulation, prescribing norms and guidelines of a wide variety in case of all types of financial institutions; (xiv) A new Department of Financial Supervision set up within the RBI to strengthen the supervisory system for banks and other financial institutions.

The belief underlying these reforms has been that the regulatory framework developed during the planning period has done an incalculable harm to the IFS, and that such a framework is no longer adequate and relevant today. At the same time, it has been argued that deregulation does not automatically imply no regulation at all; instead, regulation would assume sophisticated level in the form of prudential, supervisory and regulatory structure which would "protect financial system without unnecessarily restraining it". The reforms are said to be directed towards "stringent prudential regulation" in a "deregulated environment" giving autonomy, flexibility, and transparency to banks and other financial institutions.

Apparently, the reforms are guided by the Narasimham Committee Report (RBI, 1991). How far this Report was a mere systematisation and formalisation of the decisions already made under foreign guidance and pressures has remained a moot point. Event if not dictated externally, reforms can still be said to be following (imitating) the trends or "fashions" abroad. It is interesting to note here that many analysts in the USA describe the process of marketisation, liberalisation, globalisation in other countries as the "Americanisation of finance."

Deregulation X-rayed

After having presented the context of reforms, let us now turn to a systematic examination of deregulation philosophy and the dangers it poses to the financial structure in India in coming years.

Did Regulation Harm the Financial System?

The argument that the regulatory framework harmed the IFS is only partially valid, and, whatever the failures of regulation, they do not automatically establish a case for deregulation in the conventional sense, and without other suitable changes in the organisational and value framework. During the period of regulation, while the financial system suffered from certain drawbacks, it also simultaneously achieved phenomenal growth, innovations, and diversification. Many of the drawbacks were more due to politicisation and wrong pricing policies than due to regulation *per se*; to treat the two synonymously would be an error. The sectoral targets for credit allocation, in themselves, would not have lowered the profitability if politicisation had not infected their implementation. The preemption of funds for the government need not have been harmful if the suitable interest rate policy was pursued. Thus, the case for deregulation in this context reflects a convenient or biased use of facts and evidence.

Is Deregulation Really Taking Place?

It is also pertinent to ask whether deregulation is really taking place in India? Because of the fear of instability and understandable lack of desire to shed power, what is really happening these days is more a redesigning, reorganising, recasting, remaking, restructuring, regulation, supervision, control, which is being projected as deregulation because to do so has become politically expedient. To separate the supervisory functions of the RBI or to replace CCI by SEBI are the misleading examples of deregulation.

While "deregulating", the authorities are busy with constructing a regime of detailed, complex, wide-ranging, and widely reaching norms, guidelines, regulations, restriction and directives. The knowledge of a plethora of norms which have been recently issued for underwriting, foreign institutional investors, brokers, banks, mutual funds, insurance companies, share trading, etc. would immediately convince any perceptive and objective person regarding the fakeness or hollowness of the deregulation plank. Similarly, the real deregulation of interest rates is yet to take place; most of the interest on debt instruments are still administered, with the result that differentials between rates of return on these instruments and on equities or units have widened and have gone against debt instruments.

The authorities are also closely regulating how much global depository receipts would be issued, who will issue them and at what interest rates they will be issued. In the regime that set out to create a level playing field and an environment for fair competition there have been many instances of glaring, unjust discrimination, of "Stinking double standards" practiced by the authorities. For example, in August 1994, while a foreign power company (Enron) was allowed to issue global depository receipts at a higher cost (12%), the domestic companies and financial institutions such as IDBI, and ICICI were not allowed to issue them at a lower cost (6%). In respect of capital gains tax, lock-in period for purchased shares, and the extent of foreign equity participation, while some investors (FIISs) are being favoured, others (NRIs; domestic companies) are being discriminated.

The talk of reducing preemption of resources by the Government has gone hand-in-hand with devising a policy to prescribe SLR for all non-bank financial companies, and with disinvestment of equity capital of public sector units (PSUs). Disinvestment of shares is basically, actually, primarily a strategy of the State to have a greater share in community savings and not an anti-crowding out step. The reality of preemption does not depend on the form in which the Government appropriates funds; equity capital does not reflect less preemption than debt capital. The true colour of this step was exposed in a starkly naked manner when the sale of PSU shares miserably flopped in 1992. Following this failure, the Government made it compulsory for mutual funds and financial institutions to participate in the bids for PSU shares. This policy forced the said financial organisations either to off-load their holdings of industrial securities or to subscribe less to the new issues of these securities. This, in turn, has tended to depress both the primary and secondary markets for industrial securities.

Fuzzy Concept of Prudential Regulation

Realising that it has not been possible to liberalise the system in the real sense and spirit of that term, a diversionary notion of "prudential regulation" has been invented and made popular for justifying the present policy. Let it be realised that what is prevalent in India today is the regulation proper, dirigiste policies, the state intervention which goes far beyond nominal or indicative state policies. Moreover, the case of prudential regulation reflects an admission that the deregulated, competitive system, by itself, is incapable of promoting prudence, viability, stability, and efficiency.

Infeasibility of Deregulation

The policy of financial reforms has disregarded the historical, evolutionary, and current reality of IFS which, as it is, is ill-suited, ill-equipped to become competitive in the text book or neo-classical sense or as perceived by the IMF-World Bank combine. The IFS has been nurtured, promoted by the Government; it is characterised by concentration, market imperfection, and almost complete Government ownership. It is worth recalling that it has evolved to such a state as a result of a systematic, conscious, deliberate policy pursued to avoid competition, to weed out weak units, to achieve social goals, to check concentration of economic power in private hands, to own commanding heights of the economy. Admittedly, it was wrong to try to check one type of concentration by another type of concentration, and to prefer State monopoly to private oligopoly. As we shall argue later there is no merit in reverting back to private oligopoly; what we need is to free the system from the monopoly of any kind whatsoever. In any case, the point of argument at the stage is that the IFS is unsuitable for competition unless the whole structure is dismantled, which is not contemplated by the votaries of liberalisation.

In the present set up, the competition will mean competition between the old, big and government units on the one hand, and new, small, private units on the other. Can a new private insurance company compete with LIC or GIC? Can a new private mutual fund compete with UTI? Can competition be real when UTI, LIC, IDBI, etc., are going to grow still bigger on account of their becoming "Universal financial institution"? The level playing field is a pious hope in India right now. One doubts whether, except a few foreign and Indian giants, there will be many takers for privatisation, the instances of still-born private sector ventures support such a doubt.

Given the nature of the Indian economy, the public sector and the Government will continue to have interest in using the financial system for their own purpose. It may also be unwise to liberalise the system suddenly and significantly because it would unduly expose savers and investors to unaccustomed levels of interest rate risk in addition to credit risk. The system may not be capable of withstanding the domestic and international market forces suddenly, sought to be unleashed by the reforms. Similarly, the authorities can hardly practise the hands-off policy when so much of tax payers' money has been locked in banks and financial institutions for clearing their portfolios and for meeting capital adequacy norms. Further, equity considerations are very much valid and financial markets must contribute to achieving greater inter-personal, inter-sectoral, and inter-regional equity. All these complex considerations cannot be brushed aside by referring *ad nauseam* to the virtues of competition or the so called inherent magic of the market place (Patel, 1993).

Dangers of Deregulation

The inapplicability of the philosophy of competition to the modern, organised financial sector is not specific to India. An important school of thought abroad consisting of scholars like Keynes (1961), Tobin (1987), Kaufman (1994), and others has cautioned the public against such a philosophy. Since the current excitement about or wave of deregulation in India is inspired by foreign thinking, it is essential to grasp this other viewpoint also so that a more balanced stance on deregulation emerges.

It has been argued that the justification of deregulation simply by pointing at the optimality of the outcomes of free competitive markets is highly flawed. The two functions—as a payments mechanism and as a credit allocation mechanism—of the financial system are no longer distinctly separated; they are now intertwined to a very high degree. Therefore, unlike in the past, it is now not enough to safeguard only the payments mechanism; the regulation is now needed to increase safety and soundness of both.

The financial institutions are entrusted with other people's money, funds, savings; they have an extraordinary public responsibility; they perform a fiduciary function as guarantors of credit; they have large liabilities and small capital base; they are engaged in allocating credit to activities which are crucial, vital, and critical to the health and stability of the economic system. Therefore, financial institutions and markets cannot be treated as private activity, they have never and nowhere been treated strictly as private activity. The Government regulation has always and everywhere been regarded as valid in their respect.

The special role and inherent character of the financial system also requires that the aggressive, zealous entrepreneurship to exploit growth—the lauded virtue of competition—should be avoided in its working. The zealous financial entrepreneurship or financial engineering encourages short-term rather than long-term investment; it results in the continuous creation of debt; it creates vested interests against slowing down the availability of credit; it necessitates raising interest rates to very high levels if credit restraint is required; it increases the risk of bad debts; it harms the solvency, soundness, safety, and stability of the financial system.

The debate on deregulation, therefore, cannot be decided primarily on the basis of considerations of productivity, efficiency, profitability, and flexibility of individual financial units. Such a debate must also address itself to wider issues. For example, how are the deregulated markets to be disciplined and how to ensure that they will compete on level playing field? What should be the policy regarding loss-making and insolvent institutions? Should they be closed down at the earliest or should they be helped by the authorities to come out of the red? Can we really close down the loss making banks and other financial institutions? The logic of market discipline, *i.e.* the survival of the fittest and the death of the weak, is not relevant, suitable, desirable, and easy to practise in the case of financial institutions because of their special character. The market discipline would burden households and businesses with ever greater over load of debt; it would make institutions weaker rather than stronger (Kaufman, 1994).

Danger of Greater Volatility

One of the ways in which financial institutions can become weaker in a deregulated environment is the increase in volatility they would face. More and more systematic evidence is now becoming available which shows that the potential for extreme volatility or financial trauma in the world financial markets has certainly become magnified due to deregulation and due to factors engendered by deregulation.

The galloping debt burden of all types of economic units, an increase in the role of mutual funds in determining the level and composition of investment, an increase in securitisation, an increase in the use of derivatives and new trading techniques, an increase in the presence and activities of "high octanes" and "hard driving" portfolio managers who roam in and out of currencies, bonds, equities, commodities, precious metals, the building up of a tremendous financial infrastructure comprising compulsive units who are outside the regulatory ken of monetary authorities, and globalisation would create a hazardous environment in which financial excesses, bouts of turbulence, and progressively greater fluctuations in security values would become inevitable.

Emergence of Conglomerates

Financial reforms are aggravating the present structural concentration and centralisation by promoting big financial, commercial, national, international, private sector, and public sector conglomerates. Like in other countries, the earlier distinctions or traditional boundaries between different types of financial institutions have begun to disappear in India also. Banking, merchant banking, investment banking, development banking, broking, insurance, mutual funds, and non-financial firms are getting affiliated, integrated, interlinked, interpenetrated with one another; they are entering into one another's business. Specialised, separate institutions, or mono-functional mode are giving way to multi-functional mode, product line diversification, "one-stop", one-statement, one-location institutions. What has come to be known as "universal banking" or "universal financial institutions" or "universal financialism" is taking shape across the financial and industrial sectors.

In India, this trend reflects a return in a far bigger way to the earlier structure in which industrial houses used to own captive banks and financial companies, and in which interlocking directorships prevailed. This structure was thought to be unhealthy, unfair, undesirable, and it has dismantled over the years. But now, the formation of colossal financial giants is being allowed through permeating diversification, mergers, combinations and acquisitions. One can easily see on the Indian financial horizon a monolith, giant ICICI, UTI, LIC, SBI, Mahindra and Mahindra, Tatas and many others. The state and private monopolies are getting further entrenched through this trend.

Universal financialism is sometimes justified by saying that it would increase profitability, reduce risk, enhance stability, and lower the costs to the consumers through synergies in joint production and management. It appears that non-banking financial organisations want to enter banking activities for accessing deposit base, Government safety net, payments mechanism, and for avoiding certain legal provisions which are specific to them. Banks want to enter non-banking services in order to increase profitability, to achieve large size to be able to compete internationally, and to follow customers. Manufacturing business organisations want to enter banking and finance in order to develop captive sources of funds, to access payments system, to avoid regulation, and to pursue bigness.

Such a structure opens the financial system to numerous abuses; it increases the fragility of the system. The non-price cut-throat competition, differentiation, advertising, and Chamberlian wastes of monopolistic competitions would be rampant in such a system. There is nothing in Smith or Arrow or Debreat that justifies the naive confidence of deregulation ideology that the unfettered growth and unrestrained combinations of firms will yield socially best allocation of resources. That combinations will be made in society's interests is simply an ideological article of faith. The economies of scope and scale do not justify mega financial institutions. The combinations are made, financial empires are built not so much for synergies as for managerial remuneration, prestige, power (Tobin, 1987).

It has been rightly stressed that allowing commercial firms to own and control banks breaks the social compact under which banks are given certain privileges in return for fulfilling certain responsibilities. The companies owning banks may transfer risk of failure of their business on safety nets provided to banks by the Government, Central Bank, and

Deposit Insurance organisation, and this is a "moral hazard". The inherent public character of financial institutions demands that their relationship must be kept separate from that of business and commercial enterprises (Tobin, 1987).

In this context, it is pertinent to ask whether financial supermarkets are desired, perceived to be necessary, demanded by the consumers or customers. It appears that there has been little pressure from customers for integrating diverse institutions. The combinations are being pushed through by businessmen, bankers, financers to serve their money-making interests. They are neither theoretically justifiable nor do they serve any compelling economic, social, public purpose. Therefore, the authorities and social scientists in USA, UK, Canada and other countries in the West are worried about the emergence of this 'brave new world' of conglomerates. While restructuring the IFS, this must be borne in mind.

Some Evidence Against Deregulation

The deregulation in India cannot be said to have a happy or encouraging impact on the IFS. The reform period has witnessed an exacerbation of the worrisome features of the system. The insatiable appetite and populism have tended to mark the setting up of too large a number of institutions. The absence of positive relationship between financial development and economic development has become all the more marked. Foreign exchange reserves have increased, but the major part of this increase is due to borrowings from abroad. There has been little relationship between the hankering after foreign exchange resources and the absorption capacity of the economy, with the result that a significant part of these resources has remained unutilised. The globalisation has increased the uncertainty, risk, volatility, complexity in the system.

The banks have continued to face a host of problems : mutual funds are suffering from innumerable ills. The financial system is being hurtled from crisis to crisis. The excessive or lunatic speculation, gyrations in stock market prices, the series of scams, increase in internal and external debt, and persistence of inflation characterise the system. The hopelessness and helplessness of genuine investors are reflected in ever-mounting thousands of complaints lodged with the SEBI.

The things are not much different abroad. The stock markets have often crashed in marketised economies; the recent world-wide crash being in 1987. One-quarter of the banking sector in USA is in the red. Non-performing loans of 21 big banks in Japan were at 12.3 trillion yen at the end of September 1992. Britain's big four banks had to set aside a record 3.34 billion pound sterlings for bad debts in 1992, bringing the total of provisions for bad debt to 22.23 billion pound sterlings during 1987-92. The failure of banks and financial institutions has been a common experience across USA, UK, Canada, France, Japan, etc. The competitive, entrepreneurial zeal to exploit growth has led to a sharp deterioration in the quality of credit increase in bad debts, insolvencies, and bankruptcies in these countries. The present condition of the US financial system is described in these words : It is sitting on a ticking time-bomb with an uncertain ting device. It has become similar to the rotting frame of an old house which miraculously stands but one day a brief but intense gush of wind will take it down with a crash (FRBKC, 1987). Many experts abroad confess that deregulation has failed to create a viable, stable, efficient financial structure. The quest for such a structure must transcend the conventional regulation-deregulatión duel.

Towards Decentralisation

We have argued so far that if regulation had harmed the IFS, the deregulation of the current type can harm it more. If there was a "regulation failure", a "deregulation failure" can be greater and worse. The set of goals of social interest, self-sufficiency, self-reliance, equality and social justice of the regulatory model was certainly superior to the set of goals of competition, profits, self-interest, economic efficiency of the deregulation model. The real failure of the earlier model consisted not so much in the lower profitability or bad debts as in its moving away from the people, its centralisation, its tremendous scope for corruption, politicisation and distribution of largess, and its creation of a culture of dependence. The deregulation model contains little to remedy these evils. Deregulationsans its harmful consequences and inconsistencies requires decentralisation, conscious promotion of ethical finance, and elimination of competitive greed. Let us now discuss briefly these prerequisites or liberalisation.

The deregulation objective of reducing or eliminating concessional lending to priority sectors may become acceptable if effective steps are taken to stop the drain of resources from rural areas. And this requires decentralising financial structure (Bhole, 1978). As it has been forcefully argued, given the validity of regional and other equity considerations, given the fact that credit markets are imperfect in which big banks are allergic to simple rural folk, and are not inclined to take time and trouble to discover and nurture real investment opportunities among small and weak borrowers, the need for private local banks or institutions run or mediated by non-government organisations or private entrepreneurs becomes important. The question of spawning a large number of small private banks in rural as well as urban areas needs to be considered seriously, and various ways must be found out to make this possible. While the question of adequate access to credit on the part of the poor and weak cannot be swept under the carpet, this must be achieved by encouraging a large number of small private banks to mushroom in cities and villages alike (Patel, 1993).

It must also be realised that inspite of a great growth of formal, organised, modern financial institutions so far, a sizable part of the capital market in India is still in the unorganized or informal sector. A good part of private savings are still invested in one's own businesses or in the enterprises of one's friends and relatives. This investment takes place informally, without paperwork, and it reflects the predominance and vitality of the small scale sector in industry, trade, and agriculture (Patel, 1993). Everything must be done to preserve, protect, rebuild, promote this informal, decentralized sector.

Thus it is not advisable to eliminate or consolidate the existing network of rural banks. The penchant for creating large public institutions must be discarded. There is no justification for a national apex body of regional rural banks. It is totally wrong to promote or allow the growth of universal financial conglomerates. Instead, there is a great merit in promoting, nurturing a financial structure comprising hundreds of small, specialized, area-specific, local financial institutions which pursue the goals of enough, sufficient margin between income and expenditure, and of social responsibility. Such a structure would not require much external regulation and supervision because its capacity or potential for abuse, corruption, exploitation, instability, etc. would be little. All this would be eminently in tune with the philosophy of privatisation, deregulation and level playing fields, it would mean promoting right kind of privatisation. Decentralisation is the only alternative which is superior to both private oligopoly and State monopoly.

Social and Ethical Dimensions

The discussion on financial reforms, like any other reforms, cannot be complete without referring the philosophy of money, capital and finance. The legitimate role of financial markets is to offer an opportunity for re-evaluating financial investments in order to facilitate real investment. As Keynes used to say, the social object of skilled investment is to defeat the dark forces of time and ignorance which envelop the future. Further, it is the long-term investor who most promotes public interest; and socially advantageous investment does not necessarily coincide with investment which is most profitable. There must be a close correspondence between the volume of business (activity) in financial markets and the volume of real investment, output, and employment. These markets are not meant to function purely or even primarily to serve the purely money-making interests of the brokers, traders, dealers, jobbers, speculators, financial professionals, financial engineers, financial wizards.

In India, like elsewhere, all this has become irrelevant today. Instead, the whole economic and financial scene has become characterized by the "forward stampedes", *i.e.* by the beliefs that "more is always better". That enough is not enough, that the only thing wrong about our financial sector is that our financial progress is still less, that "avarice and greed should be our guides" for quite some time to come. The new economic policy has whetted the frenzy of greed, fury of money making passion, and mindless financial obsession. The atmosphere is laden with the spirit of lotteries and casino finance. The game players and games with popular zest to make money quickly have come to dominate the system. Contrary to what Keynes had said, the money making passion is not canalizing, diverting dangerous human proclivities into comparatively harmless channels; instead, it has unleashed the forces of cruelty and the reckless pursuit of power and authority. Today, man is "tyrannizing over his bank balance" as well as "over his fellow-citizens". The dishonesty, cheating, frauds, misappropriations, self-enrichment in financial markets have reached unbelievable, legendary, stunning, conclusive proportions.

Regulatory, supervisory measures, necessary as they may be, are woefully inadequate and unsuitable to eliminate the above-said poison from the body-finance, unless the ethos, culture of ethical finance is systematically, consciously nurtured, unless the public is educated in the virtues of "just finance" in place of "high finance". The universality of the financial crises proves that essentially they are not of structural, or cyclical, or regulatory nature, that they are of ethical or moral nature. The disclosure requirements, norms, guidelines, accounting standards, forms to be filled have been extant for decades, and we should not be guided into believing that every thing will be all right if their number is increased, or a new authority is set up to administer them, or a slightly different way is adopted to administer them. It is not the generalised procedures for regulation that matter so much in the end as the very high standards of integrity, honesty, vigilance of all professionals and everyone are concerned.

The stock market scam in 1992 reflects, apart from the administrative and regulatory failure, the authorities' propensity to use any and every indicator to justify the ideological and power game. The speculative rise in share prices before the scam broke out instead of being used as a warning signal, was actually used to claim that the liberalisation policy was showing a quick and big success even when the greed, avarice marginal affairs was an aberration. Specious arguments that the scam should not be allowed to arrest our thought processes, that the "scam is not the end of the world", were put forth to be little what scam really stood for. The Action Taken Report of the Joint Parliamentary Committee on the scam has nakedly revealed once again the nation's moral failure.

Everywhere, the volatile financial structure has gone hand-in-hand with the glittering high finance in which the 'successful' and dishonest have amassed large fortunes only in a few months or years; where finance graduates are receiving salaries which must be termed as distorted. Neglecting the basic health of the financial system, the people's imagination is going wild with computerization, globalisation, electronic funds transfer, 24 hour banking, and other seemingly endless stream of basically frivolous innovations. In the present world of high finance, everything is possible and nothing is prohibited.

The pertinent question to ask is how far the preoccupation with the "brave new world" of portfolio management is right. The risk-return trade off as the supreme value is dangerous. There is an urgent need to develop morally, socially responsible attitudes to investment. The question whether the activities in which people invest are morally repugnant cannot be brushed aside as irrelevant. The belief that financial marketeers cannot exist without speculation is a blind, irrational superstition. To amass financial wealth by causing price fluctuations must be condemned.

The earning of income by the individual is not an isolated activity arising out of some individual values; it is of a piece with social communication. Therefore, investors should consider refusing to buy debts of governments which are racist, repressive, autocratic, etc. Similarly, investments in organisations producing armaments, liquor, cigarettes, drugs, etc. must be considered taboo. The societies cannot save themselves from oscillations between unthinking euphoria and enervating pessimism; moral sanctions and mandates are obeyed by everyone in matter of finance also (Simmel, 1978. Frankel, 1977).

Since neither the visible hand nor the invisible hand can automatically and magically reconcile the private and social interest, the ideals of social investments, social responsibility, moral and just finance will have to become a part of common life even in areas from which they have been traditionally excluded. The world of finance cannot be rescued from its present cataclysm unless people's 'mind-sets' change in such a way as to accept the possibilities, uses, indispensability, imperativeness of the "martyrdom or the market place" (Ruskin, 1862).

Summary and Conclusion

We have examined in this paper various aspects of the current policy of financial liberalisation in India. It has been argued that there has been little actual liberalisation. In fact, the increase in volatility, financial excesses, and speculative bouts in the wake of the announcement of liberalisation has compelled the authorities to tighten the regulation. It is difficult to believe that the modern State would, on its own, shed its power; power-shedding goes against the grain of bureaucratic and political establishment. What is really happening is the further entrenchment of the powerful combination of the pursit of profit by private business and the pursuit of power by the State. In any case, deregulation with the conventional forms of economic organisation and management, and with the conventional motivational foundation can result only in the loss of stability and well-being of the society. It is only when deregulation, decentralisation, and ethos go together that a stable, sustainable, safe, sound financial system can be created. Unit banks, micro credit agencies, and informal credit arrangements emphasizing self-help, self-reliance, public participation, and loan-savings linkages should constitute the core of financial structure.

REFERENCES

Beauchamp, T.L., and Bowie, N.E., (eds.), *Ethical Theory and Business,* Prentice Hall, 1979.

Bhole, L.M., *Financial Structure for Rural Development : In Retrospect and Future Perspective,* The Indian Economic Journal, October-December 1978.

Bhole, L.M., *Financial Institutions and Markets,* Tata McGraw-Hill, New Delhi, 1992.

Bhole, L.M., *Proposals for Financial Sector Reforms in India : An Appraisal,* Vikalpa, July-September 1992.

Federal Reserve Bank of Boston, *The Regulation of Financial Institutions,* New Hampshire, 1979.

Federal Reserve Bank of Kansas City, *Restructuring the Financial System,* Wyoming, 1987.

Frankel, S.H., *Money : Two Philosophies,* Basil Blackwell, Oxford 1977.

Government of India, *The Economic Survey,* 1993-94, New Delhi, 1994.

Kaufman, Henery, Structural Changes in the Financial Markets : Economic and Policy Significance, *Economic Review,* Federal Reserve Bank of Kansas City, Second Quarter, 1994.

Keynes, J.M., *General Theory of Employment, Interest and Money,* Macmillan, London, 1961.

Patel, I.G., Indian Capital Market—Emerging Trends. *The Journal of Indian Institute of Bankers,* January-March 1992.

Patel, I.G., Some Reflections on Financial Liberalisation, *Discount and Finance,* Dec. 18, 1993.

Rangarajan, C., Financial Liberalisation and Reforms, *Discount and Finance,* January 30, 1993.

Rangarajan, C., Indian Financial System ; The Emerging Horizon, *Discount and Finance,* June 18, 1994.

Reserve Bank of India, *Report of the Committee on the Financial System* (Narasimham Committee Report), Bombay, 1991.

Ruskin, John, *Unto This Last,* 1862.

Simmel, G., *The Philosophy of Money,* Routledge and Kegan Paul, London, 1978.

6

National Stock Exchange: Re-Engineering of the Securities Markets

Neeraj Prakash

NSE : THE ORIGIN AND THE PRESENT FUNCTIONING

Another Study Group to Suggest Desired Reforms

With liberalisation emerging as the gateway to success for the Indian economy, it was obvious that the financial sector would not be left behind and that financial sector reforms would be taken up in right earnest. In fact, it was not just liberalisation, but the various loopholes in the existing system of trading also which prompted the authorities to give securities market trading a face lift. Lack of computerisation and inadequate telecommunication facilities on the existing stock exchange, a settlement system incompetent to deal with the enormous amount of business leading to leading delays and abrupt closure of the market for a few days, made the bourses inefficient in servicing the large investor base.

With a view to overcoming these hurdles, a "high powered study group on establishment of stock exchanges" was appointed under chairmanship of the late M.J. Pherwani which submitted its report in June, 1991. The Committee recommended the setting up a "model exchange", *viz.,* the National Stock Exchange (NSE) which would play a complementary role to the BSE by listing medium sized companies and which would also permit trading in debt instruments. Thus, the NSE of India was incorporated in November 1992 with an equity capital of Rs. 25 crores and promoted by the IDBI, ICICI, IFCI, all insurance corporations and selected commercial banks.

Although NSE has emerged as a "Votary" of the security market modernisation and automation in keeping with Pherwani's intent, the present form of NSE is substantially different from what was originally conceived by M.J. Pherwani study group. It is actively pitching as a competitor to the BSE especially with the commencement of the operations of NSE in the capital market segment. Given the public character of NSE it is reviving immense support from the Government and the regulators and this could ultimately lead to NSE emerging as a "beneficiary" of the security market modernisation process in sofaras it becomes the largest and the nodal exchange of the country relegating BSE to a secondary level force.

NSE operations could be broadly classified into the Wholesale Debt Market (WDM) Segment and the Capital Market (CM) Segment. While trading in debt instruments commenced on June 30, 1994, that in equity started only recently on November 3, 1994.

The WDM segment is the same as the money market operations where institutions and corporate bodies enter into high value transactions in instruments like Government securities, Treasury bills, PSU bonds and commercial paper.

The Capital Market Segment of NSE started the operations on Nov. 3, 1994. Initially 200 scrips had been allowed for trading which recently went upto 400 and it is proposed that NSE would list shares of 525 companies by the end of December 1994. The NSE has two groups, listed shares and permitted shares but the scrips are not segregated into the specified and the non-specified categories as in the case of regional exchanges. Interestingly, BSE is following suit and plans a merger of securities groups. As most often scrips to be listed presently figure in the list of permitted securities, the group of permitted securities will become short. It is likely that the list of permitted securities will be expanded in stages after the listing process is completed.

Listing the Upper-end

For listing, the exchange has selected companies which have a minimum paid up capital of Rs. 10 crore and minimum market capitalisation of Rs. 50 crore. The listing norms on the NSE are slightly different from the norms followed by the other established stock exchanges. In case of NSE all the listed companies have to provide unabridged balance sheets to the shareholders of the company; all the listed companies have to compare the actual financial performance with that of the projections made by them at the time of becoming public and thirdly, necessary provisions for immobilisation of securities, once depositories come up, are also incorporated. The above conditions, being more stringent are definitely a pointer towards the fact that the larger and the better companies would be listed at the NSE.

Membership, Professionals Please

Members desirous of operating on the WDM should have a net worth of Rs. 2 crore and have at least two years experience in banking or financial services or treasury. Individual players on the equity market seeking membership on the NSE must have a net worth of Rs. 75 lakhs while the corporate members will need to have a net worth of Rs. 1 crore. The common eligibility criteria for both the segments are that the applicants must have been engaged only in the securities business and not in any fund based activities. Brokers, who are members of other stock exchanges have also been encouraged to become NSE members, and at present, they constitute about 50 per cent of total membership on the NSE. At present there are approximately 250 members on the NSE with SEBI registration. It is noteworthy that NSE is equipped with professional staff who do not have any equity stake in the organisation. In other stock exchanges the major controlling interest is in the hands of brokers. Hence it could be expected that the observance of the rules of the game at NSE would be superior in comparison to other exchanges.

IT in Operation

The emphasis on transparency and settlement has meant that the system had to be order-driven and that is exactly why the NSE is not a computerised version of the quote-driven BSE. Order-driven trading means that traders on the NSE simply feed their buy or sell orders into the system, and not like the two way quote exchanges the BSE and other exchanges run on. Try system then matches the best buy orders with the best sell orders and finalises deals automatically. Orders that offer the same price prioritised by time, which means all deals are made always at the best possible price at the time.

The NSE trading system software, National Exchange for Automated Tracing (NEAT), allows "trading members" (essentially brokers) and "participants" (basically large operators who will be directly responsible for settlement of deals among themselves) to trade either from the NSE premises or remote offices through a communications (satellite based) network. All that a trader has to do is switch on his terminal, log in, enter his password and begin trading.

The communications network is the backbone of the NSE. Trading members in the wholesale debt market segment are connected by high-speed telephone lines. Capital Market traders are linked by Very Small Aperture Terminals (VSATs). Presently trading is restricted to Bombay but will soon be extended across the country. The NSE's screen based trading facility for wholesale debt is the first of its kind in the country. Subsequently, options and futures and other derivatives are also expected to be introduced.

Settle and Clear, Weekly

The NSE finalised its settlement and clearing mechanisms for trading in Capital Market segment in the month of September 1994. The following are the main features of the NSE settlement and clearing system:

- Mandatory weekly settlement, *i.e:* no postponement or clubbing of settlements.
- Uniform settlement cycle for all scrips, *i.e.* no separate specified and non-specified groups.
- Payments within 15 days of transaction.
- Members to get complete report of trades after each trading period.
- Final settlement statement to be sent to each member to specify delivery of securities.
- Securities settlement to be handled through a clearing house.
- Funds to be handled by clearing bank.
- Every delivery to be made in sealed envelopes.

Interestingly, though the BSE is also supposed to follow the weekly settlement system it has, till very recently drawn flak from the SEBI for frequent complaints in cash group scrips and for not adhering to the weekly settlements.

Advantage, NSE

With the above understanding of NSE's origin and the present functioning, the following, in brief, may be pointed out to be the major successes of the NSE system :

- Nationwide access to the traders.
- Caters to the investment needs of various categories of investors.
- Automated screen based trading with real time response.
- Anonymity of the trading member which helps in obviating the influences of large order on prices through sentiment.
- The precise details of the rates, time and counter-parties on the trade confirmation slip ensures complete transparency.
- Orders are matched by price priority which means all deals are made at the best possible price.

- Since the settlements are weekly any bad delivery is auctioned the very next week.
- The system has been designed for book-entry settlement and as and when the legislature gives the go-ahead and custodian and infrastructural supports are in place, physical delivery can easily be scrapped.

The Emerging Structure of the Securities Market

Speculation has always been and will continue to be the mainstay of securities transactions. It is "excessive speculation" that the regulators get worried about. The subsequent discussion in this section of the paper speculates on the possible structure of the securities markets in India that is likely to emerge in the next couple of years. Whether it is an excessive speculation or not may be judged by the readers of this paper themselves. In order to make a reasonable forecast it is essential that some existing facts be considered and analysed. It is in this context that the following are noteworthy.

The Favoured Lot

NSE and OTCEL are the only exchanges where the Government has a stake through the holdings of financial institutions and other public bodies such as insurance corporations and commercial banks. This is bound to result in positive support to the two exchanges by the Government and the regulators (particularly SEBI). We have already seen it in the speed at which these exchanges have grown. Besides, there have been some hard hitting rulings for the BSE such as the ban on renewals in the 'B' group; ban on Government securities broking; the embargo on forward trading (without the introduction of an alternative system); and SEBI making it compulsory for all interbank securities deals to be conducted through NSE brokers. These would indirectly turn into positive benefits for NSE's business volume in the future.

A Strong List

If the present listing of securities, and the criteria of selection thereof, in the Capital Market Segment of the NSE is any guide then we can expect that the larger and the better of the Indian Companies would ultimately find their way on the scripcard of NSE. This would result in high volumes and turnovers at the NSE in the not-so distant future.

A Good Start

The first session of trading at NSE gave it a turnover of approximately Rs. 9 crores. Presently, the average daily turnover amounts to Rs. 7 to 8 crores. All this has been achieved only with approximately 200 scrips being traded and even when the national trading network has not yet commenced its operations. Given the expected expansion (both of the number of scrips and the network) the NSE could definitely witness volumes as large as BSE if not larger. Also consider the shift of business from BSE to NSE.

The "Multi-segment" Exchange

In the words of Dr. R.H. Patil, the managing director of NSE, there are going to be multiple segments, debt, hybrids and later, options—where NSE could be like a departmental store. Add to this the fact that NSE would be accessible nationally for almost all categories of investors. That definitely is a pointer towards increased volumes for the NSE in the future.

Inclination of BSE Members

Fifty percent of the membership of the NSE presently consists of those who are also members at BSE. This may be a pointer towards the expectation of the traders about NSE's pivotal role in the securities markets in the days to come.

A thoughtful consideration of the above facts about the present functioning is certainly suggesstive of the on coming revamp of the securities markets.

NSE A'LA NYSE

Firstly, the NSE may emerge as the nodal and the pivotal stock exchange of the country which provides nationwide (and later globe wide) accessibility to investors in the scrips which are most frequently traded. At the same time, OTCEL is likely to emerge as the nodal national (and later global given its agreement with NASDAQ of US) exchange for scrips at the lower end, essentially performing a complementary role to NSE. These developments would mean that the BSE is relegated to a lower level SE in the country (may be a strong regional exchange)—a reversal of fortune for the BSE. These changes would imply that we could be looking at three tier securities markets structure: NSE, OTCEL, BSE and other regional exchanges (such as DSE, MSE, ASE and others). This would be a structure very similar to that in the US, *viz.* the NYSE,

OTC, NASDAQ, AMEX and other regional exchanges (such as Midwest Stock Exchange, Pacific Stock Exchange, Philadelphia Stock Exchange, Boston Stock Exchange and Cincinnati Stock Exchange). That definitely shows that NSE stands to be a major beneficiary of the process of modernisation in the securities markets.

Automation Wouia Come of Age

Secondly, with screen based trading in stocks already in place on the NSE and OTCEL, and phased introduction likely on the BSE, the face of the Indian securities markets is likely to see a major change. A higher degree of transparency, better and faster liquidity, national access (in the case of NSE and OTCEL) on a real time, on line basis, trading in stocks stripped of delays in settlement and ownership transfers, reduced transaction costs and eradication of risks associated with physical handling of securities (once depositories come into place) would be the benefits of screen based trading, and that is as broad a canvass of benefits as any investor could have desired for. With NSE and OTCEL giving a high quality alternative, the other exchanges would also have to fall in the fast, and given the raw deal to the investors till now, that would be a most welcome change.

Global Networking Likely

Thirdly, the emerging structure could well become global. For instance, globally, trillions of dollars are transacted through computerised trading systems. These connect all the major financial centres of the World—New York, London, Tokyo, Frankfurt, and Singapore. Similarly, networks facilitate global transactions in securities as well. With NSE and OTCEL pitched as the network markets, it is only a matter of time (given the changes required for capital flows across the borders) when they could provide for a creation of global markets in India and for India.

Derivatives May not be Far

Fourthly, the days may not be far when the new structure of the markets in India gives a rise to trading in equity and debt derivatives (such as options and futures). Today derivatives account for over 75 per cent of financial market activity in Europe, North America and East Asia. The main advantage of such derivatives markets is seen as the transparency they bring to the speculative activity and the scope they provide for hedging and limiting risks. With the creation of screen based transparent trading systems in the securities markets of India, the derivative instruments are bound to see the light of the day in our country.

THE EFFICACY OF THE EMERGING STRUCTURE

Active Trading and Market continuity

One of the most valuable services performed by securities markets is to maintain active trading so that investors can buy or sell securities immediately at a price that varies little from the previous selling price. Although the creation of a new exchange such as NSE would, in the short run, increase price arbitravges, once the national system is in place, a continuous and nationwide market would emerge which would support active and continuous trading.

Prices Closer to Intrinsic Value

The existence of securities markets also facilitates the price discovery process. Price is determined by buy and sell orders that flow from investor's demand and supply preference. In addition, when securities markets publicly disseminate their prices, this information helps the nation allocate its financial resources more efficiently. With the advent of screen-based trading and on-line, real-time information transfers across the country through the telephone/satellite network, the security prices would be more reflective of the underlying intrinsic value rather than being largely affected by the market sentiment as is the case now. This then would be an obvious economic benefit for the nation.

Liquidity and Choice and New Financing

Securities markets indirectly aid new financing. If it is easy for investors to trade securities in a liquid securities market, they are more willing to invest in Initial Public Offerings (IPOs) which finance the economic growth. As is proposed by NSE and OTCEL, and as is also substantiated by a reasonably good start for these exchanges, the evolving structure could be expected to greatly enhance the liquidity (and also the depth and the breadth) and the choices in the securities markets for the investor. Obviously, then the investor finds it much easier to hold and transact securities resulting in increased financing towards economic growth.

Addressing the Investor

Investors in the Indian Stock Markets have been beleaguered by numerous problems such as execution of transaction at 'not the best price', clubbing of price and brokerage making it impossible for them to check out on the correct price of transactions, a long delay in realisation of sale proceeds, forged certificates and delays in delivery of certificates to name just a few. It would be crucial for the securities markets structure to address these problems and seek solutions, if they are to be seen as efficient and useful structures. With the idea of screen based trading catching up (with the advent of NSE and OTCEL) and depositories likely to emerge in the near future, the investors may be in for better times. This definitely suggests an improved securities markets structure and system, the way it is evolving.

7

Recent Trends in the Primary Markets: An Overview

M.R. Murthy and K.S. Chatapati Rao

The period since 1991 has witnessed a tremendous growth both in terms of market capitalisation of listed shares and the activity in the primary market. The withdrawal of restrictions on fresh investments in a number of areas and the booming secondary market appear to have contributed to the fast growth of the primary market. The profiles of investors, promoters and intermediaries are also changing over the period. In this paper an attempt has been made to identify the major characteristics of the primary market in 1993-94 and the emerging trends. The analysis is focussed mainly on the public issues made during 1993-94. For purposes of this exercise rights issues were not taken into account unless these were also accompanied by public offer of shares or debentures, etc. Data for the tabulations was taken from the various issues of the *Prime Annual Report*.

Growth of Primary Capital Market

The primary market has witnessed a phenomenal increase during 1993-94 both in terms of amount raised through public issue and the number of issues as compared to the previous year. The total amount planned to be raised by the companies during 1993-94 was Rs. 17,226.23 crores. Out of this, an amount of Rs. 2424.62 crores were allotted on firm basis. An additional amount of Rs. 2257.50 crores was to be mobilised on rights basis. Thus the amount offered through prospectus was Rs. 12544.04 crores. The total public issue (TPI) amount analysed here is the amount issued through prospectus and it excludes amounts reserved on firm allotment basis and as rights. While the number of companies which entered the capital market increased from 528 in 1992-93 to 770 in 1993-94 there is more than doubling in the amount offered through prospectuses. The amount offered through prospectuses during 1993-94 was more than twice the corresponding figure for 1992-93. *Table 7.1* shows that the amount raised through public issues during 1993-94 exceeded the combined figure of the previous four years which works out to Rs. 12,449.80 crores.

Table 7.1—Growth of the Public Issue of Capital

Rs. Crores

Year	*Total No. of Cos. which went to Public Issue*	*Amount offered through Prospectus*
1987-88	122	1627.7
1988-89	150	1291.74
1989-90	187	2793.26
1990-91	141	1704.35
1991-92	196	1711.36
1992-93	528	6060.83
1993-94	770	12544.04

Status of Issues

Of the total 770 companies which entered the market during 1993-94, 473 were existing companies and the remaining 297 companies entered the market for the first time. More than 60 per cent of the total public issues amount was raised by the existing companies. The quarter-wise analysis suggests the market showed a buoyancy in April and moved downward between May-August. During the first six months 244 issues entered the market with an amount of Rs. 4,742.66 crores. The turn around came during the last two quarters as 526 companies went to the market with an aggregate amount of Rs. 7,801.38 crores.

Instrument-wise Analysis of Issues

Of the total 778 instruments issued by 770 companies during 1993-94, which sought to raise Rs. 12,544.04 crores through public offer of capital, almost one-third was through equity at premium. As many as 199 issues out of 778 instruments were issued at premium.

The share of equity at par issued was 17.2 per cent and only single issue of Triple Option Convertible Debenture (Reliance Petroleum Ltd.) accounted for 17.3 per cent of total amount offered through public issues.

Taxable Bonds accounted for 11.38, Partly Convertible Debentures 9.58, and Fully Convertible Debentures, Deep Discounted Bonds, Optionally Fully Convertible Debentures etc. have accounted for the balance 48 per cent of total public issue amount. (*See Table 7.2*).

Table 7.2—Instrument-wise Issues made during 1993-94

Instrument	*No. of Instruments 1993-94*	*Total Issue Amount 1993-94 (Rs. Cr.)*
Equity at Par	514	2,154.13
Equity at Premium	199	4,033.56
TOCD	1	2,172.00
Taxable Bonds	6	1,420.00
PCD	24	1,188.00
FCD	23	1,067.60
Deep Discounted Bonds	1	150.00
NCD	1	150.00
Other Instruments	9	208.75
Total	**778**	**12,544.04**

In the new era of liberal free pricing it was observed that the companies have charged premium on the issues accordingly to their ability to market the issues. Out of 199 premium equity issues 87 issues charged premium upto Rs. 10, 84 issues between more than 10 rupees and upto Rs. 50.00 and 24 issues charged premium ranging from more than Rs. 50 to 100. The companies which charged more than Rs. 100 as premium were: Ballarpur Industries Ltd. (Rs. 165.00), Core Parentarals (Rs. 140.00), Godrej Soaps (Rs. 130.00), IPCA Laboratories (Rs. 120.00) and BPL and Triveni Engineering (Rs. 100.00) each.

The average size of the public issue in 1993-94 was Rs. 16.29 crores compared to Rs. 11.49 crores in 1992-93 and Rs. 8.73 crores in 1991-92. It is significant to note that 122 companies were for Rs. 10 crores and above. These issues accounted for four-fifths of tne total public issue amount. On the contrary, 250 companies with public issue amount of less than Rs. 3.00 crores accounted for only 4.59 per cent of total public offer.

Table 7.3—Size-wise Distribution of Public Issues

Public Issue Range (Rs. Crs.)	*No. of Cos.*	*% age of Col. 2*	*Public Issues Amount (Rs. Cr.)*	*% age of Col. 4*
(1)	(2)	(3)	(4)	(5)
Rs. 1 & below	12	1.56	8.37	0.07
Rs. 1 to Rs. 3	247	32.08	567.57	4.52
Rs. 3 to Rs. 5	236	30.65	886.91	7.07
Rs. 5 to Rs. 10	153	19.87	1,020.59	8.14
Rs. 10 Cr. & above	122	15.84	10,060.60	80.20
Total	**770**	**100.00**	**12,544.04**	**100.00**

Industry-wise Analysis

The companies were grouped using the Reserve Bank of India use-based classification. The results of this exercise are given in *Table 7.4*. It can be seen that intermediate goods industries accounted for nearly 30% of the total public issue amount. next importance is the financial services sector. Of the total public issue amount more than 25% of the amount raised from the public has gone to companies engaged in financial services. Consumer non-durable industries like personal care products, drugs and pharmaceuticals, textiles and food processing industries etc. are those which proved to be attractive for investment purpose. (These industries accounted for more than 21% of the total amount raised through public issue). On the other hand new investment in capital goods, consumer durable industries through public issues was very low (*i.e.* 2.62% and 1.76% of total Public Issue) during 1993-94.

Table 7.4—Industry-wise Distribution of Public Issues

Description Range (Rs. Crs.)	*No. of Cos.*	*%age of Col. 2*	*Total Public Issue Amount*	*%age of Col. 4*
(1)	(2)	(3)	(4)	(5)
Basic Industries	76-	9.87	1,890.87	15.07
Capital Goods Industries	57	7.40	328.17	2.62
Intermediate Goods Industries	220	28.57	3,756.43	29.95
Consumer Durables	18	2.34	220.48	1.76
Consumer Non-durables	296	38.44	2,658.67	21.19
Financial Services	71	9.22	3,191.15	25.44
Miscellaneous (NES)	32	4.16	498.28	3.97
Total	**770**	**100.00**	**12,544.04**	**100.00**

Even if one looks at from individual industry point of view, financial services topted the list of industries in terms of amount offered. Next in importance was Oil Refining and allied activities. The high of intermediate goods can thus be explained. Next in importance were textiles, power generation, iron and steel, drugs and pharmaceuticals. However, if we look from the number of companies point of view, textiles stood at the top with 95 companies followed by financial services (71), drugs and pharmaceuticals (55), iron and steel (42).

Regional Distribution of Issues

Regional distribution of companies which went to public can be analysed either by plant location or according to the place of registered office. Of the 770 companies which came to the public during 1993-94., 160 companies' plants were located in Gujarat followed by Maharashtra (141), Andhra Pradesh (76), Madhya Pradesh (54), Uttar Pradesh (50), Tamil Nadu (47) and Haryana (38). If we take registered office addresses, Maharashtra accounted for the highest number of companies followed by Gujarat (137), Delhi (102), Andhra Pradesh (75), Tamil Nadu (57) and West Bengal (45). In terms of plant locations, Western Zone accounted for 448 of the total issues followed by North Zone (298), South Zone (238) and East Zone (48). On the other hand, in terms of registered offices of companies west and north zones accounted for more than 708 of total public issues made during the year.

Firm and Preferential Allotment

The total capital issues off by a company may be of firm and preferential allotment to promoters, promoters group companies, financial institutions, foreign collaborators, NRI's and employees etc., and general public in addition to rights issue to the existing shareholders of the company.

Firm Allotment : The total amount planned to be raised by the companies during 1993-94 was Rs. 17.226.23 crores. Of this an amount of Rs. 2,257.56 crores was issued on rights basis, Rs. 6,472.35 crores through firm and preferential allotment basis and the balance 8,496.31 crores was to be raised from the general investing public (*see Table 7.5*). The share of private promoters or their group companies in the issues through firm allotment aggregated to Rs. 1,872.27 crores during 1993-94 against Rs. 1,271.28 crores in 1992-93 and Rs. 272.87 crores during 1991-92. Thus, the net amount offered to general public after preferential allotment was Rs. 8,496.31 crores constituting more than two-thirds of the TPI. This was considerably lower than the amount offered to general public during the last two years (83% in 1992-93 and 82% in 1991-92). The amount reserved on preferential basis for promoters/shareholders of promoter companies was Rs. 411.28 crores (3.28%) of the total amount offered through public issue. Employees had a share of only 0.8%. Foreign banks/FIIs had a preferential reservation in 60 issues amounting to Rs. 439.73 crores (3.5%). Mutual Funds and Financial Institutions had accounted for a significant share of Rs. 2,233.74 crores in the issues constituting 17.8% of the total public issue amount. In all 450 issues had reserved an amount of Rs. 867.72 crores for non-resident investors (*i.e.* a share of 6.8%) in total public issue amount offered during 1993-94.

Issues Involving Offers to NRIs

The Non-Resident Indians (NRIs) participation in the primary capital market through both firm and preferential placements has been increasing over the last three years. During 1993-94 NRIs had a preferential participation in 405 out of the total 770 companies as compared to 125 in 1992-93, and 32 in 1991-92. The 405 issues involving NRI participation in 1993-94 included 288 equity at par issues, 90 equity at premium issues, 14 fully convertible debenture issues, 11 partly convertible debenture issues and 2 CCPS issues. The total amount offered to the NRIs in 1993-94 was higher by 170% at Rs. 867.72 crores compared to Rs. 322.70 crores in 1992-93. The corresponding offerings in 1991-92 and 1990-91 were only Rs. 71.70 crores and Rs. 92.76 crores respectively. The share of NRIs in the total public issue amount was 6.92% in 1993-94 against 5.32% in 1992-93 and 4.19% in 1991-92 (*see Table 7.6*).

The largest amount offered to the NRIs was that in the issue of Chambal Fertilizers (Rs. 42.40 crores). This was followed by BSES (Rs. 42.00 crores), Madras Refineries (Rs. 33.17 crores), Core Parenterals (Rs. 31.55 crores), Jindal Iron (Rs. 27.00 crores) and Modern Syntex (Rs. 25.50 crores). As many as 328 of the 405 companies had reserved less than Rs. 2 crores for NRIs.

Looked from a lightly different angle, one finds that the total inflow of funds from foreign sources (collaborators, financial institutions, banks, and NRIs), through promoters contribution or preferential allotments in 1993-94 was Rs. 1575.12 crores against Rs. 572.41 crores in 1992-93, Rs. 172.46 crores in 1991-92, and Rs. 148.71 crores in 1990-91. NRIs was the single largest source of foreign investment through public issues aggregating to Rs. 965.32 crores followed by foreign financial institutions and banks at Rs. 523.74 crores. Direct participation by the foreign collaborators was only of the order of Rs. 86.06 crores. 53 companies out of the total 770 had foreign financial collaboration as compared 29

Table 7.5—Firm and Preferential Allotment of Shares

Year	*Private Promoters*	*Private Placements*	*SFIs*	*FCs*	*MFs/FIs*	*FFIs/ Banks*	*NRIs*	*Emplo- yees*
Firm								
1990-91	219.85	—	26.69	21.57	41.14	4.51	27.48	21.49
1991-92	272.87	32.70	51.21	57.41	31.53	5.41	26.42	9.99
1992-93	1271.28	50.65	52.28	196.69	69.19	7.73	30.86	25.34
1993-94	1872.27	10.00	61.87	86.07	203.96	84.00	97.60	8.85
Preferential								
1990-91	178.77				145.58	2.39	92.76	105.12
1991-92	63.88				59.63	11.52	71.70	105.71
1992-93	395.57				134.28	6.84	322.10	182.48
1993-94	411.28				2233.74	439.73	867.72	95.26
Total : Firm and Preferential								
1990-91	398.62	—	26.69	21.57	186.72	6.90	120.24	126.61
1991-92	336.75	32.70	51.21	57.41	91.16	16.93	98.12	115.70
1992-93	1664.85	50.65	52.28	196.69	203.47	14.57	361.96	207.82
1993-94	2283.55	10.00	61.87	86.07	2437.70	523.73	965.32	104.11
Percentages								
1990-91	23.38	—	1.57	1.27	10.95	0.40	7.05	7.43
1991-92	19.68	1.91	2.99	3.35	5.33	0.99	5.73	6.76
1992-93	27.47	0.84	0.86	3.25	3.36	0.24	5.97	3.43
1993-94	18.20	0.08	0.49	0.69	19.43	4.10	7.70	0.83

Note : The row totals do not add up to the total because the net public offer is not shown here.

Table 7.6—NRI Participation in the Primary Issues

Year	*No. of Companies*	*Public Issues*	*No. of Issues NRI Participated*	*Reservation Rs/Crs*	*Col. 3 as % of Col. 1*	*Col 4 as % of Co. 2*
	(1)	(2)	(3)	(4)	(5)	(6)
1989-90	187	2793.60	32	183.00	17.11	6.55
1990-91	141	1704.35	22	92.76	15.60	5.44
1991-92	196	1711.36	32	71.70	16.33	4.19
1992-93	528	6060.83	125	322.70	23.67	5.32
1993-94	770	12544.04	405	867.72	57.86	6.92

in 1992-93, 22 in 1991-92, and 18 in 1990-91. On the other hand, as many as 146 companies had foreign technical collaboration/assistance agreements in 1993-94. The corresponding figures for 1992-93, 1991-92 and 1990-91 were 100,65 and 67 respectively.

Participation by Mutual Funds

A major development during the year was that the reserved categories were gaining importance over the general public. One of the important constituents of the reserved categories was the mutual funds. In as many as 450 companies, one or more mutual funds participated either on a firm basis (prior to public issue) or on a preferential basis (reserved out of the issue amount). The total amount reserved for the mutual funds under firm/preferential basis was Rs. 2437.77 crores compared to Rs. 203.47 crores in 1992-93, Rs. 91.16 crores in 1991-92 and Rs. 186.72 crores in 1990-91 (*Table 7.7*). Of this, Rs. 203.98 crores was on firm basis and Rs. 2233.74 crores was on preferential basis. During 1993-94 the highest participation by mutual funds was made in the cases of Reliance Petroleum Ltd. (Rs. 868.80 crores), followed by the State Bank of India (Rs. 490.00 crores), Sardar Sarovar Nigam (Rs. 200 crores), Madras Refineries Ltd. (Rs. 94.77 crores), Modern Syntex (Rs. 73.20 crores), BSES (Rs. 52.50 crores), IFCI (Rs. 52.50 crores), ATV Petrochem (Rs. 35 crores) and Metazinc (Rs. 29.78 crores).

Table 7.7—Extent of Participation of Mutual Funds in Public Issues

Amount in Rs. Crore

Year	*No. of Cos.*	*Public Issue*	*Reservation for MFs*		*Col 3 as % of Col. 1*	*Col. 4 as % of Col. 2*
			No. of Amount	*Amount*		
	1	2	3	4	5	6
1990-91	141	1704.35	91	186.72	64.54	10.96
1991-92	196	1711.36	48	91.16	24.49	5.33
1992-93	528	6060.83	118	203.47	22.35	3.36
1993-94	770	12544.04	450	2437.72	64.29	19.43

Trends in Underwriting of Issues

The primary capital market is slowly moving towards zero underwriting commission. Although the underwriting of issues is no longer mandatory, companies in general prefer underwriting since it creates confidence in the minds of investors. Smaller companies accessing the market cannot afford to dispense with underwriting as they are either new or little known to the investing public. Even the larger companies who charge high premium on issues may not have guaranteed success and hence may prefer to get the amount underwritten. The contingent underwriting of issues ensures that merchant bankers take up the issue in case of development.

In the emerging new policy environment, the Development Financial Institutions/banks (DFI) have been facing stiff competition to underwrite issues from merchant bankers and brokers. Though the merchant bankers do not have adequate capital base as compared to the DFIs, they have better placement power and are able to get higher premium to their customers through extensive broker network. While the brokers are still receiving underwriting offers, there have been a significant reduction in the volume of amount underwritten. *Table 7.8* shows that the share of underwriting by private merchant bankers and brokers increased from 6.29 per cent to 20.14 per cent and 43.94 per cent to 49.31 per cent respectively, during the period 1991-92 and 1993-94. The combined share of the two categories of underwriters in total public issue amount underwritten was 70 per cent in 1993-94 against 50 per cent in 1991-92. The role of merchant bankers and brokers in underwriting new issues has increased sharply from 30 per cent to 70 per cent during the last two years. On the other hand, the share of DFIs and banks in underwriting of new issues declined from 34.06 per cent in 1991-92 to 23.72 per cent in 1993-94. The share of banks declined from

Table 7.8—Public Issues Underwritten by different Categories of Underwriters

(Amount in Rs. Cr.)

Category (1)	*1991-92* (2)	*1992-93* (3)	*1993-94* (4)
1. All India Financial Institutions	244.87	1440.55	1812.94
	(14.31)	(23.78)	(14.45)
2. State Level Institutions	3.38	45.19	48.49
	(0.20)	(0.75)	(0.39)
3. Nationalised Banks & Subs.	337.95	1313.34	1161.20
	(19.75)	(21.68)	(9.26)
4. Foreign Banks	184.75	325.04	384.71
	(10.80)	(5.36)	(3.07)
5. Private Banks	80.81	233.09	124.54
	(4.72)	(3.85)	(0.99)
6. Private Merchant Bankers	107.59	606.58	2526.72
	(6.29)	(10.01)	(20.14)
7. Brokers	751.99	2094.84	6185.43
	(43.94)	(34.58)	(49.31)
Total Public Issue	1711.36	6058.63	12544.04
	(100.00)	(100.00)	(100.00)

Note : Figures in brackets are percentages to the respective column totals

19.75 per cent to 9.26 per cent during the same period. It is possible that financial institutions may be underwriting those issues to which they have extended either project finance or bridge loan.

Response to the Public Issues

The public response to the issue is an important factor determining the promoters' ability to mobilise funds from the investing public. Public issue amount refers to the amount which is being offered to general public through prospectus leaving aside all firm and preferential allotments which may be referred to as net public offer. During 1993-94, 770 companies made the net public offer of Rs. 8,496.31 crores. Of these data on issue responses was available to us for 757 issues.

It appears that response from the investing public to new issues was low during 1993-94 as compared to previous period in terms of over subscription. Nearly 12 per cent of the 757 issues were subscribed more than 10 times and 27 per cent issues by more than 3 times. On the other hand, in case of large number of issues, subscription was less than 1.5 times. If one takes this as poor response, besides 18 cases of development on underwriters, *i.e.* more than half, as many as 403 issues fall in this category during 1993-94. The issues which got poor response had increased from 4.35 per cent in 1991-92 to 53.24 in 1993-94 (*Table 7.9*).

Table 7.9—Overall Response to Public Issues

No. of Times Subscribed	*1991-92*	*1992-93*	*1993-94*	*% Share in total* *1991-92*	*1992-93*	*1993-94*
Development Issues	—	38	18	—	7.24	2.38
1.5 times & below	9	155	403	4.35	29.52	53.24
1.5 to 3 times	13	89	126	6.28	16.95	16.65
3 to 10 times	60	154	120	28.98	29.34	15.85
More than 10 times	125	89	90	60.39	16.95	11.89
Total	**207**	**525**	**757**	**100.00**	**100.00**	**100.00**

Note : Response data for the available issues only given.

There can be various reasons for poor response to issues. The possible reasons for this may be depressed secondary market, free issue pricing, bunching, large number of issues and poor quality of issues. Investors enthusiasm for equity at par issues also seems to have declined during the year. Nearly 63 per cent of equity at par and only 39 per cent of premium issues were subscribed less than 1.5 times. On the other hand 65 per cent of the partly convertible debentures, 45 per cent of premium issues and 19.56 per cent of equity at par issues got response of more than 3 times. Size-wise analysis shows that out of 21 mega issues worth Rs. 50 crores and above, 9 issues got less than 1.5 times, 46 per cent of the issues in the size range of Rs. 10 to 50 crores, were subscribed more than 3 times. Of the lower size issues (below Rs. 10 crores), 89 per cent got poor response. Surprisingly, the response to the existing companies (463) and new companies (294) was almost similar. Industry-wise response to issues reveals a mixed trend except for the financial sector which had a better response rate.

8

Some Quaint Facets of Management

R.P. Billimoria

Management has many an erudite definition. We shall define it simply as that function which formulates policy and gears the organisation to achieve its mission-objectives motive. 'The emphasis is on Mission-Objectives' not on minor objectives. But is this abundantly clear?

In our experience we found that in many of the organisations in public sector (where later on work was done by FORE) even the top management was not clear about the mission and objectives. In fact in one of the public sector organisations an exercise was out by FORE Researchers and it was observed that 12 managers provide 12 different definitions of mission. In terms of FORE's theory this is known as mission confusion which led to great deal of Fittering of effort, working to counter objectives and finally adversely affecting the integration.

Issues of Concern

Another quaint facet is on the perceived prioritisation of major issues. A recent survey was conducted among 34 organisations in the public sector —25 centrally owned and nine owned by State Governments—and 31 from the private sector out of which 20 were limited companies, 10 multinationals and one, a family business. The survey revealed that among the top-level executives there is a high concern with the growth of individuals in terms of their appraisals and reward systems (n = 50) and for career planning (n = 15), but no mention was made by them of any concern over growth of the individuals in other areas, Training and Development, for example, found no mention.

The top executives identified major issues of importance to them, in the order given in Table 8 :

Table 8.1 : Issues in Organisation Structure

Issues	*No. of responses out of a total of 181*
Distribution of Authority	47
Basis of Accountability	37
Coordination and Control	33
Line and Staff	20
Roles and Positions	19
Level and Span of Control	16
Expansion and Growth	6
Miscellaneous	3

It is interesting to note in this table, that 'expansion and growth' features last. Why is this so? It is lamentable but it is no use lamenting it. What is the weakness in our system which makes our top executives concern themselves primarily with authority and accountability and put such low value on a factor like expansion and growth which is the raiseon d'tre of their existence?

These are some of the issues you would like to think about. In doing so you are likely to come across the problem of keeping up with the newer methodologies and techniques as also the newer concepts of the younger generation on their own role in business, industry and Government.

Harnessing Creativity

In this exercise you have also to ensure that technical or managerial obsolescence does not catch up with you and those working along side you. And then as per the definition given earlier, you have to 'gear' those working under you to achieve the 'mission objectives'.

We now ask the question, are we taking all possible steps in getting the maximum out of those working within our orbit? Take for example, the harnessing of suggestions and ideas of employees and supervisors.

Let us see what is happening elsewhere. Toyota's example is before us; it is recorded that during 1981, 1.4 million suggestions were submitted by Toyota employees corresponding to about 30.5 per worker per year, and of these, 94 per cent were accepted. You will agree that in India, with the best of organisation either in the public sector or in the private sector the number of effective suggestions per year would not even touch the level of 0.1 per worker per year. You would do well to interact among yourselves in order to discover what more can be done to harness this great power that rests in your hands.

On the Training Conundrum

There is so much lip service and so little actual service provided by training programmes that Foundation for Organisational Research conducted a study covering 50 organisations in the Central public sector. This was a perceptional study among executives all of whom agreed that there is a certain base level of knowledge, skills and attitudes which all executives must have. Those mailed the questionnaires were asked to express the extent of gaps existing in knowledge, skills and attitudinal aspect of the existing training programmes across top, senior, middle and junior management levels.

The ranks in the areas perceived to have gaps in order of importance are given in the Table 8.2 :

Table 8.2 : Gaps in Existing Training Programme in Order of Priority

1 = Largest gap;
6 = Least gap

	Levels of Management			
Gap Areas	*Top*	*Senior*	*Middle*	*Junior*
Knowledge in the functional area	6	6	1	4.5
Leadership & Human Relations	4	2	3	2
Managerial skills (Planning Organising Coordinating)	2	1	2	3
Job-related attitudes (Responsibility, ability to manage boss and shop floor workers)	5	5	5	1
Attitude-General (Relevance of Attitudes & Value of Indian Culture, Social Responsibility)	1	3	6	6
Team Work	3	4	4	4.5

Findings of perceptions reveal that

- Irrespective of the areas, gaps increased mostly with the decrease in level from top to junior. Is this real or is it wishful thinking on the part of the respondents?
- Major gap was in the attitudinal training, development of team spirit and leadership among top level.
- Developing managerial skills, leadership and human relations was the major gap for the senior level.
- Major gap for the middle level was in the functional areas, develop-

ing managerial skills and in team building training.

— Major gap for junior level managers was knowledge and training for job related activities.

These findings of FORE's Research study, were discussed at a National Seminar and the Working Groups suggested the following action plan which I commend for your consideration.

Suggested Action Plan

In order to make the training a success, the training function must be supported with commitment from those who are running the organisation. Indeed it needs to be an integral part of the running of the organisation since training is a major factor in establishing the levels of effectiveness of component parts of the system, its people.

A systematic approach to programme planning of analysing training needs is the need of the hour so that all the training activities in an organisation are integrated, namely they take place in the right perspective in terms of the needs of the organisation, needs of the trainee and the availability of resources. Thus a Human Resource Devclopment Cell needs to be created which has a scientific orientation towards training and which undertakes research work on a regular basis to bring about innovation.

Most stress should be laid on the training for attitudinal change of the managers at all levels.

Training aids and methods need to be modernised.

Emphasis on training of trainers should be given.

In fact a National Institute of Trainers should be set up which holds seminars and workshops on a regular basis to keep them updated in all areas.

Pooling of training programmes and faculty among the public sector units should be encouraged.

Being able to respond to the need for change is a matter of concern for the training department. It is the responsibility of training to monitor the changes in the organisation and the environment and help the organisation to deal with them effectively, causing minimum of disruption.

Performance appraisal system should have a development outlook and it should reflect the training needs of the organisation.

The study and findings apply not only to the public sector but to all other sectors where, you may be sure, similar studies in detail have not been conducted. May it be reiterated that in training as in all other functions those who wield power in another organisation play a critical role. Unless they support the activity it will not achieve its objectives.

On Wiedling of Power

Talking of wielding power, herein lies not only a quaint, but one of the most serious weaknesses of normal managers. I would like to acquaint you with the little experiments that I had made and other research done in the world in this dangerous area of self-hypnosis of power.

What happens to a manager, when he gets into the seat of power? I was going through my old diary. In the late forties or early fifties when I was a worker as supervisor and a line manager in a large undertaking, I have written about certain aberrations in the attitude of those who look to be normal decent people, the moment they sat in a seat of power. Alright, keep that at the back of the mind. And then, in 1951-53 when I was doing my research in a British University, I spoke to some of my colleagues about the attrocities that were reported widely in the press during World War II supposedly in concentration camps and elsewhere by the Germans and the Japanese; and my colleague in the research department said, that is what we have read in the papers, "but do not forget the Americans and we the British, were not totally free of guilt during this period". And he also pleaded some personal guilt when he was in the army of occupation. I asked him why? What made you do it? And I quote his answer; he said, "It was some kind of compulsion, some Hyde in me, which made me find a massochistic outlet, an urge to exhibit and exercise my power". Keep this remark in mind.

Then in August 1971, there was a publication by Stanford, *Prison Experiment : A simulation of the study of the Psychology of Imprisonment"*. What happened was this, White and Zimbrardo collected a random group of people who were considered as normal human beings. They told them that we are conducting some prison experiments. "Half of you on a random basis will be prisoners and half of you will be guards". And simulated prison surroundings were created in certain area of the Psychology Department in the University Campus. Mr. Zimbrardo assumed the role of the "Warden". The 'prisoners' and the 'guards' were let loose on each other. This was on a Saturday, and by Sunday evening, the 'guards' started behaving abnormally and unduly cruelly towards the prisoners. Conditions became so chaotic that within four days the experiment had to be promptly terminated not only because of the behaviour of the 'guards' but Zimbrardo said that he was himself very adversely and mentally affected in his capacity as the 'Warden'.

Three years later, Yale University conducted a study called *"Obedience to Authority—An Experimental View"* published by Harper and Row, New York and there, Stanley Milgram of Yale University again collected a group of normal people and told them that he wanted their participation in some tests on obedience. He told them that he had collected a random group of people and an 'authority figure' will order each of them to give electricshocks to members of the random group. These shocks will be either mild, severe, or very severe. Ninety percent of them in writing said that they were agreeable to this experiment but were not going to obey anyone asking them to give very severe electric stock to fellow human beings. Milgram said, alright, start the experiments.

The trick in this was that people who were to be given the electric shock were not a random group but the University's own men, and there was no electric current in the shock giving apparatus. When the Man of Authority asked a man from the first group to start giving mild shocks to the second or planted group, they not only obeyed, but started giving severe shocks as well. Yale changed the experiment, by putting a transparent screen partition started shouting and screaming when the 'current' was turned on. Even so, the shock giver enjoyed inflicting pain and torment.

Milgram could not come to a specific solution and asked the following questions : Is this something genetic in a human being? Is there species survival value in heirarchy? And does authority lead us all to submit or are people simply sadistic? He concluded most generously that our culture has failed almost entirely in inculcating internal controls on actions that have their origins in authority.

Why I went into all these details is to emphasise that something does happen to us when we sit in the official chair of power. Once you realise that something abnormal is happening to normal people when they sit on this chair, then you are prepared to guard against this abnormality creeping into you. You become a little more of a decent human being, to your peers and your subordinates. How do you do that? It is in this area of behavioural sciences that I have said our post graduate institutions, research institutions, should conduct more and more research and I am sure, you will be able to give valuable inputs to them in the study of the quaint facet of the self-hypnosis of power that takes place in managers and actions of industry.

On Quaint Facets of Appraisal Systems

It is not power alone that causes aberration. Recent studies on appraisal of bomber crew by the Commander of the aircraft gives some interesting side-lights. Some years ago, it was found that whereas the cluster of crew located around the Commander got high ratings, the person in the 'tail' consistently got a relatively lower rating. Raising of recruitment standards, increased training effort and higher emoluments did not result in any change in the rating pattern over a period of time. Did the Commander give the relatively lower rating to the tail gunner because he was physically farther away from him? If so, what are the implications for multi-unit companies where the appraiser in the Head Office is sitting far away from the appraisee in a distant unit?

Another interesting study was made in which the future prowess and success factor of research scholars, was forecast by the Professor in-charge; the group consisting of other researchers; and by their Assistants. Over a period of time it was found that the Professor and the Assistants to the researchers, were a little over 50% correct, whereas the peer group scored over 70% correct forecasts. What lessons do we learn from this in industry, business and Government?

To make appraisal a meaningful, development system and to harness employee creativity, referred to earlier, one needs to have second look at our formalised systems of worker participation.

On Creating a Reacting Participative Base (RPB)

In our own country and elsewhere we have observed and acknowledged the need for closer association of workers in order to make management effective.

To understand this need for a new look on human resource development we should get back to some fundamentals a little mathematics, perhaps. A number of natural phenomena as also the distribution of a large work force in terms of its effectiveness, are covered by, what is called normal probability distribution or simply normal distribution. The normal distribution or the normal probability curve is the famous bell-shaped curve. A number of natural occurences of normal distribution have been shown in the curve such as heights and weights of individuals and I.Q. As indicated in the bell-shaped curve, in every organisation, there are a few employees who are below standard and there are a few who are high fliers. In between is the 'hump' of the bell curve covering the large majority of average workers.

Since the onset of the industrial revolution our endeavours, generally copied from the Western countries, have been to eliminate the sub-standard and to put the high fliers in a position of power and authority with the greatest speed and despatch, as the total solution for effective management, leading to higher productivity and prosperity. Modern research has, however, indicated that in addition to weeding out the worst and encouraging the best, excellence is only reached by those organisations which concentrate mainly on the 'hump' or the large number of average workers, by training them, motivating them and making them associate or participate with management problems and processes.

But do we ensure this in the existing worker participation schemes of different kinds; with worker directors on the Board or elected or nominated worker representatives on joint bodies? No, this does not happen because irrespective of the method of selection of the workers' representative by election or by nomination, the level of representation at the Board level or at the unit level, the average workers' participation is vicarious or at best through periodic one way communication from the joint body. The hundreds or even thousands of other workers, nay, even supervisors and managers, are not involved and therefore, have no chance of reacting continually or being motivated, individually or en block, in the decision making or problem solving participative process. Hence the need for setting what I would call a Reacting Participative Board (RPB) to supplement and complement formal joint bodies set up by the organisation. The Reacting Participative Base will not be a formalised body meeting at regular intervals on a permanent basis to discuss items on a set agenda. Whenever there is a specific problem in a section or a department, not covering matters pertaining to collective bargaining or matters coming within the tradition management prerogatives such as relationship with shareholders, Government and top management, an RPB group will be constituted for action.

The head of the unit or department concerned will select a group of workers and supervisors, not necessarily in hierarchical sequence, who are acquainted with the problem and the environment in which it exists. The team may consist of six to ten people working together, in a given area against specific objectives such as reducing rejections, improving productivity, cost reduction or other aspects of work. The emphasis for this team is to get the job done and not to manufacture bulky reports. The team not only looks into problems and provides a solution but once the solution is discussed, modified and approved by management, it will also be associated in implementing it. Once this is done, the team is disbanded and so, on to the next problem and another group of people. Some teams may succeed and a few may not but if, say in a large organisation 50 such teams work for short durations in the year, you have about 500 employees feeling motivated in being associated with the problem solving and decision making process, as against hardly 40 or 50 who may be associated in formal joint committees.

This experiment has been tried out successfully in few foreign organisations and a couple of organisations in India as well.

The Myth of Consistency

Finally, we have also to get away from our two-dimensional attitude of mind. For example, we assume a consistent pattern of management, a consistent pattern of effectiveness or failure in an executive, over a period of time. Factually, this is not so. In the quality of performance and even the style an executive varies depending upon the interplay of several factors, in different time phases. Thus, variations may be effected by

Time cycles or bio-factors;

The environment, *vis-a-vis,* his home and emotional life;

The environment, *vis-a-vis,* his life at work and his interaction with his superiors, peer group and subordinates; and

The broad spectrum of total external environment.

Thus, even the neat curve of normal distribution may also take turns and twists in different plans and at different periods of time. We have to accept this and plan strategies for ourselves and the organisations accordingly.

Prof. David Mc Clelland of Harvard University who was recently in Delhi, emphasised yet again his theory that people are better achievers if they are thinking always of doing things better. He said that even low achievers can be transformed into high achievers if this thought could be implanted in their mind. The Japanese offer outstanding examples of how this theory works. Most firms have company songs and hymns which their employees sing before getting down to their job every day. This would raise guffaws among many Indian managers but believe me this has worked, even in India, in certain cases.

Prospect and Retrospect

Our own priorities as we see it and others see it; the external struggle with the onset of managerial obsolescence; the struggle with the self in avoiding the aberration of power; our limitations in appraising others; making workers' participation a live and all-pervasive system, and motivating ourselves and those who work under us.

The primary contribution of our getting together will be the input of synergy, rather than any pearls of wisdom spelt out by me. The grand cross-fertilisation of ideas among yourselves will surely generate scenarios of progress for the future.

9

Strategic Management and Managing Innovation : The Indian Challenge

Dharni P. Sinha

Homo Sapien, the wise man, arrived as the ultimate product of biological evolution, over 500,000 years ago. However, it is only in the last 10,000 years that human beings learned to conquer nature and create a new social order. The first major invention which transformed the life of human beings in this world was about 7000 B.C. when they discovered the art of domesticating the plants and animals. The consequence of this was a real change in the life styles of being nomads to settled communities. It gave rise to economic security; created a new form of social life based on cooperation rather than competition; group life instead of individualism; but most important was that it triggered a series of innovations which culminated in Alvin Toffler's 'second wave' towards the close of 1800 A.D. and what is called today, the industrial revolution. This revolution speeded by inventions in natural sciences, had equally far-reaching implications; changes in the world view from village self-sufficient economy to the market economy. No longer every village had to produce everything. Large-scale production of goods and services as a consequence of industrial revolution, converted isolated societies into inter-dependent communities. The social world further shrank and living standards further improved and values changed for *gemeinschaft* to *gesellschaft*. This was the beginning of a great transformation. This has further been speeded up by the third wave triggered by the inventions of micro chips; electronic and information revolution; which held its sway by 1970s. This wave has broken the barriers and the borders between societies, facilitated networking of nations and brought the globe within the reach of every human being. And now, when we are about to move into the twenty first century, human beings have almost perfected

Artificial Intelligence, perfected biotechnology; whereby it will be possible to create a human mind, generate human thoughts on computer, and create plants, animals and even human being to order. It is very difficult to visualise what all this will do to human society but it is certainly definite that it will have a far-reaching impact on the way human beings will live, grow, and perceive the world around themselves. Perhaps, three centuries ago, nobody could visualise the world we are in today. This is because of the human ingenuity to innovate, human beings' ability to convert resources into wealth, science into technology, imagination into reality; it has been a great leap for mankind.

One may ask the question that as an Indian citizen, are we touched by these? One can keep debating it but we cannot afford to escape it; we need to skip the stages and make a quantum jump to join the new world order.

Global Scene

The world is shrinking. Isolation which gave strength to some nations in the early part of this century has given way to interaction. The Soviet Union today is a good example of dismantling barriers between East and West. The 'Iron Curtain' is no longer desirable, perhaps not possible. What was good yesterday is no longer good today. In the fast changing world, the ideas and concepts, beliefs and values, and strategic thinking need to change.

In the last century, the size of a country, territory at its command, made a nation powerful. England became a great nation because it went on adding new colonies; so did Germany and France, and Soviet Union which added one Switzerland every year until World War II. However, today territory by itself no longer gives power to a nation. Canada and Argentina are alike in terms of territory but in terms of economic power, Canada is at least four times ahead of Argentina. What has made it so? Not the size of its territory but the use of technology. Technology is the emerging symbol of power today.

Towards the end of the last century, economists believed that capital was the most important determinant of the wealth of a nation. Today, capital in itself is of no consequence. What is of consequence is the productivity of capital, the capital-output ratio. I wonder if you know that India needs ten units of capital as against one unit of Japan to manufacture a watch, a radio or an automobile or steel. What gives today an edge to a society is not capital but the productivity of capital. And, productivity comes through management of human resources. It is the effectiveness of the management that gives the edge to a nation.

Some years ago, cheap labour was considered as an important asset for a nation; today it is not an important variable. Indian labour is cheap, a maximum of Rs. 15 an hour; Japanese labour costs Rs. 150 an hour; American labour costs Rs. 250 an hour; and yet, we are a low performing nation. We need 2,500 people to run a power plant which can be managed effectively by 250. What is required is not cheap labour but skilled labour, efficient labour, intelligent labour, motivated labour, committed labour, and achievement oriented innovative labour.

Likewise, there has been a radical change in the last 200 years in the concept of power. Before industrial revolution, muscle power was the real power. Soon, it was replaced by horsepower which was later translated into mechanical power, electrical power and nuclear power through harnessing of energy. Now, with the advent of artificial intelligence, even the brain power is being replaced by information power. By the turn of the twenty-first century, the whole concept of power would have undergone change. It would not be the size of the population or the size of the army or the number of warheads that one would have, but the sophistication of human intelligence and human ingenuity to process information that will determine the nature of power that one will enjoy. Strategic thinking will have to undergo change.

Science and Technology : Invention and Innovation

Let me make one more point. In the past, great societies have invested a lot of energy and resources in the development of science—basic science. However, science has not alone ensured development of society. In the 18th century, all great inventions took place in Western Europe including England. Yet, highest economic development was registered in the United States. Distinguished sociologist, Alex Tocqueville while writing about the American society, said that Americans were a nation of copiers; they copied what was invented in Europe and made better products than those who had invented them. He added that Americans borrowed science, converted it into technology and produced quality and more efficient goods and services which contributed to the rapid development of its society. Innovation was the key to the development of American society. The Japanese also received the epithet—a nation of borrowers and imitators. The Japanese commodities were marketed as "imitation goods, not worth their value." But today, the Japanese society, like the American society of yester-years, has captured the world economy; not by engineering scientific discoveries but by innovation, converting the scientific knowhow developed by others into useful technologies, which produce cameras, better watches, better automobiles, and better radios. What is required today for a developing country like India is not necessarily the discovery of basic truth, germane to science, but better technologies. There is no longer a negative value added to borrowing; borrow by all means but improve upon what you have borrowed from others. Great nations today are those who have focussed on the application of science, development of technology, which produce quality goods, competitive goods and thereby wealth for the nation. We in India need to get away from the luxury of science and invest ourselves in adopting innovating technologies which can directly influence the life and living of our people. We need to value application of science rather than science *per se*.

The growth of different societies in the past has come through different strategies. Western Europe through basic research and some development of technology; United States through defence research and widespread application of science and innovation, Japan through application of research, innovation and adaptation of technologies and production of a wide variety of high quality, competitive products. Some say imitation, but I think innovation has been the key to the rapid development of these societies.

If one notices carefully, one also sees that throughout history, there has been a gradual shift in the centre of economic power in this world. In the 19th century, England was the centre of world economic power; sterling was the world currency. In the early 20th century, US emerged as the great industrial power and the centre of the world economy. Dollar emerged as the world currency. As we near the end of this century, Japan is emerging as the major industrial power in this world; the centre of world economy has moved to the Pacific-Asia Basin and the Yen is emerging as the world currency. One wonders whether this trend will keep shifting in the next century as well. If it does, it is bound to move to the Asian mainland where India has to play the major role. India has the making of a great economy; a great society. It holds the key to the world's future but one wonders, where is the key? I believe it is in promoting a culture of innovation, moving from lab to land, from the ivory tower to pragmatic problem-solving and continuing education. May I now move to India and the Indian scene and the Indian challenge?

Indian Scenario

Every Indian agrees that India had a great past. Most Indians imagine that India has a great future, but what about the present? India is at the cross roads. It has the making of a great nation but it has not made it. In 1950s, Walt Rostow, the great American economic-historian built his 'take-off' theory of economic growth, and he described the Indian economy as one of the first in the developing world at the 'take-off' stage. Forty years have passed; we have not 'taken off'. We are still struggling to get away from the 3.5 per cent growth syndrome, what jokingly one of our well-known economists, Dr. Raj Krishna, used to call as the Hindu rate of growth. In the last two years, there have been signs of breaking away from this Hindu rate of growth; we have achieved 5 per cent growth and we are poised for still higher growth in the Eighth Plan.

Let us look at the Indian balance sheet. In the five decades of independence, India has created the world's third largest pool of scientific and technical manpower; it has developed infrastructure unparalleled in the developing world; be it transportation, communication, energy, research and development, financing, etc. It has built-in manufacturing capabilities, which span the production of a pin to a satellite.

Anything you name, India produces and manufactures it; 18 per cent of the world's irrigated land is located in India and Indian agriculture has done wonders during the last 15 years. Its agricultural production has more than doubled from 70 million tonnes to 170 million tonnes of foodgrains today; it has the world's highest savings rate—an Indian citizen saves Rs. 22 out of Rs. 100 which goes towards the development of the society. In fact, nearly 90 per cent of India's development expenditure is internally generated. No mean feat; it has skipped the debt trap that many developing nations have unfortunately succumbed to, it has kept inflation within the one digit figure, and on top of it. India has enjoyed political stability with small tremors here and there. With widely endowed natural resources and scientific establishments dotted across the country. India has all the ingredients to make it a high growth economy and a great society.

On the debit side, India is stuck with 2.23 per cent growth in population which obviously offrets the real growth of economy. Although it has developed a wide infrastructure, its maintenance is one of the poorest in the world. Any sector you take, energy, communication, transportation etc. the maintenance gap is glaring; there is more down time than up time. It has manufacturing enterprises in our country whose productivity is one of the lowest in the world. The productivity of the Indian enterprises is as distant as it could be. The same is with agriculture. In spite of achieving commendable growth, its productivity is almost half of China and two-thirds of the world's. India has large R and D establishments; it has large scientific establishments which have already acquired the reputation of being white elephants. They are caught in the brahmanical dilemma of purity and pollution, the purity of basic sciences unable to pull themselves up to meet the challenges of development.

Development of technology and application of science has become as though a polluting task, for Indian scientists. It is said that Indian entrepreneurs prefer the easy option to buy and replace technology from overseas rather than encourage innovations within. Indian savings have been ploughed into high, capital-intensive industry whose productivity is low, return is poor, whose ability to provide employment is limited. And if you employ large manpower on capital intensive industry, you engage in a self-defeating exercise—three legged race of the Indian public sector. Indian home market being large, there are 100 million in the middle class market, Indian manufacturers do not like to face competition, improve quality, bid for external trade, generate foreign exchange, which, in turn, could be ploughed back to update technologies. Last but not the least, while numerically we do have large scientific and technological manpower, but one wonders if they are relevant, they are motivated, they are concerned, they are committed. In spite of four decades of experience in managing large enterprises, Indian managers have yet to learn how to manage growth. Productive use of manpower, improving quality of products and services, being competitive in the world market remain a distant dream.

The Indian Challenge

Indian society, if one looks at is closely, has grown from Vedic times by absorbing external influences brought by Huns and Persians, Moghuls and Zoarostrians, Protestants and Catholics, and evolving indigenous innovations through Buddhism and Jainism, Sikhism, Arya Samaj and various reformist movements culminating in the contemporary India blending a culture of secularism, socialism, and humanism. History has taught us how to absorb external influence, and innovate social technologies to deal with the changing environments. It has enabled to retain social identities while absorbing new values, ideas, and technologies. However, it appears that this process has almost stopped during recent years.

In 1896 A.D., Al Beruni, the Persian—Uzbek scholar, who travelled through the length and breadth of India wrote : "Indians know everything. They are the most knowledgeable people in the world". By 1950s, John Lewis, an equally perceptive scholar, wrote : "Indians think they know everything". He was impressed by the pompousness and pervasiveness of the Indian mind. He was struck by the decadence that had crept in the Indian society, although he was full of praise of individual Indians who had made their mark in different walks of life.

As we are coming close to the end of the 20th century we are caught in the real dilemma; even though we have everything, we have nothing. We have all the ingredients of making of a great society, but we are unable to make it. The question is how will India make a real breakthrough and move with speed to occupy its rightful position as a truly developing nation of the world. One has no alternative but to search for the strategy which will turn the course of history. In the Indian context, the strategy is with our people, in our ability to make human resources work, in the process by which human potentialities will be realised, in enabling our people to innovate and, perform. The Indian society respects performance; the skills of Arjun, the power of Bhima, the tolerance of Gandhi, the vision of Nehru. It is also a society which has low value for work. On an average, an Indian works 4 hours a day, as against 7 of French, and 9 of the Japanese. It requires an Indian miracle to integrate work ethics with the culture for performance and excellence. To my mind, having world's third largest technical man power is not enough, we need the right manpower. Knowledge is not enough, we need skills; criticism is not enough, we need action. Development of right human resource, capability and commitment, and a culture of innovation is what we need today.

What does it really mean in operational terms; a massive educational strategy for development of appropriate skills and fostering an attitude of innovation. This will come through continuing education to the educated, to those who have already entered the life of work, who need to update their ways of doing things and to learn to do things better. This is a must for every Indian citizen whether he is a carpenter, plumber, engineer, teacher, manager or a scientist. Ultimately it is the people who will convert the resource into wealth, and put the infrastructure to its optimal use, create processes for improved products, transform potentiality into reality. If I may make a definitive statement, continuing education should have one basic objective, that is to update competence, capability, and commitment to enable them to make things cheaper, better, and more useful. Continuing education should foster a culture of innovation, a culture of improving technology, a culture of application of science. Science is a creative venture but what we need today is a pragmatic, productive, innovative venture.

In the area of capability building we have done a lot in enlarging the knowledge industry; but we have done little to build a reservoir of skills. For example, many students of science know what electricity is, but they do not know how to handle an electrical appliance; how to repair an electrical switch. What is required is development of skills, skills through action learning; skills through continuing innovation.

Building culture of innovation is the key to India's future. Culture is a way of life; culture is a guide to human behaviour; culture is an expression of values and ideals, culture is what one would like to stand for. Too long, the Indian society has been caught in the trap of purity and pollution; sacred and profane; social stratification and caste hierarchy; dependence on fate and faith; we have to get out of this trap by discovering and recognising human potentialities, through confidence in our people's ability and action. Indian culture has to move from its purist stand to a pragmatist one; from science to technology; from criticism to action; from dependence to growth; from invention to innovation. This will happen if our scientists forget about "reinventing wheels" and launch themselves to adapting and innovating on what is already discovered elsewhere. We have done this in agriculture. We have to do this in industry, education, and other sectors of society. If I may venture to suggest that in the emerging culture we must learn to borrow from others, incorporate the analytical and systemic approach of the Americans, technology thrust of the Japanese, relevant and skill oriented education of the South Koreans, social justice of Scandinavians, managing with low overheads of the Swiss, participation, accountability and performance of the Japanese, the Perestrioka and glassnost of the Russians, besides our own values of consultation, concern, tolerance, and absorption. Innovation is an exercise in culture building, in creating an awareness, of what is ideal and real; what is desirable and feasible; moving from energy to synergy; from competition to cooperation; from concern for self to concern for others, organisation and society, creating a culture of performance, quality, and productivity, creating a sense of partnership between people, management and union, scientists and technologists, teachers and students, administrators and citizens.

Successful societies and economies begin with people. Like revolution, innovation begins in the minds of men. Men have to be galvasnised; human resources have to be channellised; people have, to he empowered—empowered through new skills, challenging jobs, open, trusting and demanding relationship. In the Indian context, Government has to be a partner in facilitating the culture of innovation. Government should not be a donor, it should be a facilitator. It should intervene where it is necessary and refrain where it must. In the depression of the 'thirties, when free economy was in peril, Government became the planner in the United States with its New Deal policy; in the 'forties, it introduced the Marshall Plan for the reconstruction of Europe's war devastated societies, and in the 'sixties it launched a planned attack on poverty through the great society programme. When India became independent, the State took upon itself the reins for economic planning. It was needed. A time has come when fresh search for alternatives has to be initiated; when one could explore new avenues, anticipate new obstacles, and plan new actions. We have for four decades focussed on non-human variables, with the hope that these will contribute to the benefit of the people but today we stand disillusioned. We have to examine squarely our human assets; make human resources innovative, productive, committed and performing. Unless we are able to meet the challenges of innovation in the country, no matter what we do in the field of economic planning, energy planning, financial planning, environment planning, we will not get results.

I trust, I have argued enough to make one simple point; that India does not suffer from resource gap, not technology gap, not planning gap, the real gap is the human resource management gap, to be precise the innovation gap. To create a strategy of borrowing, innovating and building is India's greatest challenge. We have no choice but to meet it. I am personally sure that we will, and by the turn of this century, through innovation and innovative strategies, India will emerge, as one of the key centre of the world economy, polity, and society.

10

Emerging Trends in Marketing

Francis Cherunilam

The emerging business scenario in India, fostered by the liberalisation, is characterised by the expansion and intensification of the competitive dimensions and an explosion of business opportunities making marketing management a multi-dimensional strategic game. The conspicuous factors of this marketing epoch include;

i Redefinition of the market;

ii Extensive market segmentation;

iii Pace;

iv New dimensions of promotion and distribution; and

v Globalisation.

Redefinition of the Market

The new business environment, characterised by a general dismantling of entry barriers (and of exit barriers to a certain extent), growing competition and opportunities has prompted many corporates to redefine their markets. This entails the modification of the product mix by modifying any one or more of the following, *viz.,* the width, depth and consistency of the product mix.

In a broader strategic parlance, redefinition of the market of a company means a change in the portfolio strategy, *i.e.,* the business of the company.

In the pre-liberalisation era the restrictive government policy (like licensing, MRTP and FERA restrictions) often did not, generally, permit companies, particularly the large ones and foreign firms, to pursue the type of growth and diversification strategies they would have followed in an environment of business freedom. The restrictive regime, thus, resulted in a distorted portfolio strategy, including synergy. Yet, many of them were successful because the Government policy ensured them a protected market.

The liberalisation has, however, upset the applecart. In the new environment, with the protection gone, a firm has to survive fighting the competition and quite naturally a firm which does not have a definite competitive advantage may not be successful. Many companies have, therefore, been redefining their markets or portfolio strategies. In other words, several companies have decided to leave off some of the businesses where they would not be successful, and to concentrate on the core business where they have competency. Many, on the other hand, decided to enter new business to exploit the opportunities thrown open by the liberalisation.

The Glaxo India, for example, has decided to focus on its core business (prescription medicines) and to retrench its food products business. Similarly, Voltas, which went in for a broad diversification in the past has decided to concentrate on four broad categories (consumer durables, industrial products, textile machinery and agro-chemicals) and to withdraw from the rest (like agro-foods and beverages and distributing others' products). The Tatas have sold off their soaps and oils (Tomco) business. There are a number of such companies which have taken the decision to retrench the business portfolios where they lack competitive edge and to focus on core competencies or where they could become dominant players.

While several firms are contracting their portfolios, a number of firms are expanding their portfolios or product mix. The Godrej group, for example, is adding a range of white goods such as microwave ovens, cooking ranges, washing machines, etc. It also plans to enter the insurance business when it will be opened up. The Modi Xerox has repositioned itself by transforming from a photo-copier company to a document company reflecting the redefinition of its business.

The redefinition of the market encompasses not only the portfolio change but also the geographical coverage, change in the market segments served and modification of the product mix of any particular portfolio. To take on the competition a number of companies have been adding new product lines and new items in existing lines.

Market Segmentation

The growing competition has given rise to extensive market segmentation and concomitant brand positionings. While such extensive segmentation has been necessitated by the competition, it has been facilitated by certain socio-economic trends favouring market development.

The Mirc Electronics Ltd. (the makers of Onida) entered the TV market with the idea of 'one brand, one product, one model'. However, in due course, it realised that it is a fragmented market and that market segmentation and differentiated marketing are vital for survival and has come up with new models. In quick response to the Star TV multiple channel phenomenon, *Onida* began selling the idea of a second, 14 inch screen, colour TV, targeting at the teen-ager who would want to watch different channels from the oldies. In 1991, it entered the Black and White TV market, cold-shouldering its earlier haughtiness in this regard. It has recently launched a 29 inch CTV at Rs. 59,000 and a 25 inch CTV for Rs. 36,000. Quite contrary to its original policy of one product, it has added new lines like VCR, audio items and washing machines.

In the detergent powder market, the Hindustan Lever, which had earlier only the Surf, introduced the Wheel to counter the Nirma challenge in the large low-quality low-price segment. When Procter and Gamble introduced the premium product *Ariel,* Hindustan Lever fitted *Surf Ultra* against it. In the medium segment, *Rin* competes with *Ariel Supersoaker*. The *Sunlight* with colour guard is targeted at a specific segment. The USP of *Surf Easy Wash* is that it does not lather much and requires less water to complete the washing process. It is promoted as a product suitable to situations where there is water shortage and for use in washing machines.

Several companies try to expand their market by carving out new segments and niches. For example, the Malayala Manorama Group which already had, like several other Malayalam publishing groups, a periodical for the children, has recently identified a new segment, *viz.,* nursery school children, and launched a bi-monthly called *Kalikkudukka*.

The intensification of competition in the wrist-watch market is characterised by very extensive and fascinating market segmentation and positionings.

Such trends have been becoming more and more pervasive encompassing even the services sector. The HDFC, for example has tried to tailor schemes for every financing need that the middle class may have when buying or constructing a house. The UTI has a range of products to suit different socio-economic segments. And the LIC and commercial banks try not to lag behind.

In short, market segmentation and positioning have been gaining greater importance and new dimensions in high-touch to high-tech products. With the multi nationals in and competition hotting up in the Indian market, companies are busy working out permutations and combinations to introduce the right product for every purpose, purse and personality and beyond that.

Whilst many companies are trying to flank and consolidate their markets by line filling and extensions, a number of companies are also redefining their market segments in the light of the emerging competitive environment. Unable to successfully compete with the multinationals in the premium segments, several Indian companies have decided to concentrate on the middle and low segments or in markets where the MNCs do not pose a threat. Several companies focus on niches. For example, faced with severe competition from global megabrands like Sony, Panasonic and Philips as well as Indian majors like BPL and Videocon in the consumer audio electronics market, the small Indian firm Sonodyne has decided to retreat from mass market into premium segment. The strategy is to concentrate on products that the big players ignore because those markets are too tiny for their scales.

Pace

In the highly competitive market, pace, *i.e.,* the speed with which a company acts, is a key factor for success.

Pace implies the following :[1]

- i Increasing the speed of new product launches;
- ii Cutting the gap between one launch and the next;
- iii Responding quickly to changing customer needs; and
- iv Stepping up frequency of promotions.

The pace is managed by :[2]

- i Launching brands without elaborate trials;
- ii Occupying new segments before rivals;
- iii Creating systems designed for quick responses; and
- iv Compressing product manufacturing cycle.

The pay-offs of the pace are the following :[3]

- i The thunder is stolen from competitors' launches;
- ii Being first helps achieve leadership in a segment;
- iii Quick launches make up for late entries; and
- iv Rivals are denied precious shelf-space.

According to an Indian Market Research Bureau poll of the marketing heads of 100 companies, 50 per cent of the country's marketing men rate speed as extremely important in strategic terms while another 37 per cent rate is as very important.[4]

The strategic importance of pace is that when competitors can match the four Ps of marketing, the ultimate differentiator is speed to market.

The great importance that pace has come to assume is evinced by the flood of launches of new products, brands and brand extensions in quick succession. The pace setters include Hindustan Lever, Procter & Gamble, Britannia Industries, ITC, Philips India, Videocon International, Coca-Cola India and International Distillers.[5]

The pace game is contributing to the fast fragmentation of the markets into sub-segments and new segments to such an extent of creating or aggravating the consumer confusion. This could even degenerate into a vicious circle—the confusion calling for more promotion and enhanced promotion causing more confusion. The pace game also tends to make products and brands less enduring than the past. In other words, many products and brands will have to content with short life cycles.

New Dimensions of Promotion and Distribution

The advent of Cable TV, the increased presence of foreign ad agencies, flood of new products and brands, growing competition etc. have added new dimensions to promotion.

One of the recent developments in developed nations, particularly in the US, in promotion and distribution is the growing popularity of *direct marketing.*

There are two kinds of direct marketing, *viz.,* direct relationship marketing and direct order marketing.

Direct order marketing has shot into prominence in some advanced countries like USA. Goods sold this way range from lubricants to machines and magazines to tea.

Direct relationship marketing has as its main purpose the stimulation of sales at retail by establishing direct contact with prospects and customers in their homes. It may result in the generation of some direct sales, but that is not its main purpose.

Direct relationship marketing is a reaction to the ineffectiveness of mass advertising and other promotional means that have been becoming increasingly evident. Consumers are bombarded with an infinite number of advertisements in the electronic, print and other media to such an extent of consumer aversion that they skip time or space slots of advertisements. Further, there is no guarantee that a company's products can attract the attention of the consumer in the overcrowded advertiscenario. Again, mass advertising lacks focus and may also miss the target making the lavish ad spent wasteful.

Against this background, Stan Rapp and Thomas L. Collins in their best sellers *Maxi Marketing,* the *Great Marketing Turmaround* and *Beyond Maxi Marketing* have highlighted the power of direct relationship marketing. They point out that winning marketers are adding the *Double D*—dialogue and database—to the classic four Ps of the marketing mix.

In short, as Peter Brabeck, worldwide chief strategist at Nestle, observes, "Advertising is out. Credible communication with the consumer is in."

Catering to specific marketing characteristics evolved through market segmentation, the niche marketing has been further fine tuned, substantially, by the power of the Double D to *individualised marketing*. Individualised marketing does not literally mean a company addressing a special advertising message to just one individual, although there may be some such cases. It is rather a very personal form of marketing that recognises, acknowledges, appreciates and serves the interests and needs of selected groups of consumers whose individual identities and marketing profits are or become known to the advertiser.

The elaborate database needed for the individualised marketing is provided by the power of the computer which, as Rapp and Collins observe, by capturing, storing and combining bits of information about who we are, where we are, where we live, what we like, what we need, what we buy, is making countless niches in the market place identifiable and accessible—creating what economist Robert J. Samuelson has dubbed "Computer Communities". In the U.S. the number of computer companies or niche markets of people with common marketing characteristics are mind-boggling. This enables, point out Rapp and Collins, the smartest advertisers to establish direct contact with the consumer, whether before or after the first sale, and use the contact to gain customer loyalty and market share by building a mutually rewarding relationship. It means placing more importance on close involvement with individual prospects and customers than is now devoted to (a) increasingly inefficient image advertising, and (b) promotional discounts aimed solely at improving the immediate sales performance regardless of the long-term effect. This involvement covers not only direct contact and inter-active communication between advertisers and identified consumers by direct mail, phone, audio and video cassettes or computer but can also mean contact with the public through event marketing, public relations and personal encounters between company personnel or representatives and consumers in the market place sites such as stores and service establishments.

To succeed in the new era of individualised marketing, Rapp and Collins suggest the *Maxi Marketing* concept according to which people are actually or potentially the company's best customers are identified, contacted, activated and cultivated in a way that maximises sales and prospects. In their *Beyond Maxi Marketing* they chronicle the success stories of companies who have employed daring new ways to improve the quality of life of those who purchase what the company has to offer, adding value to the sales transaction by exceeding expectations and developing an on going involvement with the customer

In short, marketing leadership is shifting to the *caring and daring* companies.

In India, direct marketing has not been able to make even ripples except in respect of industrial goods (which has been traditionally so) and a few consumer durables like vacuum cleaners and fire extinguishers.

Certain developments on the distribution front in India are noteworthy. One of the emerging trends is that the growing competition for the retail shelf-space is enhancing the retailer power.

Multiple channels have been becoming more popular . New channels have been added for many products. For example, several convenience goods like toffees, chocolates, pan masala are sold through taxies and autorickshaws and ice creams, cigarettes etc. are sold through telephone booths etc. In short, there is an effort to sell products through unconventional channels like joints of one type or other visited by potential customers. For example, a video cassette lending library may sell head cleaning cassettes or liquids and a beauty parlour may sell select cosmetic items.

Another recent development, particularly the developed markets, is the popularity of the concept of *extra value proposition (EVP)*. In a mature market, where competitors are able to quickly imitate any special advantage a company may introduce, competing products move ever closer to parity and it becomes ever harder to carve out the perception of a unique difference. The answer to this problem lies, suggest Rapp and Collins, not in turning away from the idea of USP but in adding to it—in turning to EVP. They opine that in the 1990s an EVP can be the best way to have a unique advantage. Several companies, like Nestle and Cadillac, have very successfully employed the EVP. Back home, the Malayala Manorama Group of publications has been using the EVP; very useful booklets are supplied free of cost with the publications like *The Week* and *Balarama.*

Although Rapp and Collins advocate the EVP as a strategy against the imitation of the USP by the competitors, one finds no reason as to why the EVP also is amenable to imitation. Further, one may also wonder, whether EVP itself is not an USP.

Globalisation

In the case of a growing number of Indian companies, the marketing strategies are no more based on the domestic marketing environment, rather they are shaped by the emerging global environment as well as the domestic environment.

The on going liberalisation makes the Indian market increasingly open making foreign competition a very powerful force to reckon with.

Quite awake to the realities of the emerging environment, many Indian companies have given a global orientation to their marketing and other business strategies. These strategies are designed not only to fight the foreign competition in the domestic turf but also to expand their business horizon beyond the national borders.

The foreign business increases the strength of the Indian companies in several ways. It helps improve their overall image. The increase in the volume of business may help improve the cash flow. The foreign business familiarises them with the relevant business developments abroad and foreign competition. The foreign exchange earnings and familiarity of the foreign market trends would help them to obtain the state of the art technology and to upgrade quality so that they can more efficiently compete with the foreign firms in the Indian market. At the same time Indian firms can make gradual inroads into the domestic market of the foreign firms putting them on the defensive in their own home front.

Some companies go international as *counter-competitive* strategy. For example, one of the strategic considerations behind the plan to substantially increase the company's exports is that instead of waiting for the global onslaught into India, we will fight them in their playing field.

Several Indian companies like Balsara, Vicco, Pricol, etc. have successfully employed the niching strategy in international marketing. Niching may be used as a market entry strategy. After consolidating the position in the niching and gaining experience it may be possible to expand the market.

A number of large and small Indian companies are investing abroad as part of their globalisation strategy. The pioneer of this move is the Aditya Birla group. The group's drive to set up business overseas is that : "We want a predominance in the industries that we enter. The objective is to be a low-cost, high quality and global standard player."

Several of the overseas investments aim not only at establishment of production base and business abroad but also at consolidation of the domestic business. The Ballarpur Industries of the Thapars are setting up a giant paper mill in Indonesia at an estimated cost of Rs. 1800 crores. A plantation put up on 2,50,000 hectares will feed the paper mill. Any surplus pulp may be exported to India to feed Thapar Paper mills here.

The significance of it should be viewed in the background of the projected wood and pulp shortage in future in India. The Ceat expects that when the tariff barriers come down, part of the South Indian market could be served by its type plant in Sri Lanka.

Recently many Indian companies have resorted to acquisition of companies abroad to gain a foothold in the foreign market and to increase the overseas business. Mergers and acquisitions (M&As) have certain advantages. It may be used to acquire technology. M&As may have the effect of eliminating or reducing competition. One great advantage of M&As in some cases is that it provides instant access to markets and distribution network. For example, the acquisition of the small British firm Wiltshire Brewery by the Vijay Mallya's U.B. Group has provided it with a chain of 300 pubs throughout Britain which can be used for marketing of U.B.'s brands of beer like *Kingfisher.* The acquisition of 32 per cent stake in the Ilva Lamini Piani, an Italian state owned steel major, by Essar Gujarat gives it a global steel presence and access to downstream steel technology and Ilva's marketing network worldwide.

A number of companies have taken the joint venture route to foreign markets. It is an important strategy adopted by pharmaceutical firms like Ranbaxy, Core Parenterals, Lupins Labs etc. In several cases, joint ventures, as in the case of foreign subsidiaries, help Indian firms to establish and consolidate their domestic business, besides the expansion of the foreign business. For example, Essar Gujarat's joint ventures in countries like Indonesia and Bangladesh to manufacture cold rolled steel have resulted from a strategy to create an assured market for its hot rolled coil mother plant at Hazaria.

Several Indian companies have been using licensing and franchising for international marketing. For example, Ranbaxy has licensing arrangement in countries like Indonesia and Jordan.

Another important international marketing strategy employed by several Indian firms is strategic alliance. Also known by such names as *entente* and *coalition,* this strategy seeks to enhance the long-term competitive advantage of the firm by forming alliance with its competitors, existing or potential, in critical areas, instead of competing with each other. The goals are to leverage critical capabilities, increase of innovation and increase flexibility in responding to market and technological changes. Several factors like high risks and costs of R&D, fast changes and complexities of technology and the resultant imbalance in the in-house technological capability, high costs of marketing; the need to acquire complementary technology and skills, the need to achieve economies of scale, the need to overcome market entry barriers etc. make alliance, instead of competition, the competitive strategy. The Procter and Gable-Godrej alliance seeks to combine Godrej's well-developed marketing infrastructure and intimate knowledge of the Indian market and the technological and marketing strength of P & G.

Conclusion

With the liberalisation and the emergence of a largely free and competitive market in India, marketing management is becoming a multi-dimensional and global strategic game. The following observation of Kotler is becoming true of India and Indian companies : "Entire markets are disappearing as a result of managed trade policies, advances in technology and innovative competitors. Mass markets are fragmenting into micro markets. Power is shifting from the manufacturer to the retailers, multiple distribution channels are replacing single channels."

REFERENCES

1. Adite Chatterjee, "Pace", *Business Today,* December 7-12, 1994, p. 78.
2. *Ibid.,* p. 79.
3. *Ibid.,*.
4. *Ibid.,*.
5. Cited by Adite Chatterjee, *ibid.,*.
6. Stan Rapp and Tom Collins, *The Great Marketing Turnaround,* (New York; Plume, 1992).
7. Stan Rapp and Tom Collins, *Maxi Marketing,* (Singapore : McGraw Hill International Edition, 1987).
8. Stan Rapp and Tom Collins, *Beyond Maxi Marketing. The New Power of Caring and Daring.* (New York : McGraw Hill Inc., 1994).
9. Cited by Dr. Stephene Johnes et al, "Marketing Your Own Brand", *World Executive Digest, June,* 1994.

11

New Dimensions in Personnel Management

M.L. Jha

In the past few years, personnel management has gone through a sea-change, adhering to certain pre-conceived policies with its various interpretations and occasional dilution from time to time under pressures from within or outside.

Personnel functions have emerged from welfare concept in our country. They date back to the Report of Royal Commission on Labour, 1929, which recommended appointment of Labour Officers or Labour Liaison Officers. But, with the enforcement of Industrial Disputes Act in 1947, the personnel department was viewed from a negative approach. A personnel man was expected to control labour and bring the recalcitrant workers in line or get them out. Contrarily, our Government made a remarkable progress by enacting numerous laws to protect the interests of labour.

Quite recently and even now in some private organisations, the personnel unit is deemed inferior to others, the personnel man lacks the due status and recognition, and personnel functionaries are no better treated than glorified clerks of a post office. He has little intervening powers but he has to implement the policies laid down by his super bosses on all facets of personnel management. Of course, the situation worsens if powers are confined to one or two at the top whose major decisions are based on impressions rather on facts and natural justice. Often, their state of indecision or delayed decisions devoid of human considerations, procrastination and undue pressures lead to high turnover and contagious demoralisation.

Today, personnel management has several off-shoots, say, Manpower Planning and Recruitment, Training and Development. Human Resource Development (H.R.D.), Industrial Relations and so on. A successful personnel man has to be well-versed in Behavioural Sciences, a plethora of laws and H.R.D., industrial relations, etc. His multiple roles include of a theoretician, a diagnostician and an experienced practitioner.

Personnel management has recently shown several new dimensions, as detailed below.

Impact of Applied Behavioural Sciences

Behavioural Sciences have considerable influence on selection, induction, placement, training and development through appropriate job designing, necessary instructions, learning opportunities and suitable incentive plans. It has also contributed to leadership role, communication skill, inter-personal relations, decision-making and problem-solving areas. Again, it has enough scope for improving resolutions of group-conflicts and integration of various groups, healthy team-spirit and maximum efficiency. In human engineering too, it has helped in proper designing of instruments and machines to the convenience and efficiency of workers and executives. Similarly, the knowledge of physiology makes one possible to better understand the functions of various limits, their interactions, sensory inputs and their coordination with the psycho-motor activities, effect of self-pauses on fatigue and efficiency.

Thus, Behavioural Sciences enables a personnel man to attain the best adjustment and satisfaction from his job to enhance better prediction of his subordinates' job-behaviour and capacity.

Human Resources Development becoming Popular

H.R.D. helps people to acquire necessary competence on their job, leading to efficient functioning of organisations. It inculcates higher work commitment, better teamwork and higher job satisfaction. H.R.D. programmes result in trust, collaboration, role-clarity, pro-action and risk-taking tendency which influence optimum efficiency and productivity. Its practices develop participative styles of leadership which harmonise inter-personnel relations and also facilitate the functioning of Joint Consultative Committees for canteen management, production boosting, grievance handling, safety and welfare. Yet, for an H.R.D. man, to be truly successful top man, must show sincere involvement through related appreciation programme.

Strikes and Gheraos

Strikes and gheraos are often viewed from a negative angle, though strike, unless specifically prohibited, is a legal right under the Industrial Disputes Act, 1947, within the free trade unionism. It is the strong pursuasive tool of employees for expressing and redressing grievances, inducing reasonableness, compromise and agreement; and ultimately controlling the employers. Most people often callously oppose strikes and search for some panacea or doctrinaire approach as a quick solution. Recent thinking in this regard is gradually changing, since both the personnel and operating managers do honestly try to diagnose the real causes *ab initio*, followed by some agreeable just solution in a congenial atmosphere. In addition, precautions are also taken to avoid re-occurrence of similar causes which may result in strike in future.

Human Resources Information System (H.R.I.S.)

H.R.I.S. is an integrated computerised system designed to improve information to be used for various personnel decisions. Proper storing of information and timely retrieval thereof by a personnel man are assets for efficiency. Yet, proper designing of an H.R.I.S. programme requires a strong data-base, its types, its uses and specific purposes. Hence, a good HRIS programme would certainly result in effective H.R.D. scheme in any personnel department.

Personnel Research and Allied Areas

Research, statistics, records, auditing and computer's use in the H.R.I.S., have brought objectivity, accuracy and reliability in personnel management. Scientific and systematic enquires by employing questionnaire, surveys, interviews, case and comparative studies, historical and explanatory studies, reliance on facts and their analysis rather than on personal opinions and experiences, personnel records, statistics and auditing (*i.e.* evaluation) of personnel programmes, all facilitate analysis and appraisal of human resources and manpower management. With the help of records and statistics, information required by the Government can be supplied, other departments can be communicated, pay-rolls and succession plans may be prepared, and training needs can be assessed followed by evaluation of training programmes.

Similarly, a personnel auditor helps in preparing and maintaining job-wise comparative data about wages, perks, employees' turnover, grievances, accidents, suggestions and activity-wise cost figures. In fact, various reports based on auditing can be presented when so required and certain indicators for action plans can also be clearly derived from them.

Better Quality of Work Life

With increasing importance of job design and job analysis, a good work relationship would develop between people and their jobs, leading to better human resources planning, affirmative action and better staffing. Quality circles, consisting of small groups and meetings at regular intervals to discuss ways and means to cut costs and improve productivity, would enhance greater workers' involvement, effective communication, shared decision-making, and better self-discipline among the employees.

Objective Appraisal System and Better Compensations

Appraisal system would be better designed and implemented with the cooperative efforts of personnel and operating managers on objective reliable bases, thus replacing the old, conservative and biased approaches in practice.

Besides, the employers are expected to think about better retirement benefits, *e.g.* pension, contributory fund, gratuity, medical facilities and providing service to one dependent of the employees.

In short, personnel department is henceforth expected to get better status and recognition by the employees. To serve its various off-shoots, specialists would be obviously needed. And, the emphasis is likely to shift from the mechanical (static) approach to an ever-emerging developmental tool of the organisation so as to positively improve the organisation effectiveness.

12

Information Management Policy Framework in India

Utpal K. Banerjee

The gradual emergence of complex scientific, engineering and other technological disciplines today are helped by management techniques, to cope with data and information more systematically, without losing sight of their wider social, economic and cultural contexts. This complex of disciplines is referred to as informatics which can be described as "totality of disciplines and technologies for the systematic treatment (particularly by computer) of data and information scene as the medium for knowledge with a view to its conservation in time and its communication in space"

Informatics can be regarded as a technology where human energy is transferred in physical form using mainly computer as a tool to produce the change needed in the society. According to Yohan Galtung (1978), informatics can be visualised to have techniques plus structure as follows :

(a) *Techniques*

- (i) Hardware components (computers as tools);
- (ii) Software components (human skills and programming knowledge).

(b) *Structure*

- (i) Economic structure (in terms of capital intensive labour extensive, research intensive and organisation intensive factors);
- (ii) Socio structure (in terms of factors which create lasting demand for information, knowledge and skills and for new technologies);

(iii) Cultural structure (in terms of dependency on a Western Centre based on analytic rather than holistic insight and inducing man-over-man and man-over-nature relations);

(iv) Cognitive structure in terms of assumption that whenever the technology is developed, deployed or transferred, a structure is being built, whether it is a technique for production for distribution, or for consumption).

The policy-making for informatics involves intelligence, design and choice activities. The first phase of policy-making process, according to Herbert Simon (1960), is searching the environment for conditions calling for a policy which can be called intelligence activity. The second phase—inventing, developing and analysing possible course of action—can be called design activity. The third phase—selecting a particular course of action from those available can be called choice activity.

Strengths of the Policy Making System

In a Third World country like India, the Government is concerned with a variety of issues whose origin can be different from each other. The normal strengths of the policy making system are as follows:

(a) The data-base of the Government of India is massive and is available for use in policy formulation. There are experts and competences available on most economic and socio-political issues of the country;

(b) The technical experts base in the natural, biological, social and mathematical sciences and in technology has grown over the years and a sustained effort to develop universities and special-purpose institutions by the Government has opened up a knowledge-base for policy formulation;

(c) An extremely vast institutional frame has been developed for consultation with an involvement of the concerned people in the examination of policy issues;

(d) The policy frame is primarily prepared at professional and executive levels with appropriate reactions and support from the Prime Minister and the Minister-in-Charge, the Planning Commission and the constituted bodies for the purpose;

(e) Systematic review of the policies is held by the Ministry concerned along with the Planning Commission. Such reviews are instrumental in taking corrective action by the Centre and the State Governments irrespective of their policy plans and programmes.

Weaknesses of the Policy Making System

The weaknesses of the existing approach to policy formulation of the Government of India are perceived to be as follows :

(a) The available data are meant for general purposes and are refused both over area and content for specific purposes of policy formulation. Much of the data have no continuity for policy making purposes;

(b) A fast selective and participative network in policy formulation development may be a necessary condition for acceptability but it does not seem to be a sufficient condition for achieving results intended in the policy. The consequences are as follows:

   (i) Most often the modus operandi through committees find it difficult to depart radically from the previous frames. Therefore, improvements are suggested instead of innovative solutions;

   (ii) Although the Government uses experts in policy formulation, no sharp difference is intended to be made between acceptability and optimality;

   (iii) There is seldom any clarity in defining a specialist and a techno-administrator;

   (iv) Schemes and policies are examined often in isolation, of other related fields. Hence perspective is a segmented one, not of the totality.

(c) In the complex inter-locking system developed for policy formulation, where the premier inputs are provided by the administrative personnel, the political inputs are confused. At best this is a reactive process and the political system generally underplays its role in policy making function in development.

Informatics Policy Programmes : Analysis of Cases

India has made an early beginning in applying information technology for the benefit of the Indian society and a number of project plans have been drawn which are under implementation.

Five such cases are taken up here for a SWOT analysis—their strength (S), weakness (W) from the technology side and opportunities (O) and threats (T) for their societal impact. The SWOT analysis is based on general assumption and can be taken as only indicative but not predictive.

(A) Public Administration Informatics

National Informatics Centre, as a premier national organisation for the Governmental information in the country, is setting up NICNET as a wide-area computer network on a nationwide basis. At the apex level,

NICNET will have five regional computers of very large configuration at Delhi, Bhubaneswar, Pune, Hyderabad and Madras using four NEC and one ND computers. At the second hierarchical level, there will be 22 State capital computer centres, based on ECIL mainframe computers. At the third hierarchical level, there will be 390 district headquarters computer centres using PC and super micro computers. While the number of State and district computers may go up further, the above network would be for hierarchical distributed processing, concentrating upon agricultural information system, health information system, educational information system and statistical and mathematical planning models. NICSAT satellite is ear-marked to provide the data communication facilities for NICNET, while 10 districts have been selected for initially developing complete district-level information systems. Orissa and Karnataka have also entered into an agreement with NIC for developing State level information system and providing turn-key support for the State computerisation.

Technology Strength

- Creation of wide-spread employment opportunities for programmes, analysis and data-entry operators at Centre, State and district levels;
- Standardisation of data collection, storage and information retrieval procedures;
- Uniformity in administration of Central, State and district information systems.

Technology Weakness

- Likely deficiency in the necessary leadership;
- Prevalent lack of subject area knowledge;
- High cost of using dedicated satellite.

Societal Opportunity

- Better planning environment for Central Planning Commission and State Planning Boards;
- Vastly improved information exchange between Centre and States on subjects belonging to Union List, State List and Concurrent List;
- Large spin-off in employment creation in the user community for public administration.

Societal Threat

- Likely conflict between "Top down" approach (Planned by NIC from regional centres downwards) and "Bottom up" approach (Planned by States from district level upwards in terms of user needs);

- Likely undesirability in observing uniformity of developing district information models with conditions of district situation being extremely uneven within the States as well as from one State to another.
- Likely information monopoly arising out of the Centre's access to the State information with possible effect on Centre-State relationship;
- Likely creation of dependence on the Centre for information purposes with an impact of India's federated structure.

(B) Natural Resource Informatics

National Natural Resource Management System (NNRMS) is being planned by Department of Space for a large number of natural resources by using remote sensing satellites and image-processing computers. The resources include glacial water storage, riverine water-flow, overground crop, overground forest canopy, underground mineral, sea fishery and sea-bed minerals. While IRS-1 and IRS-2 are the satellites to be used for this purpose, eight image processing computers are to be located at IIT at Kharagpur, National Institute for Remote Sensing at Dehradun, National Arid Zone Research Institute at Jodhpur, Geological Survey of India at Bangalore, National Soil Survey and Soil Research Institute at Nagpur, Madras University at Madras, Indian Council of Agricultural Research at Delhi, and National Remote Sensing Agency at Hyderabad. In order to utilise the vast amount of data that would flow from NNRMS, National Resource Data Management System (NRDMS) is being planned by Department of Science and Technology for five districts using data from National Sample Survey Organisation, Census Commission and field survey in the district itself. The chosen districts are Visakhapatnam in Andhra Pradesh working with National Coastal Research Institute at Visakhapatnam, Koraput district in Orissa working with Operational Research Group (ORG) at Baroda, Gurgaon district in Haryana working with National Institute of Science and Technology Development Studies at Delhi, Sultanpur district in UP working with Aligarh University at Aligarh and Baroda district in Gujarat working with Indian Institute of Technology at Bombay.

Technology Strength

- Immensely rich data-base of varied types of natural resources;
- Possibility of any kind of information in time and space for natural resources;
- Possibility of any kind of forecast in time and space.

Technology Weakness

❒ Possibility of poor administration for a new approach;
❒ Likely dependence on personal motivation and initiative in the micro-level district planning.

Societal Opportunity

❒ Definitive improvement in district planning;
❒ Definitive improvement in resource planning on a national scale;
❒ Better allocation of resources, giving the knowledge on their availability and distribution.

Societal Threat

❒ Likely rivalry among States for relatively scares resources;
❒ High social cost of incorrect usage of resource information;
❒ Likely information monopoly by power groups in a federal structure of the country.

(C) Environmental Informatics

Indian Meteorological Department is acquiring CRAY super-computer to conduct meteorological calculations for Numerical Weather Predictions (NWP). NWP is based on a complex SACRAMENTO model, among other techniques, which involves a vast array of variables relating to cloud, dust, micro climate, soil and sub-soil vegetarian and so on. The detailed resolution of NWP in space and time grid is important for achieving production confidence and efficiency,—being looked for by India.

Technology Strength

❒ Tremendous assistance for complicated calculations through array processing;
❒ Possibility of very high resolution in terms of spatial distance and time intervals.

Technology Weakness

❒ High cost of acquisition and operation;
❒ Strong dependence on overseas support for spares and maintenance at the cutting edge of technology.

Societal Opportunity

❒ Better quality of civil administration with confident knowledge on climate situation and variations;
❒ Better emergency planning and disaster management for cyclones,

flash floods, tidal bores and sea storms;

- Better adoption of agricultural, forestry, animal husbandry and a fishing practices.

Societal Threats

- High social cost of unreliable and inaccurate predictions;
- Likely aberration in information usage by power groups in a federal structure of the country.

(D) Social Justice Informatics

Starting with Tamil Nadu, 13 Indian States have ECIL computers used by police authorities in their Home Departments to administer social justice. Broadly, these comprise crime-criminal information system, maintaining records on individuals, past apprehensions and convictions, modus opearndi of crimes and territorial distribution of crimes. These also comprise finger-print information system maintaining classified and codified records on finger-print indices. From the Centre, National Crime Records Bureau coordinates in the matter. The plan is to eventually put the above computers in a POLICENET for rapid, appropriate exchange of data on suspected individuals.

Technology Strength

- Useful availability of massive crime data and finger-print data;
- Availability of tested and proven model for social justice information management;
- A high degree of uniformity in social justice administration.

Technology Weakness

- Likely lack of motivation in systematic data capture and data management;
- Likely distortion in data quality leading to poor data management;
- Likely absence of proper leadership due to wrong policy on posting and administration;
- Likely usage of data to satisfy individual "ego"

Societal Opportunity

- Vast improvement in crime detection and criminal apprehension;
- Substantial improvement in criminal conviction in the face of scanty evidence;
- Efficient exchange of information through POLICENET when realised;
- Better social environment and reduction in crime.

Technology Threat

- Likely threat to individual liberty when practised on large scale as has been the Western experience;
- Likely wrong usage by the power groups in a federal structure of the country;
- Possible lack of Centre, State and Inter-State cooperation leading to information stalement.

(E) Economic and Development Informatics

Planning Commission in India has been using INTER DATA Computer for working out the detailed material-flow balance in more than 80 sectors using input-output relations, investment, financial resource, import, employment and perspective planning. This is done through VIDHATA Model for agriculture, export, demography, investment and deciding long-term objectives. Macro level district planning, in turn, is being done in Gujarat by using SUNRAY computer for district waste land reclamation, water supply and monitoring of Integrated Rural Development Projects (IRDP). Similar exercise in district planning is being done in Uttar Pradesh using SPERRY-UNIVAC computer for grass-land location and mounting irrigation schemes under Drought-Prone Area Projects (DPAP). These applications have considerable potential for diversification in other areas which are being slowly realised by other States like Karnataka.

Technology Strength

- Need of small computing power of PCs, being the "latest, the cheapest and the best";
- Utility of local language as done in Gujarat;
- Great commitment to data quality and information usage by local people.

Technology Weakness

- Possible lack of leadership when needed at district level;
- Possible lack of specialised knowledge to meet the user need.

Societal Opportunities

- Tremendous potential for extension to orchard locations, afforestation, sericulture cultivation and a host of other administrative policies;
- Possibility of highly improved technology transfer from blueprint stage to field stage ("Labs to land").

Societal Threats

- Likely social cost of incorrect usage;
- Likely information monopoly by power groups.

Broad Implications of Informatics Policy

Informatics policy programmes, as outlined and analysed above reveal a number of common features. It would be useful to consider these features together and consider their implications in the broad policy context.

The basic point is that the informatics technology has 'arrived' in the developing country scene and has the potential in bringing about qualitative changes in the process of development. It is, therefore, imperative that the policy choices are exercised now and here in terms of both contents as well as consequences to make it more meaningful and remove its maladies in relation to the society.

Possible Implications

These are summarised below

(a) Informatics technology need not remain gender specific. Technology has remained far too long and in too many developing countries the special preserve for men in terms of all benefits. This has been the legacy of the past where muscle-power had male domination. Later, male preference had continued for technology usage in a situation of general poverty of the multitude.
Informatics policy can change drastically the above situation by recognising women as end-users. In the new profession of software engineering, women are already emerging as systems and programming professionals all over India and the same can be easily replicated in the Third World. As a fall-out from the technology, new business ventures are sprouting up where again women can play a vital role as entrepreneurs,—as is already evident in India.

(b) Currently, social institutions seem to be failing the emerging technology scene, including informatics. For instance, educational institutions are not moving beyond the blackboard stage while easy availability of audio-visual technology, supported by micro-computers, can bring in sea-hange in education. Similarly, while irrigation technology through minor irrigation schemes is in for a revolution, the village institutions are yet to develop an ethos for just sharing of irrigational water.
The informatics policy should mobilise opinion leaders of all shades and from all walks of life in order to put technology for the greatest good. Informatics is an incipient area where there are large fears and distrust still. It is necessary to create social support by restructuring social institutions in that direction.

(c) Informatics technology has often a poor delivery system. Informatics and telematics, for instance, were combined in India under the Centre for Development of Telematics (C-DOT) which produced sophisticated digital exchanges. But, despite its successful trial in the Karnataka State, the rural exchange did not reach the field more than one year later. Again, although 8-bit micro-computer technology has been available with the supportive "Courseware", the same has not reached the majority of schools for providing computer literacy at all stages of education as provided for in the new education policy.

Informatics policy should be supported by suitable official support and clearance, strengthened by teaching entrepreneurship and modicum of management practices. Only in this way the technology can reach the masses fast for their ultimate benefit.

(d) Quite often, marginal additions to technology are needed to improve existing practices and to usher in a better quality of life. Embedded micro-computer and micro-processor systems, for instance, can bring in a quiet revolution in industrial process machines, railway signals, automative engines and so on.

Informatics policy should emphasise intensive and extensive studies needed on marginal use of technology in our plan for balancing equipment and facilities.

(e) Self-reliance and employment generation are often emphasised at the cost of competence and productivity in informatics technology. Self-reliant technology often ends in poor quality at a high cost, and as a result, does not generate high employment. There is a "Zero-Sum" gain in the field of technology which favours high employment only when high quality can be produced at a low cost. This would apply to the example of producing personal computers in the small scale sectors without high skills, appropriate machinery and R&D support and resulting in poor quality at a high cost.

Informatics policy can redress the above situation by a judicious mix of self-reliant, appropriate technologies on one side and competent and highly productive technologies on the other.

(f) Informatics technology often shows no concern for the societal value system. For example, indiscriminate adoption of informatics technology can augment the mass media. But this can also result in the wiping out of the enduring values as is happening to the eastern hills of India. On the other hand, the Japanese have adopted information society by integrating the information technology with Eastern value-base. Thus, high technology efficiency has been coupled with tradition, grace and strong humanitarian concerns.

The informatics policy needs conscious inculcation and careful vigil about the traditional value system. Trans-border information flow allows for informatics crossing one border and reaching another in our "global village". This flow brings in its wake its own value-imperatives in the diffusion and absorption process. Informatics policy needs to cater for conscious protection of a value-environment germane to the developing country.

Conclusion

To summarise, we have attempted to look at the genesis of technology and its impact on the developing society as far as informatics is concerned. Five concrete cases have been considered for enumeration and analysis from the angles of technology strength, technology weakness, societal opportunity and societal strength. Thereafter, we have analysed the overall implications of informatics policy in terms of choice and adjustments so that course-corrections can be implemented in using informatics policy in a developing world. While examples cited are primarily Indian, they are valid for other countries as well for two reasons. First, India has been an early starter in informatics field is forging ahead. Others will face similar problems sooner or later. Secondly, India's being primarily democratic society, much of the debate can be waged to arrive at the best acceptable policy solution. The final point remains that informatics is a powerful tool and should not be allowed to be abused in the hands of major power groups in any Third World country.

13

Towards a Power Policy in a Liberalised Economy

C. Gopalkrishnan

The electricity sector in India has been passing through turbulent times recently. The eye of the storm has been private participation, especially with reference to foreign investment in the power sector. Though the topic has been debated very widely in the recent times, very little effort has been made to understand the real issues and problems facing the electricity sector in India. As a result, it is felt that in the maze of controversies and recriminations, the real issues will be buried deep and incalculable damage will be done to the interests of the Indian economy. The focus of the paper, therefore, is an examination of some of these issues on the basis of available published data, at the same time keeping ideology away.

A Critique of the Current Debate on Power Policy

The common thread in the antagonism to private participation in the power sector, according to the papers published in various economic newspapers and journals, could be summarised as follows :[1]

(a) Cost of power generated by the private sector is said to be considerably higher than that of SEBs. It is said that the tariffs could be Rs. 2.40 per unit or above in the case of power generated by the private sector, whereas the average cost of present generation by the State sector is about Rs.1.40 per unit.

(b) The Government has allowed a guaranteed rate of return of 16 per cent, and according to some writers, the rate of return could even reach 50 per cent in the case of some of the private projects.

(c) The Government did not resort to international bidding and as a result, there is no transparency so far as certain deals are concerned.

(d) The Government has allowed import of capital equipment. This action adversely affects the interests of organisations such as BHEL.

(e) There are counter guaratnees offered by the Government in the case of foreign investment in power sector.

The plan of this paper is to analyse the important issues in the overall context of the working of the power sector, instead of examining them individually without looking at the present problems of the power sector. Data for this analysis come from various reports, including the Fourteenth Electric Power Survey (EPS) and the various articles which appeared in the recent times.[2]

Demand for Power

According to the 14th EPS, the peak and energy demand over a period of next seventeen years beyond the end of Seventh Plan would rise from 42,000 MW and 241 BUs to 1,44,300 MW and 824 BUs respectively. This simply means, according to the report, an addition of 1,42,000 MW capacity if accelerated hydro development takes place and 1,57,000 MW otherwise. The above figures, if must be stated here, may look very large, but in actual fact, this will result in a per capita consumption of about 590 units of electric power only.[3] According to another report, funds needed to achieve the above target would be Rs. 6,60,000 crores, which means an investment of Rs. 4.5 crores per MW approximately at present day constant prices.

Further, according to yet another report, the total outlay in the 8th, 9th and 10th Plans may not be more than Rs. 2,50,000 to Rs. 3,00,000 crores (at constant prices), which of course, means a very serious power crisis in the coming days, unless arrangements are made otherwise. In other words, the crisis is basically a crisis of capital to meet the growing needs of the power sector.

In this connection, the performance of the power sector could also be examined. According to the various reports, the Sixth Plan could add only 14,228 MW against a target of 20,000 MW. Similarly, the achievement during the Seventh Plan was only 21,406.6 MW against an original target of 48,000 mw, which was revised downwards many times because of financial constraints and finally brought down to 24,000 MW. According to the most recent reports, the shortfall in the Eighth Plan is going to be to the tune of 10,000 MW. In short, according to Mr. S. Venkitaraman, a former Governor of RBI, "additions to generating capacity have stagnated around 4,000 MW power annum in the recent past. To be precise, 4,000 MW per annum was achieved in 1985-90. But in the recent period the annual addition has been around 3,200 only."

The following questions emerge from the above analysis :

(a) Without private participation, including foreign investment is itpossible for the SEBs to meet the above demand?

(b) How did the country get into this quagmire of SEBs not being able to finance their own growth? Why did nobody question when SEBs were not able to meet even their own revenue requirements, leave alone future expansion?

(c) Has BHEL got the capacity to supply equipment to meet the above requirements. If they have, then import of foreign equipment is unnecessary But do they have the capacity?

Can the Indian Private Sector fill the Gap in Supply?

After having discussed the demand and the question of capital costs and availability of capital for investment and the related crisis, as a next step we will examine the ability of the Indian private sector to fill the gap in supply. For example, to establish a power plant of moderate size of 2,000 MW, the total capital outlay needed is approximately Rs. 9,000 crores. Assuming a debt equity ratio of 4:1, the organisation needs to meet the balance of requirements. How many organisations in India today are in a position to get into the power sector on their own? This illustration only goes to show that a large number of power plants in the Indian private sector are not going to materialise. If this is so, then to meet the growing demand, foreign investment in the power sector would become essential.

Capital Cost

As stated above, the capital cost estimates show a requirement of about Rs. 4.5 crores per MW. In the recent times, however, capital cost of the Independent Power Producers (IPPs) has come under scrutiny and they have been attacked for quoting a capital cost which is in the neighbourhood of Rs. 4.5 crores. For example, Enron's Dabhol Project, Cogentrix's Mangalore Project and Neyveli Zero Unit, all have come under attack by various writers on the issue of capital cost. Therefore, this issue needs further examination.

According to Mr. S.N. Roy, a former chairman of the Central Electricity Authority, "The present day investments per MW of installed capacity for nuclear, gas, coal-based thermal and hydro power stations range between Rs. 5 crores and 2.5 crores. For the purpose of working out the cost of energy, an average investment of Rs. 4 crores per MW can be considered for generation." The above estimate has been further supported by various advisory committee reports. In the light of the above, the investment cost by private sector seems to go in line with the above estimates.

Further, according to the 26th report of the Parliamentary Standing Committee on Power, capital costs incurred by the public sector power plants are not any different. For example, the capital cost of NTPC's gas-based 650 MW Gandhar plant which became functional last year was Rs. 3.8 crores per MW. Similarly, UPSEB's 1,000 MW coal-based Anpara B Plant, which was commissioned in 1993, cost Rs. 4.7 crores per MW. Similarly, NTPC's proposed 420 MW gas-based Kayamkulam plant is expected to cost 3.4 crores per MW. According to the annual report of the Ministry of Programme Implementation, the average cost escalation was on an average about 47.7 per cent. In the case of NTPC's Kahalgaon thermal plant, cost escalation was, according to the report, more than 100 per cent. According to the *Economic Times*[4], BHEL's costs are similarly under-estimated. Although, equipment costs for thermal plants are between Rs. 2.5-2.75 crores per MW, when developmental charges, consultancy charges, construction and supervision costs are added and on capitalising interests costs, the final costs come to Rs. 4.7 crores per MW. Therefore, capital costs have been, it must be stated here, more often abused to state a cause.

Cost of Electricity per Unit

By obfuscating facts on cost of generation, the opponents of private generation of electricity have made any intelligent discussion difficult. The major thrust of their arguments on cost of generation is as follows :

> The cost of private generation is Rs. 2.40 or upwards per unit, whereas the cost of generation of SEB is less than Rs. 1.50 per unit. The implications, according to them, are that the SEBs would not be able to sustain by purchasing the high cost power generated by the IPPs.

One of the greatest half-truths perpetrated has been on cost of production per unit. No doubt, a statement such that the private sector power would cost Rs. 2.40 or upwards per unit whereas the SEB's cost would be in the region of Rs. 1.40 or Rs. 1.50 has a great mass appeal. But does this statement reflect the reality? When costs are compared what costs are taken for comparison : average costs of one sector with marginal costs of the other, or marginal costs of one sector with the marginal costs of the other? When we talk of Rs. 1.40 or Rs. 1.50 as the cost of generation of SEBs, it is the average cost of present generation, whereas Rs. 2.40 per unit reflects actually cost of production by a marginal plant on a future date. These in fact, are strictly not comparable.

Because of low costs of investments in the past, the average costs of generation of SEBs is going to be considerably lower, whereas both the average and incremental costs are the same for new generation. In other words, when SEBs add to their capacity, their marginal costs are the same as private generators, say Rs. 4 crores per MW. Therefore whether new investments take place in SEBs or in private sector, the impact on SEBs is going to be the same.

According to Anil Upadhyay, assuming an SEB buys 10 per cent of its requirements of power from the private sector, the implications on cost per unit would be to the extent of 11 paise per unit[5]. As stated above, if the SEB, on the other hand decides to invest, the impact on cost of power per unit is going to be the same. Threfore, whether new investments take place in SEBs or private sector, the impact on SEBs is going to be nearly thc same as seen earlier.

Rate of Return

Let us now examine costs from another angle. Stating that electricity per unit would cost such and such amount under different options is meaningless unless we examine the elements that get into cost calculation. For example, if the marginal investment costs are same or nearly the same for both the sectors, as we have noted earlier, the difference in per unit cost can arise due to :

(a) Rates of return are different for both the sectors. For example, private sector has been allowed a rate of return of 16 per cent. In this connection, it must be stated parenthetically, that the Working Group on private participation of power in 1987 had recommended a rate of return of 15 per cent, though the private sector had asked for 20 per cent.

(b) Plant Load Factor (PLF) could be different for both the sectors.

The first point needs to be examined more closely to be fair to the argument. What exactly is the actual cost of capital at the margin to SEBs and to the independent power projects (IPPs). Is capital available to the SEBs any cheaper? If not, a prescription of lower return would only mean a subsidy. It is, therefore, essential to remove the element of capital subsidy if we have to make any meaningful comparisons.

The impact of capital costs under two rates of return (assuming the same plant load factor) has been worked out as follows :

Investment cost per MW	Rs. 4.5 crores
Expected life of plant	20 years
Rate of return	12 per cent

Capital recovery factor	0.13388
Annualised cost/MW	Rs. 60,24,600
Cost per kWh at 68% PLF	Rs. 1.01.
Alternatively :	
Rate of return	16 per cent
Capital recovery factor	0.16867
Annualised cost/MW	Rs. 75,90,150
Cost per kWh at 68% PLF	Rs. 1.27

As can be seen the difference in capital cost is merely 26 paise per kWh. However, it must be noted that the final figures would change, if we change the assumptions. For example, PLF plays an important influence in the determination of capital cost per unit. With higher PLF, lower would be the capital cost per unit. The above calculations have been made for illustrative purposes. Also, whether front loading is done or back loading or a levellised tariff, the figures would be different.

Further, it has been argued that the rate of return would not be merely 16 per cent, but much more than this because of the incentive payments for capacity utilisation beyond 68.5 per cent of PLF. Here it must be stated that two opposing forces operate : when PLF goes up, incentive payments will push up the rate of return, but at the same time the capital cost per unit will decrease. When a system of incentives is determined, the net effect of these two mutually opposing forces has to be reckoned with.

The question of rate of return is more complex. The rate of return also depends upon perception of risk. S.P. Kothari has examined this aspect in detail in his article on 'Economics of Investment in Power' in the *Economic Times*. According to him the average rate of return on equity investment is about 20-25 per cent per annum. One therefore cannot think of obtaining investments at a rate lower than this. The rate of return of the Indian corporate sector would also be an eye opener in this connection. The dividends that they pay to their equity shareholders is a good indication of their rate of return.[6]

On the other hand, it has also been argued that foreign investment in power is riskless in view of the assured rate of return, counter guarantees, power purchase agreements etc.

As Mr. Kothari writes, "the new Maharashtra Government's decision to re-examine the Dhabol power project contract suggests that, despite all the guarantees, investors face uncertain prospects."[7]

On the other hand, if the power sector has been such an attractive investment proposition, we would have been flooded with offers. This does not seem to be happening, which means we need to re-examine the problem more incisively.

The Problems of the Power Sector

This raises questions with regard to the real problems facing the Power Sector in India. The recent debate and criticism on Enron Corporation actually shows lack of understanding why the Indian Power Sector was not in a position to bargain a better deal with IPPs. These facts have been repeated *ad nauseum*, but it needs restatement here, so that we may be able to develop strategies later on in the paper.

There is one thing in the argument against foreign participation, that is, the fear of what will happen to the finances of the SEBs, which are already in a precarious condition. Whether IPPs or not, SEBs are already in serious trouble with an accumulated loss of about Rs. 70,000 crores. In 1992-93 alone they had a loss of about Rs. 5,000 crores and according to the estimates, during the Eighth Plan period the loss is expected to be in the region of Rs. 30,000 crores.

With the increasing consumption, especially by the agricultural sector, which is highly subsidised (even to the extent of Re. 1 or more per unit on an average and much more at the time of peak loads), SEBs' problems are going to be compounded further, irrespective of whether SEBs invest in new generation or they buy from the private sector. It is, therefore, this problem that needs attention.

The concern expressed by many on the costs and prices of power reminds one of the observations of K.N. Raj in *EPW* in 1973 and the Rajdhyaksha Committee more recently. K.N. Raj states :[7]

> A common experience is that the more "basic" the investment undertaken by the State, the lower generally is expected to be the price charged for the product relatively to the price that might be fixed by the usual economic criteria. This is a reflection of the biases of the ruling class in the sense that it tends to judge the comparative advantages of the system to a large extent in terms of prices alone. . . .Whether it is irrigation, water, electricity or steel, the main argument against the higher price is that it would hurt "the small man" (even when it is the large enterprises that are the main beneficiaries).

And the Rajdhyaksha Committee observes :[8]

> In actual practice, however, the (electricity) Boards are often regarded as promotional agencies to be used to subsidise different classes of consumers and with little or no control over their tariff policy.

Certain categories of consumers had been enjoying large subsidies for a long time and it is this fact that comes against looking at the problem on the face of it. Under the changed circumstances, when the economy is going through the pangs of liberalisation, we may have to examine the question of costing and pricing electricity or for that matter any utility from a different framework.

Counter Guarantees

Another point of controversy has been on counter guarantees. To understand the circumstances behind counter guarantees, we need to restate the problem facing the SEBs.

As stated above, in 1992-93 alone, the SEBs incurred a loss of about Rs. 5,000 crores, which means a negative rate of return of 13 per cent on assets. The high losses are due to, among other things, high line losses (about 23 per cent) and low PLF (about 55 per cent). In most cases, their tariffs do not reflect cost of generation at the margin. This has resulted in their inability to meet their current revenue requirements and to finance growth of the system. SEB's inability to meet their revenue requirements is reflected in their payment crisis. For example, some time ago, it was reported that NTPC had yet to recover Rs. 3,135 crores from SEBs. Coal India also was compelled to start a cash and carry system. And they are all state owned enterprises.

Further, very recently, the World Bank decided to cancel loans to all SEBs, except Maharashtra and Kerala, and told them that to be eligible for loans, they would have to come out of their present precarious financial crisis.

We, therefore, need to examine the counter guarantees in this context. Let us first see the experience of other countries in this connection. The case of Latin American and Carribbean countries presents a very similar picture like that of ours in India. According to Saud Siddique, an Investment Officer in the Capital Markets Division of IFC :[9]

> In Latin America and Caribbean countries electricity was produced and delivered at a high cost, which ultimately proved unsustainable. For political reasons, major projects were built without full consideration of their economic costs and benefits. For example, rural electrification was extended to areas where it was financially viable, electricity tarrifs were set below long run marginal costs, and many utilities were used to generate employment without considering implications for efficiency. Poor management of the sector was also reflected in neglected

> maintenance, high transmission and distribution losses, brownouts, and electricity rationing. By the late 1980s, the electricity sector, like other state controlled sectors, was in a weak financial position... and large operating deficits.

As seen above the case seems to be very similar in every respect. Their experience, according to Siddique shows that IPPs are comfortable with projects which have;[10]

(a) Sales contracts denominated in US dollars or indexed to changes in the exchange rate to mitigate devaluation risk.
(b) Power purchase agreements directly with multinationals or with local exporters that have access to offshore hard currency accounts.
(c) Performance guarantees from the Government.
(d) International arbitration for resolution of disputes.
(e) Insurance for political violence, expropriation etc.

In this connection, according to Siddique, until a state owned utility has established a track record of financial viability and operating independence, it will be difficult to attract investors without Government support.

We, therefore, need to understand counter guarantees in the light of the above.

The above analysis shows that most of the criticisms are half-baked in nature. This does not, however, mean that everything is all right with the IPPs. For example, Girish Sant et. al. have done a brilliant analysis of the power purchase agreements and brought out the problems.[11] However, it must be stated that the root cause for all these problems lies in the fact that we failed to restructure the Power Sector before opening it up for foreign participation. A weak Power Sector can neither attract investment without governmental guarantees nor can it negotiate power purchase agreements from the position of strength. It is, therefore, this problem that needs immediate attention.

Towards a Consistent Power Policy

As the power policy is in the process of evolution, a lot of inconsistencies have got into it. For example, we have one pricing principle for one set of IPPs (cost plus), another set for others (16 per cent rate of return) and no policy in the case of the state sector. However, it must be added here that there is a policy with regard to rate of return, but it is observed more in its absence. We have different tariffs, as a matter of fact a variety of them, for irrigation consumers. This calls for a consistent tariff policy at National level. The multiplicity of policies have their origins in our constitutional and legal framework relating to electricity supply. As Anil

Upadhyay has noted, "the matter regarding awarding a particular project to a particular private party and connected commercial matters like finalising the PPA are entirely within the domain of the states/SEBs."[12] This has given rise to a number of problems. In addition, the present policy is not suitable for privatisation and nor for that matter consistent with liberalisation policies. Therefore :

(a) The Electricity Supply Act should be suitably amended. There should be provision for a Regulatory Authority which will examine all investment proposals, study the costs and prices, arrange for open debates before finalisation of the proposals. In the United States of America, for example, the Public Utility Regulation Act takes care of this aspect. In the absence of a centralised regulatory mechanism, the problems are bound to continue. UK also takes care more or less similarly.

Another important point relates to restructuring.[13] In the West, before privatisation, the organisations concerned were restructured. This was not done in India. As the electricity sector was not restructured before opening up for private participation they were in a very weak position to bargain. Restructuring will involve :

(a) Financial Restructuring
(b) Study of Costs and Determination of Prices on the basis of Long Run Marginal Costs (LRMC).[14] Innovations in tariff structure towards demand management, perhaps, something similar to the "price cap" to take care of the consumer interest, as they do in the UK.
(c) Determination of policies pertaining to subsidies and how to meet them.
(d) Separation of generation from transmission and distribution, introduction of competition in generation as they do in the United Kingdom.

The present unsavoury controversy and the implications could have been avoided, if we had taken these measures before opening up the Power Sector for private participation.

REFERENCES

1. A number of papers have been published in *Indian Express, Economic Times, Financial Express* and the *Economic and Political Weekly*. These were highly critical of the foreign participation in the Power Sector.
2. Government of India, Fourteenth Electric Power Survey, Government of India, New Delhi.
3. *Ibid.*
4. "Capital Confusion", (Editorial), *The Economic Times,* June 10, 1995. Please also see

Anil Upadhyay, A Mountain Out of a Molehill, *The Economic Times*, May 29, 1995, and Madhav Godbole, "Acute Affliction, Worst Remedies, *The Economic Times*, June 26, 1995.

5. Anil Upadhyay, Cost of Power : Misleading Numbers. *The Economic Times*, June 27, 1995.
6. S.P. Kothari, *Economics of Investment in Power, The Economic Times*, June 10, 1995, Please also see in this connection, Anil Upadhyay, The Holy Alliance in Power, *The Economic Times*, May 31, 1995.
7. K.N. Raj, The Politics and Economics of Intermediate Regimes, *The Economic and Political Weekly*, July 7, 1993.
8. Government of India, *Report of the Committee of Experts on Power*, (Chairman : V.G. Rajadhyaksha), GOI 1980.
9. Saud Siddique, Financing Private Power in Latin America and the Caribbean, *Finance and Development*, 32, 1, March 1995.
10. *Ibid.*
11. Girish Sant *et. al.*, *The Enron Controversy, Techno-Economic Analysis and Policy Implications*, Pune, Prayas, 1995.
12. Anil Upadhyay. The Frost after Big Bang, *The Economic Times*, May 26, 1995.
13. C. Gopalkrishnan, *Economic Consequences of Political Pricing of Power*, Nirnay, September, 1993. Please also see Swaminthan. A. Aiyar, Case for Renegotiating Dabhol, *The Economic Times*, July 17, 1995.
14. C. Gopalkrishnan, *The Economics of Electricity Pricing with Sepcial Reference to Gujarat*, unpublished Ph. D. Thesis, Gujarat University, 1988.

14

In Search of A Mother : The Missing Motherhood in a Liberalised Economy

R.P. Banerjee

With the liberalisation in the economy Indian women are coming up, at a rapid pace, in all spheres of its activity, thinking and with vision. In the process they are tending to loose the nobility of motherhood. Motherhood? What a nonsense! Indian women are rather preferring the way of life of an ultramod—the glazy scanty and transparent dressed miss, revealing her beauty and showering attractiveness to all around. Motherhood being the casualty of the process, the society is being deprived of the love and care of a mother. Women remaining a miss or girl in mind are forgetting the solemn duty of nursing and nurturing the children around. The heart of a mother having disappeared from the scenario, leads the society to the condition, as it is now. A motherless civilisation, heartless, as it is, can afford to remain indifferent to the death of millions of Ethiopian children, the crushing of the weaker masses throughout the world, the mass killing of Rwanda and the slow-poisoning of the global mind. Motherhood having been missed from the society, turns it into a rolling bio-entity that succumbs to any kind of pressure from around, and leads the same to an unpredictable destination.

In the fourth international meet on women and development held in Beijing, China, during September 1995 issues concerning the integrity, rights, and freedom of women were on the cards. Beijing Conference resolved 'sisterhood' as the achievable universal role model for the women. Yet the question remains—What bent of mind the sister is likely to possess ? 'Sister' of the health and hygiene domain or 'sister' as used in the common parlance where a bond of duty, care and love for others in a family is expected of the sister. The women activists feel that universal sisterhood would unite the women, to fight the gender enemies and to protect their rights and establish smooth existence. The issue is to identify the enemy—make appropriation and come out of the domination—the social chains arising out of gender oppressions. Male domination, as the activists identify the problem to be, seemed to be a hot matter of discussion.

But, the problem remains yet,—who mothers the society, who cares and after all who protects? The author finds it is not merely a superficial question of unnatural equalisation of establishing an universal 'sisterhood' that nurses the wounds arising out of the onslaughts. The question goes even beyond the context of women's liberation from the bondage of the society but to the realm of protecting a society.

The problem is felt more in Indian context. Indian women were known throughout the ages for their overwhelming motherhood. While liberalisation has resulted in the opening up of economy opportunities for women, the question of culture and protecting the basic fabric of the society is coming up. The problem is not new altogether but has caught up flames with the liberalised scenario in the National Economy.

The Agony of Women

It is a felt agony, at least now-a-days, that women are put in subjugation to male; in childhood to the father, in youth to the husband and in old age to the sons. But it is in particular reference to the youth phase, that is when subjected to the husband, the woman feels the best of her treasures to offer. Mature enough, as mother she has her treasures to phase out advising and nurturing. Indian women face the agony and pains throughout the entire spectrum of their life. As some have observed, the agony of Indian women mostly lies in her woman-phase that is when she lives the life of a wife with her husband.

Dowry and psychological tortures at the husband's house, in a joint setting, poses the central problem to a wife. Housewife gives a sigh when she finds the cards of a joint family are severed and transferred to a nuclear familial setting. This is reality, not a myth. Feminist scholars are trying to link the prevailing myths of Indian womanhood with reality. Jasodhara Bagchi, Director, School of Women's Studies, Jadavpur University, holds the opinion that the myth surrounding Indian women is not opposed to reality but re-enforces it. She argues:

> "Myths of Indian womanhood act on the reality of the lives of the women of India and are, in their turn, acted upon by the same reality. Systems of knowledge, belief, institutions, socio-economic

formulations born of historical encounters have contributed to this complex process"[1]

What is that myth and what is the reality becomes the question now. Scholars are giving high stress on the status of woman as mother—something noble and divine as a myth and woman as subjugate, tortured, subordinated species, always under the domination of either the father, the husband or the sons. The domination is most of the time torturous.Pains are so much that they remove the notion and reflections of pleasure even in a subtle way. Oppressions, even in the material term become so much evident that woman seldom finds the meaning of life. The agony of women is manifold. We may summarise some of them from our daily experiences:

(a) Problems arising out of marital contracts.
(b) Problems arising out of pre-marital family culture—previously, it is the conflict between two family cultures mostly concerning the rituals and related aspects.
(c) Economic problems assume social proportions and inflict on the mental world of the woman member.
(d) Ideals of life of woman.

Problems arising out of marital contracts are mostly that of dowry—the system that disturbs the sensitive minds. Yet the male population is not still so vocal against this. And the pity of the game is that behind all calculations and bargains relating to dowry there is always a woman listing and commanding so many things for her beloved son. While engaging in this sort of dowry bargaining for her son, the mother forgets the past—the amount of pain her father had to undergo to pay dowry during her marriage. Is it a case of ragging occurring in hostels or the revenge of a woman on the society by assaulting another woman to perpetuate the system ? Ashapurna Devi a reknowned woman writer puts this problem as follows :

> "Once in a while we do come across a situation where the groom has put his foot down against dowry but surely there are not too many such cases ? The reason why men never question the dowry system is that innate sense of superiority which makes them look at women with a kind of amused indifference. It is not easy to make them respect women's work and, of course, they are quite disdainful about talent in women"[2]

It's not really so. Let us look at some of the prominent literary works. Bankim Chandra Chatterjee (1838-94) had presented a few woman characters, out of whom that of Devi Chaudhurani (1884) seems to be worth mentioning here. The story says, Prafulla, thrown out of her husband's family, becomes Devi Chaudhurani, a robber queen with an almost demonic power but embraced with noble qualities. In recent times one name—that of Phulan Devi frequents as Bandit Queen. In her case also the role of a Bandit Queen traced its origin in the social oppression including sexual harassment. Faminists find their own way of protest to the male domination which they feel the root cause of all the evils confronting them. Rokeya Sakhawat Hossain (1880-1932) dreamed of a situation where role reversal between male and women took place—a world where men are confined to the murdana (meaning men's quarter in the household) and women have taken over the affairs of the country. War and crime are unheard of in this tastefully ordered world, where cooking is so simple that it is a pleasure, horticulture is a serious business, and science is used in the service of humanity.

This is a case of direct revenge in ideas. Not only does the sentiment is contained in the realm of ideas only, the author (not using the word authoress) gave a solemn call to her fellow women to stand erect and give up all symbols of male domination. To the housewives. Rokeya had argued that if the main object of wearing ornaments is to display a husband's wealth, "I could tell you a few ways in which you could do this. Why don't you decorate your pet dog with your necklace? When you go riding on your horse carriages, deck your horse with beautiful ornaments. You could use your bangles and bracelets as curtain rings in your drawing room. That would be the proper way of being extravagant with your husband's the Nawab's money..... If men want their wealth displayed, do it in the manner I have suggested. But why display their wealth on your body ?"

The question of beautifying herself is not so simple as the display of the husband's wealth. A Gujrati poem translated by Mita Ramaiya[5] gives the answer:

'I am pole with longing for my beloved;
People believe I am ill.
The sweetness of his lips is a pot of nector.
That is the only curd for which I crave;
Mira's Lord is Gridhar Nagar,

He will feed me nector again and again. Here we find, it is not the generalised state of affair to show off but a deep rooted love for the beloved makes the lady wait. And the endurance is transcended when there is element of the divine love springed in the process.

Woman protests against the atrocities are coming up. But the role of a woman of only a mere reproductive machine resulting in the birth of many children is a problem of the present world. Particular of a definite culture this seems to be the case of not only male oppression but woman permissiveness where bearing a number of children is a welcome proposition by women, the resulting situation being a world of underprivileged children and a society heavy with the hungry and underdeveloped masses. Let us visualize an incident narrated by Seabrook:

> 'In the back of the rickshaws sit a young couple. She is in orange saree, is in slacks and sandals. On their lap, they carry the corpse of a child about four years old, wrapped in white cerements and sprinkled with Jasmine and marigold petals. Their arms are around each other; they look blankly out from the rickshaw at the closed shops. No question of dowry death now—it is typical a underdeveloped dogmatic culture that gives license to multiple births without caring for the future of the on coming off-springs. This concerns her outlook, her ideals of life.'

The agony she feels, may be coming out of her own contemplation and ideals. Behavioural scientists find the clue:

> 'In the process of focussing only on being a woman, they have disowned their qualities of instrumentality with the environment. They have disowned their assertiveness, their ability to act and to give shape, form and direction to people and situations. In the name of confronting to the process of social role-taking, they have surrendered the male portion of their identity and have managed to hold anger, resentment and worth in abeyance'.

It is not only the question of fragmenting herself but also fragmenting the society as a consequence. The pain which comes from without has very much a root in the inner being. The woman-desire centers around the future, may be with the children of the husband or the beloved. Desires all around nourish them and limit their consciousness. But once liberated from the narrow domains of the family which they aspire for, women can overrun male in their pace. Liberating from the problems and pains presupposes liberating from the desire syndrome. Women thinkers like Dhruvarajan equate the point of liberation to that of asserting rights. She says 'unless women become aware of their rights and demand that they be accorded those rights there is no possibility or any real change.

Rights's assertion has its own positive aspects. But does the rights' assertion at the level of in-laws protect the rights of wives or does the rights being asserted by the wives protect the rights of the children ? The chain is that of a desire. Women activists and thinkers are tuned to think in the line of asserting rights—which is its end in itself. The workers' rights were asserted in the socialized economics' but that could not protect the whole of those economies from being crumbled down. Let us look at the current scenario keeping this rights' principle in our mind and try to see if India has anything to offer or not?

Women in Liberalised Indian Economy

The news of beauty queens being crowned to Indian ladies are sweeping the land. Various international bodies are engaged in selecting the best beauties of the world. Sen and Rai having been identified as the world's bests, the Indians dance with joy. While expressing this person's full gratitude to all individuals including the beauty queens, may I raise the question—what is the mindset that leads one to participate in the beauty contest? Is it just a serene beauty to offer nobility to the world or is it offering oneself as a product before hungry and passionate selves that wants to cash on the exposed beauty? What is the commodity here? Verily the body and engrossed mind of the beauty. 'Oh the world, look at me, I am the best commodity in flesh and scanty robes appearing before you—enjoy me with your eyes. Let your distant senses have a taste of my beauty and myself'—Is it not the mindset that provokes passion and tends to perpetuate the desire syndrome. A folk song of Orissa beautifully describes this mindset :

"You will pull me out. O Handsome,

I will become the dust on the road..."

The waves of liberalisation are hitting the society in the manner in which the hidden desire of the society takes shape. With the spell of liberalisation gaining strength, an open culture has come in, honoured and followed by millions of women who were previously trying to assert their rights only in overturning the table to the men. The culture of openness has appeared not only in the form of Culture of selling beauties but also in a subtle way selling the noble contents. The result is a field where women are competitors of male in the sphere of managing the society. The concept of women competing out men is not new but an altogether a different angle.

Now, the pursuit is that of a career. It's a competition not of acquiring knowledge and wisdom, not of including noble qualities but one of career pursuits. The idea is to establish herself in a role reversal scenario and confront the other roles. In the analysis of behavioural scientists is this new stepping out to create a space beyond her horizon. "first unleash, with fury and intensity, the residence of the male identity in themselves. They tend initially to be aggressive and seek for themselves what they perceive as being the privilege accorded to men..... Some women give themselves freedom to be impulsive. They take their freedom for granted and indulge in 'free sex' and live in defiance and with bravo. Their search for companionship leads them to social rebellion. Others however, recognize the suitability of finding meaningful relationships in such encounters. They then search for alternatives to discover fulfillment."

Now the question is, being quite one with the sense of agony, perils and pains that women encounter in their middle life where she has to resettle one situation (of living in parental residence) to another (of living with husband). Whether this sort of encountering is letting the women undergo a role reducial or role reversal. By offering herself as a beauty is not bad at all if there were no trade principle behind that. Trade principle robs the woman of her nobility and turns her into a mere product, may be intangible, to be traded in and across the boundaries of the country.

The sheer pursuit for careerism leads her to think in terms of her role in the society—as a working woman, her status, position and utility in the society. As an onlooker she now becomes exteriorized. Exteriorized life, which seems to be quite contrary to the concept of womanhood in India, becomes a phenomenon. In the industries, academy, politics, administration, everywhere a woman is not only well suited but her presence is what is highly required but the problem arises when the mind becomes highly exteriorized.

Exteriorization : The Root Cause of Disintegration

Woman at work tries to establish a new kind of balance in the society. Particularly there are few roles in organizations where women are highly wanted. For example, the role of a scientist, a researcher, an author, an analyst, a receptionist etc. Women in the realm of work even fare better than man in many cases. Some experts are saying now that with the right brain more active women are more holistic. So work that require synthesizing abilities are better discharged by women than men by definition. At this point we can mention Vivekanand II also who traced the problem of India's misery to two—one the neglect of the masses and the second non-participation by the women in the society's productive and working process. Society cannot afford to layoff half of its vital strength, the strength of women. And obviously, it is the need of the country and the society that women take active role. Liberalised economic scenario had enhanced this possibility. With the onset of liberalisation more and more avenues of work and activities are big generated for women. The question of preserving the cultural identity looms large. Liberalisation and globalisation occurring at simultaneous pace in India on the noble dimensions in life are being forgotten and economic aim is overruling. Women in organisations, on the streets and on daises—exhibiting beauty have fallen prey to the economic aims in life. The resultant effect is serious for a country like India, the advance of western industrial civilisation aggressing the Indian soil generated questions of the like in the great minds like Sri Aurobindo, who had said:

> "If we take over for instance that terrible monstrous and compelling thing, that giant asuricc creation, European industrialism—unfortunately we are being forced by circumstances to do it—we may under more favourable conditions develop it by our wealth and economic resources, but assuredly we shall get too its social discords and moral plagues and cruel problems, and I do not see how we shall avoid becoming the slaves of the economic aim in life and losing the spiritual principle of our culture."

Yes, the social consequences are the most important part of the problem of our culture confronting the aggressive western exteriorized culture.

Throughout the ages Indian civilisation has offered a beautiful thing to the world—its family system. With the family as the unit having a father, a mother. Children under the advisory control of the grand relations lived a very beautiful life. The men being the external ties, the entire locus of the systems has been on the women. Women as grandmother offering precious advices, providing the teaching to the children, that contributed to their character, woman as mother nourishing, nurturing and realming the children and caring all others with love or gratitude was the essence of the system. The hidden agenda was to establish a balance between the centripetal force of women drawing in the centre all the repulsive forces with the help of the chord of love and affection and the centrifugal men with the tendency to be exteriorized sometimes with or without tangible purpose. The resultant effect was a beautiful system that made family a unique place to live in, to have the flavour of happiness and pleasure for all concerned. That's why the Indian system of living in family was that of living in an *ashram*. *Ashram* in the sense that it had its basis on *dharmas*—the moral principles and other aspects of life were governed by the *dharmic* principles. In the pursusit of *artha* and *kama*, the men who were out on the streets seldom dared to perform activities that contravened *dharmic* principles. The accountability was not so much with the legal system of the society but to the collective conscience of the members of the family and the reigning deity who had her seat in a honoured place inside the house. A system with this perfect balance between the centripetal and centrifugal forces might have aberrations also. But the aberrations were not all the major dynamics, was the noble path followed by the members coming from a family.

Not only this, the family was the ideal centre for drawing inspirations—the roles were not conflicting, rather these were complementary. Now with the globalisation and liberalisation becoming a phenomenon—needs and wants have multiplied many times. 'Contentment' is proving to be an idiotic term. Like men, also, ladies are viewing life as something that must be fulfilled by economic and materialistic aim by enjoyments only. That is why the women are venturing out on the streets and trying to catch up with a straw. She goes out of the *ashram* in search of a career, competes with him. Now that the *ashram*-boat is without centripetality where is the balance? No where; everyone is in the pursuit of careeristic goal. Well, but at what cost?

Away from Mother's Lap

The casualty is the child. On the 19th July1995, Calcutta High Court was giving a judgment on whom to allocate the responsibility of maintaining Ayan, a 7 years old child. The case report 13 says Ayan's mother wanted to live in a nuclear family with her husband and child only and trying to break from a joint family. The problem was mentioned by her to the court. After three years of hearing etc. the judges passed the verdict that while Ayan's parent be allowed separate life, Ayan can live with the special officer where his mother may be allowed to visit him. Ayan's mother visited him at the flat of the special officer with toys and chocolates. She asked, 'Ayan have you eaten anything'? The boy answered with nothing but tears... The mother is in a hurry and leaves the boy.

The case gives a direct indication though from one angle, to the consequences. The rising pursuit of careerism by both men and women leaves the family a meaningless station-rest house where the ashramic bondage gradually shatters and in the event of either of them becoming a prey to egotism the system crumbles. The children devoid of proper love and care seldom understand the true import of love and affection and in the later life are prone to become a prey to such disvalues, as greed, lust, anger, restlessness and general cruelty. This cruelty turns into a characteristic phenomenon. Cruelty and grabbing would be the future dynamics of the society inhabited by these grown ups.

Not only the forbidden child, but also the entire society lacks in the lap of a mother of love, to nurse and to care. With motherhood gradually disappearing from the scenario creates the entire problem. Swami Vivekananda's viewpoint may throw much light on this:

> "In the west it (womanhood) found its ideal in the wife, in India, in the mother".

The problem of breaking families originates with the problem of roles, basically. The educated woman, prompted by her urge to actualise egoself and supported by the environment of liberalisation, considers her role as the prime one and tries to establish her hold. The role model of a wife dominating the role model of a man is contrary to the traditions of an enduring civilisation like India. Wife is so intolerant that she forgets her future motherhood and resulting hold and the subsystem. This is one aspect, the other aspect of the problem is the male trying to dominate woman and judging her from his own angularities. Again, Vivekananda's advice is worthy mentioning;

> "when you are judging man and woman, judge them by the standard of their respective greatness. One cannot be in other's shoes".

Judging women from male point of view is wrong. A holistic outlook is required. The question is to establish and maintain a living society where the man, woman and child get normal breathing provision and grow in their own fashion. While the child adopting an adult's role breaks the system, similarly with a woman performing the role of a man' no one's role is inferior in any respect to another. Quoting a Sanskrit poet. Vivekananda highlights the importance of the role of a woman:

> *"No griham grihamityahu grihini griham uchyte"*—"It is not the building that makes the house, but it is the wife that makes it"—says a Sanskrit poet, and how true it is! The roof that affords you shelter from heat and cold and rain is not to be judged by the Pillars that support it— the finest corinthian columns though they be—but by the real spirit pillar who is the centre, the real support of the home—the women."

But that does not mean the women remain as immobile as the pillar. Vivekananda wants woman's participation in the society's activities but with slight difference from the western outlook. He says;

> "If the women are raised, then their children will by their noble actions glorify the name of the country then will the culture, knowledge, power and devotion awaken in the land".

The difference lies in the inward seeking mind of Indian woman. Indian women have mothered and sistered-their own civilisation with the strength of their realisation and holding the divine by rituals. It was the daily rituals involving the household deity that maintained the integrity and protected the harmony of its civilisation.

Wisdom of Women

The Indian tradition has levied a very high opinion of mothers. Mother regarded as a protector, was conceived of as parallel to the Lordship of Vishnu. Woman in Indian context is considered as the *'shakti'* or energy of the Brahman and is considered as different manifestation of one and the same divinity. Brahman undertakes activities through his *Shakti*—the mother. Mother principle in India is therefore one of the most fundamental principles.

In the Rig Veda we get the name of Vac-devi and the daughter of sage Ambhrin who was one of the wisest and realised souls. Devi Vac revealed the famous Devi Sukta, which says;

> "...... I am the ruling Queen, the amasser of treasures, full of wisdom, first of those worthy of worship.
>
> In various places the divine power have set me.
> I enter many homes and take numerous forms.
>
> The man who sees, who breathes, who hears words spoken, obtains his nourishment through me alone.
>
> Unrecognizing me, he yet dwells in me.
> Listen, you who know! what I say is worthy of Believing"

The verse cited above reveals the strength of realisation and wisdom. Not only Vac alone, twenty seven truth seer women have contributed their visualisations of truth through words placed as hymns of Rig Veda, the most ancient scripture of the world. To name a few among these are Viswaghara, Ghosha, Apala, Godha, Gargi, Maitreyi etc. Amongst these wise women the dialogue that Gargi had with the Sage Yajnavalkya is very famous. Wives of sages likes Lopawmudra, Sulochana were attracted, to live a life of hermit in the *'tapovan'* (forest of austerity) leaving their rich and kingly homes, by the strength of consecretion of the sages. Maitreyi's refusal to the ownership of riches indicates the attainment of a very high level of wisdom that helped contain the desires.

The vedic sages saw woman as the divine symbolising all cosmic activities and forms. Deva Duhita or the daughter of heaven is worshiped in the Rig Veda as "See now, the shining daughter of heaven approaches, dispelling gloom of night that we may see

The friendly lady ushers in the light".

Woman is considered as the daughter of light who provides illumination to remove darkenss:

> "Her face turned toward
> this far-flung world.
> She rises, enwrapped in bright garments.
> Shining with gold.
> With rays of light bedecked.
> She sends forth the world on its course".

It's not only a world of divine freedom of women but that of men's subordination. With the rupture of the culture by aggressions from other quarters, the kind of laws and rules subjugating women as prescribed in later phases are found. Unfortunately, critics of Indian culture as also a section of woman activists try to brand India's heritage as anti-woman—which is nowhere near the fact. Not only in the case of Maitreyi but also in many other cases the same strength of character and wisdom are found. One exmple is that of Madalsha, — a queen. Madalsha herself had imparted the knowledge of the supreme and out of four sons she allowed first three to adipt thc lifc of ascctism. Woman's transcendence and wisdom is again reflected in the character of Gandhari, the mother of Duryodhan. Duryodhan had sought his mother's blessings to win the war but the mothers blessings were not directed to her son Duryodhan, rather she had said, 'Let the righteous win'.

Can we see the contrast with the present day mother-turned-ladies! The difference lies mostly in the areas of concern for self. The wise women of whom reference has been made above were common in one respect, in transcending their lower ego considerations. Deviated from this ideal, when women become instruments of selfish need fulfilment they leave the society a chance of disintergration.

Conclusion

It is out of deep compassion for the society that one is raising these issues. The question is of prioritisation one of giving importance to a particular role. Motherhood does not imply just mothering a child but it is the heart of the mother which the country needs so much. The society confronts an emerging situation where the heart of a mother is gradually withering out. 'We need the motherly heart'—the cry of inhabitants of a heartless society may reach the ear of mothers. Society can regain its motherly heart if mothers first re-emerge as persons with motherly heart. Before we debate on this issue, let us keep in our mind the fate of "Ayan" the seven year old boy trying to find peace in mother's lap but being denied.

Let the call be in tune with the Vedic sage once again;

"We yearn to be yours (O mother), partaking in your rewards.

Accept our love as that of mother's children"

Economic liberalisation should go hand in hand with Vedic wisdom and bring mother back to the centre of womanhood. The country and the civilization is groaning for the heart of a mother and not for the beauty of a woman.

REFERENCES

1. Jasodhara Bagchi, (ed), *Indian Women: Myth and Reality,* Sangam Books, 1995, pp. 1-2.
2. Ashapurna Devi, *Indian Women: Myth and Reality* ed. by, Jasodhara Bagchi, Sangam Books, 1995, p.21.
3. Susie Tharu and K. Lalita (ed.) *Women Writing in India : 600 B.C. to the present*, Oxford University Press, Delhi, 1993.
4. *Ibid*, p. 341.
5. *Ibid*, p. 92.
6. Geeti Sen (ed.), *Perceiving India; Insight and Enquiry*, Sage Publications & India International Centre, New Delhi, 1993.
7. Indira J. Parikh and Pulin K. Garg. *Indian Women an Inner Dialogue,* Sage Publications, New Delhi, 1989. p. 181.
8. Vanaja Dhruvarajan, *Hindu Women and the Power of Ideology*, Vistaar Publications, New Delhi,1989 p. 119.
9. Susie Tharu and K. Lalita, *Ibid*, p.128.
10. Indira J. Parikh and Pulin K. Garg, *Ibid* p.181.
11. Swami Vivekananda, *The Foundations of Indian Culture*, Sri Aurobindo Ashram, Pondichery 1975, p. 388.
12. Parthasarathi Sengupta, *'Bartaman'* (Bengali daily) Calcutta : 20th July, 1995, p. I.
13. Swami Vivekananda, *Complete Works*, Advaita Ashram, Calcutta 1989, Vol. 2 p. 506.
14. *Ibid*, p. 26.
15. *Ibid* Vol. 6, p. 247.
16. *Ibid* Vol. 7, p. 220
17. Raimundo Panikkar, *The Vedic Experience* Mantramanjari, Motilal Banarasidas Publishers, New Delhi; 1994, pp.96-97.
18. *Ibid* p.168.
19. *Ibid* p.169.
20. *Ibid*, p.168.

15

Globalisation, Management and Human Values

K. Ramakrishna Reddy and Lalitha Sreenath

The glaring lopsided growth and development of the countries all over the world has prompted the World Bank Group in the nineties to promote economic development and reduce poverty. To achieve these objectives, it has supported Private Sector Development (PSD). Encouraging the development of an efficient private sector and permitting entrepreneurial activity to play a greater role in economic growth is the main objective of PSD. Greater reliance is placed on private sector as a vehicle for growth in countries across a broad spectrum of economic, social and political development. Consequently, the influence of privatisation is growing fast and wide. Perhaps, privatisation of public enterprises marks the emergence of capitalistic thinking even as nationalisation made the approval of socialistic thinking. In fact, the privatisation can be construed to an expression of trust in the efficiency of markets and the distrust in the efficiency of the Government. While the conservatives have argued that the Governments have grown too fat and must be reduced, the liberals apprehend that the compaign for efficiency is indeed a camouflage to efface out the concept of Welfare State. Despite the claims and counter-claims the fact is that India is, willy nilly, heading in the direction of customer-contractor structure, with diminishing core ministries and expanding areas of privatisation, and entering into contracts with the private sector to transact heretofore Government business under the influence of market ideology. The two glaring objectives of this new ideology can be spelt out as : (i) to reduce the operational one of the Government and to liberate market forces in a variety of ways, such as deregulation, and adoption of various monetary and fiscal measures; and

(ii) to import market concepts and incentives into the operation of the Government itself.

Now, India has become a partner of globalisation, since four years its commencement, the policy of liberalisation as well as the role of the State continue to be vague and hazy till this day, Strangely, even the staunch opponents to the policy seem now to have accepted it as a *fait accompli*. This confirms the view that liberalisation if used in a planned and in a positive manner could bring about far-reaching macro and micro level changes, discernible improvement in the entire gamut of life of the average Indian citizen—with quality products, efficient services and abundant growth potential.

Ethical Values

The essence of market is the freedom of choice of the individual. The concept of public choice is based on the assumptions of 'self-interest' and 'rationality'. The basic behavioural postulate of public choice is that man is an egoistic, rational utility maximiser. The idea that self-interest is both necessary and desirable for an 'efficient' economic system has its genesis in the most famous passage of Adam Smith:

> "It is not from the benevolence of the butcher, the brewer or the baker, that we expect our dinner, but from their regard to their own interest. We address ourselves, not to their humanity but to their self-love".

In contrast, the traditional Indian idea, as popularised by Mahatma Gandhi, emphasises that restraint (*Nivriti*) is preferable to indulgence (*Pravriti*) and the distinction between 'pleasurable' and the 'good' (as explained in the Katho-Upanishad) is significant. Interpreting in the modern jargon, it would mean that 'utility' and 'welfare' are not treated synonymously, as the neo-developmental market proponents may choose to. Thus increase in consumption, beyond a point, may increase 'utility' as consumption gives pleasure but it may not be 'good' for man and society'. The traditional Indian idea thus suggests that voluntary limitation of wants is both good and sustainable.

Hence, when globalisation has led to the development of the market economy in our country, growth of output and consumption become the central concern of development. If rapid growth of consumption is the chosen objective, then there seems to be an apparent dichotomy between the traditional and modern approaches. But this can be easily countered when resort is made to other oriental ideas. As Japanese Management practices have revealed, appealing even slightly to Peoples' 'humanity' can enhance efficiency. In Japan, their values, their traditions, their culture and beliefs have been used to perform the objective, impersonal tasks of a modern economy and to harness modern technology for social and economic performance. Marketing is viewed as a technique that could be easily embedded in the deeply rooted Confucian ethics of mutual relationships. A sale to a customer thus creates a 'relationship' and with it a permanent commitment. Further, Japanese managers do not start out with desired profit, that is with a financial objective in mind. As Peter F. Drucker explains: "They begin by asking 'How much market standing need to have leadership?' 'That new market standing do we need to have?' 'How much do we need to spend to train and develop people, to build distribution, to provide the required services?'" Only then do they ask 'And how much profit is necessary to accomplish these business objectives?' Then the resulting profit requirement is usually a good deal higher than the profit goal of the Westerner. More importantly, the Japanese believe that the end of business is not "only to make money". Though money-making is essential for business survival, it is also a result of performance and measurement thereof. The purpose of business is to create a customer and perform a service satisfactory to the customer. These traditional national values of the Japanese have made them the most successful business-managed country in the world. Thus, increasing internationalisation of the ancient oriental idea (found in varied forms in Confucianism, Buddhism, Hinduism and other Eastern schools of thought), that 'goodness' in man has powerful social externalities which increase the efficiency levels in society, into modern business management would yield far-reaching results. Then it would be found that the welfare enhancing aspects of ethical development are multitudinal and actually are compatible with old economic theories. Borrowing from an Indian example, Kautilya in his *'Arthshastra'* indicates that *arjana* (creation), *vardhna* (increase) and *rakhhana* (protection) are the three important aspects of the *artha* or the 'Wealth of Nation'. He believes that wealth is the star for wealth and advises to be guided by this star along and not by the stars in heaven. And, further explains that the ruler should have the overall achievement orientation, guided not by narrow self-interest but by *Yogakshema, i.e.* well-being prosperity, hapiness and security of the subjects. If this theory is fully imported into modern business strategies and management, value-conflicts and controversies regarding the need for liberalisation policy in our national context, would all vanish.

Corporate Social Responsibility

In the light of the liberalisation process, the modern corporation has evolved into a social as well as an economic institution. Without losing sight of its need to make profit, it has obligations and responsibilities which go far beyond the profit motive. The existence of corporate is a stark reality today. Because these corporations occupy a commanding position in the industrial sector and partly because they have vast wealh at their disposal, they are in a position to materially influence the economic, foreign and domestic policies of the Government through lobbying in the legislatures, contact with bureaucracy, contribution to political parties and threats of stoppage of production. These are the means through which the economic power of the corporation is translated into political power. These corporations on which the society depends to a great extent for its survival, have an obligation to use their power responsibly without any harmful detriment to the society. This obligation rests only at the moral level, as an extension of the moral principle that every man is morally responsible for his acts in economic transactions as in everything else, and a corporation commanding vast resources should use them for the benefit of the public. It also recognises that each person is attached to an extended social system on which he is partly dependent. Consequently, certain obligations and responsibilities arise from such an attachment. After all, the business organisation is set up in response to some social need by some person who saw a way to make money out of serving that social need. So the solution is to find out how to fill the needs of the society by the use of the profit motive.

Under the classical market model economy, the behaviour of the business corporations was adequately controlled by the pressures from the market and what little regulation was necessary being accomplished within the framework of corporate laws through such devices as the doctrine of *ultra vires* and *prohibition* against corporate waste. Unless there is some tangible benefit or return to the corporation, corporate philanthropy was prohibited by Company Law. So, under the classical market model enterprise, the only responsibility of the corporation was towards the shareholders and there was absolutely no scope for the corporation to take active part in alleviation of social evils, since the prohibition against corporate waster constituted a big hurdle. Gradually, the view that a business corporation has duties to employees, consumers, suppliers, dealers, community as well as to shareholders and that it was the duty of the Boards to mediate between competing interests, gained popularity. More and more managers looked upon themselves as balancing private interests in the general interest of the longevity of the enterprise itself. This in turn has led to the emergence of professional managers occupying a pivotal role in the management of corporations. The professional manager has now to don the role of trustees balancing the interests of many diverse participants and constituents in the enterprise whose interests may often conflict with those of others, *viz.*, the demands of employees for more wages and improved working conditions, customers for lower prices and greater value for money, vendors for higher prices, Government for more taxes and shareholders for higher returns and greater capital appreciation. Thus Drucker describes management as an example of social innovation. Management is thus the specific function of today's society of organisation. It is the same practice that converts a mob into an effective, purposeful and productive group. The essence of modern organisation is to use individual strengths and knowledge productively and to render individual weaknesses irrelevant. Hence, the modern manager could well start with the following priorities in the 'ethics programme'.

1. Do Your Best

Healthy competition helps us and others to do the very best by throwing up new challenges and helping us attain newer heights of efficient performance. Healthy competition comes when we approach life and work with desire to'do my best every day'. This focusses the competition internally instead of just externally, encouraging to compete with one's own self. The following checklist would prove useful in this regard.

(a) *Purpose :* Do you have a reason to do your best?

(b) *Commitment* : Do you work tenaciously towards your goal?

(c) *Responsibility* : Do you hold yourself accountable for your choices?

(d) *Flexibility* : Are you willing to creatively adapt to change?

(e) *Support* : Do you have others on your team?

Doing one's best is a way of demonstrating commitment, the single most important factor in becoming a long-term success in both the professional and personal life.

2. Doing One's Duty

The really successful business manager would see duty as the responsibility to work for everyone's benefit, *i.e. Yogakshema.* In the organisation this would mean working to the benefit of shareholders, customers, employees, suppliers and the community. In private life it would mean working to the benefit of family, friends and one's own self. As persons of integrity, the modern professional managers may not get to choose whether or not to 'do our duty'—they would only get to choose how they would be able to discharge their duty. They are not content to just do their job, but would strive to do more than that. They would not only want to do what is right, but rather would want to do what seems right—even if they have to lose something in the process.

Modern managers often have to face 'moral dilemmas' many times during each day, over diverse issues everytime they have to decide. The following six-point test 'The Ethics Litmus Test' would help in evaluating managerial decisions:

a Does the course of action you plan to follow seem logical and reasonable? If it makes sense to you, regardless of what others may comment, it is probably right.

b Does it pass test of sportsmanship? If everyone followed the same course of action, would the results be beneficial for all ?

c Where will your plan of action lead? How will it affect others? What will it do for you?

d Will you think well of yourself when you look back at what you've done?

e Try to look at the problem objectively. Pretend that it is the problem of the person you most admire. Ask yourself how that person would handle it.

f Hold up the final decision to the glaring light of publicity. Would you want your family and friends to know what you have done? The decisions we make in the hope that no one will find out are usually wrong.

3. Evolving a Suitable Corporate Culture

Corporate culture is a system of shared values and beliefs that interact with a company's people, organisational structures and control system to produce behevioural norms. It encompasses the company's goals and the dominant ideologies and underlies much of the way in which things get done in the organisation. Corporate culture influences behaviour in three areas :

Corporate Values

Both the ends (goals) and the means (action) plans for achieving these goals are spelt out.

Organisation Climate

This refers to the working atmosphere of the organisation as preceived and experienced by its members and the general feeling and reaction of the community to the characteristics and quality of the community characteristics.

Management Style

Management style means the way in which managers behave and exercise authority as conditioned by the organisation's culture and values. A management style encouraging commitment and co-operation would tend to be democratic, relaxed, friendly, informal, open but nonetheless decisive.

It is for the manager to create a high integrity work environment that allows customers, employees and the community to have their needs met only by embracing integrity. If integrity is the main thing wanted in the workplace, then it must be made important on a daily basis. Hence, to help create a high-integrity work environment, the manager should:

(i) Communicate the organisation's expectations to employees;
(ii) Hire and pomote based on demonstration of high ethical standards;
(iii) Deal swiftly with unethical behaviour.

The following checklist for integrity rating in an organisation would be helpful to the modern professional manager in the present Indian circumstances:

1. Are decisions based on what's right for all parties and not on the basis of tradition or political positioning?
2. Do the people at all levels of organisation clearly understand what is expected of them in the area of productiviy, quality, service, job performance, and integrity?
3. Are the individuals within the organisation continually encouraged to upgrade their skills—technical and communicative besides improving inter-personal relationship?
4. Are the organisation leaders and managers held accountable for the development of their people?
5. Do the organisation's leaders set a good example of integrity?
6. Are the individuals rewarded for their performance that demonstrate integrity?
7. Does the organisation deal swiftly with individual performance that does not meet its standards of integrity?
8. Has the organisation a reputation for honesty, value, integrity among customers and the community?
9. Are both the management and non-management employees united behind the common goal of providing quality products and services to customers in a manner that communicates honesty, value and integrity?
10. Does the organisation act responsibly toward the welfare of the community as a whole?

The above checklist would help in rating the integrity level in which the organisation presently stands and in chalking out the correct future course of action to put the organisation back on its ethical rails. A key part to be played in this process would best be the chief executive, who with the support of his team would help in achieving excellence by defining the organisation's mission, getting his vision of what needs to be done across to everyone, defining and promulgating what he believes to be the right organisational values, exercising leadership in order to motivate the members of the organisation and ensuring that they are involved in and committed to achieving its objectives. An analysis of values can be made broadly on the following lines :

1. Are employees proud of the company and its products or services?
2. Does the company truly believe in producing high quality products and providing a good service to its customers?
3. Is the company innovative and acting as a socially-responsible entity?
4. Are managers and employees really interested in increasing productivity?
5. Do managers truly believe in the importance of the people with working life, providing opportunities for growth and development, giving individual attention to the needs of the employees, keeping them informed on matters that affect them and involved in decision making, and maintaining a fair pay system which rewards staff accordingly to their responsibilities and contributions?

Values will only be got across if they are believed in, acted upon and pursued relentlessly. In Matsushita Company in Japan, at 8.00 a.m. every morning all the 87,000 employees sing the company's song and recite the company's code of values.

Conclusion

Today, we sometimes see those people who violate the principles of integrity honoured as if bad were good and right were wrong. When we see such things, it is logical to ask, 'why would anyone in today's competitive environment want to follow such strong principles?' Successful business professional managers know that by following these principles their organisations will reap multiplied results. In return for their efforts, they would receive results such as increased loyalty from employees and customers word mouth advertising, fewer people problems, safer work environments, increased profits, less personal stress and increased personal satisfaction and perspective. These social benefits of ethical development would definitely spell better standard of living for the people with better corporations impregnated with a social conscience and better human beings, as an additional bonus. As the U.N. International Strategy of 1970 suggests: "The ultimate objective of development must be to bring about sustained improvement in the well-being of the individual and bestow benefits on all. If undue privileges, extremes of wealth and social injustice persist then development fails in its essential purpose. Qualitative and structural changes in society must go hand-in-hand with rapid economic grwoth". Thus in the Indian context, for better perception and appreciation of the New Economic Policy of liberalisation, we should aim at reducing economic disparities as a central objective in our endeavour for development. As President Dr. Shankar Dayal Sharma stated, "Reform and restructuring acquire meaning only when the common man is benefitted—when his quality of life improves and his burdens and worries diminish". Hence, in this transitional phase, fears and doubts about the viability of Manmohanamics and the suitabilities of economic reforms to the teeming population struggling below the poverty line could be brushed aside with one broad sweep, by converting corporate managements into responsible power structures with mandatory duties and verifiable accountabilities to respond to social needs. Consequent to these sweeping changes in Business Management in India, it would be highly appropriate to Management Programme to include a paper entitled "Business and Ethics" with emphasis on human values.

16

Economic Liberalisation and Employment

N. Shasikala Devi

Employment generation has been considered as an important policy framework in most of the labour abundant, less developed economies like India. Even though Indian planners took concise efforts to create employment opportunities for the growing labour force, our development strategies remained virtually ineffective in bringing out a structural reorganisation in terms of employment across the different sectors of the economy. Prior to independence, agricultural sector was found to be the major absorber of the ever growing labour force in India. Since the Second Five Year Plan has laid its importance for the development of industrial sector, the successive years have witnessed a steady growth in manufacturing employment. The share of manufacturing sector in the aggregate employment has increased considerably during the seventies. But the world industrial recession has hard hit the industrial sector of the Indian economy during the eighties.

Despite massive investment to increase the industrial output rather than employment, the share of manufacturing employment has declined slowly throughout the eighties. The limited liberalisation approach for the Indian industries during the mid-eighties has proved to be ineffective. Meanwhile, the economy has plunged into serious economic turbulences and the Government of India has been in a position to adopt the liberalisation policies as prescribed by the IMF and the World Bank in terms of Stabilisation Programmes. A major goal of this programme was to improve efficiency and growth through free competition in an open economy. In this context an attempt to examine the impact of economic liberalisation on employment growth in the organised manufacturing sector would serve as a useful research for planners and policy makers. But, examining the impact of liberalisation even it though has its own rationale at this stage, the data availability with a considerable time lag limits the scope of the research. Thus, assessment with the help of pre-liberalisation data is considered as a useful method for forecasting the present conditions of the Indian economy which is characterised with a large size and weaker communication system. Based on the neo-classical economic framework, the paper intends to examine the influence of the growth of manufacturing output on manufacturing employment on the organised sector during 1981-82 to 1992-93. From the estimated long run elasticity, we could forecast the number of employment opportunities to be created by every one percent increase in the income of the organised manufacturing sector.

Problem of Unemployment : The World Scenario

After the Second World War, the global economy has experienced unprecedented dimensions of economic growth leading to highly sophisticated and standardised development activities. However, these developments have been overshadowed by general failure of the economies in generating additional employment opportunities for the growing labour force. In the industrialised nations, even though labour supply has not increased substantially, the employment growth has lagged behind the growth in Gross Domestic Product. According to UNDP Report [1] "Three quarters of increase in output in these countries came from increase in the capital investment and the rest of it from Total Factory Productivity Growth". In the developing nations the rate of growth of employment has increased steadily, but it is not sufficient to absorb the growing labour force. The attention of the International Agencies and the Heads of the Government thus has been on the twin problems of unemployment and underemployment.

The data from the Human Development Report reveals that in DECD countries, the unemployment stayed above 6.00 percent in 1991. In Asian countries like India and Pakistan despite a respectable GDP growth, unemployment rates remained during June 1993 warned that the problem of unemployment would have dangerous social implications. The International Labour Office has predicted that more than 35 million workers would be unemployed in the industrialised nations at the end of 1994. In India too, open unemployment was estimated at 17 million in 1992-93 [2].

Employment : The Indian Experience

The structural distribution of labour force in the organised sector during the eighties indicates the predominance of the community and social service sector. It accounts for nearly 40 percent of the organised labour force of India, revealing the growing nature of service sector in employment generation during the last decade. Manufacturing, even though lagged behind, has employed nearly more than 25 percent of the labour force. However, the manufacturing employment in the organised sector has declined slowly throughout the eighties. Within the manufacturing sector, the share of private sector was found to be high but shows a slight deceleration. The partial liberalisation of the mid-eighties for the industrial manufacturing has reflected comparactively higher levels of output and employment than the previous years. On the whole, the employment growth has lagged behind the output growth.

Liberalisation Policies : Experience of Other Nations

Before examining the liberation policy measures adopted in India, it would be worthwhile to briefly review the experience of other nations which took the similar policy measures in earlier years. Prior to the adoption of IMF/World Bank stabilisation package, the Mexican economy had grown at a rate of 8 percent per annum and a million of jobs were created in each year. Between 1982-88, the growth rate of the economy was found to be equal to zero. However, the aftermath impact of the stabilisation package has revealed a decline of per capita gross domestic product by 15 percent, large fall in employment and cut in real wages to be the characteristic features of the Mexican economy during the late eighties. A similar experience for the Latin American countries which have undergone the SAP has clearly shown that between 1980 and 1984, the open unemployment has gone up from 7 to 11 percent. In Chile, Columbia, Peru and Venezuela, the unemployment rate has ranged between 14 to 20 percent. The experience of the Asian nations indicates a mixed trend. Most of the Newly Industrialised Countries (NICs) have aimed full employment over the last two decades. However, the South Korean economy experienced the highest rate of unemployment as 4 to 5 percent per annum. It has been believed that in the four Asian countries, *viz.*, Indonesia, Thailand, Malaysia and Phillipines, liberalisation has increased the demand for labour. The structural adjustment which has followed by the unification of the two Germanies has resulted in a job loss of one out of every three workers. Likewise, during the period of Margaret Thatcher, over one lakh workers had lost their jobs due to the privatisation of a few major industries in UK, which mainly includes the Steel and Coal Industried. In Japan too, three lakh workers were declared as surplus when the National Railways were privatised.

Liberalisation in India

Even though India realised to open up the economy during the late eighties, the process of liberalisation for the industrial sector has started from 1985 onwards. It has been branded under the partial liberalisation policies. Notable changes introduced at that time include liberalisation of import regime, exemption of certain industries from the MRTP system and raising the investment, broadbaing of industrial licences etc.[3]. Inspite of an accelerating trend in output, the period after the partial liberalisation has witnessed a fall in the share of manufacturing employment. However, during the late eighties, the Indian economy has been characterised with high rates of inflation, decelerated industrial production, fiscal indiscipline, a very high ratio of borrowing to GDP and low level of foreign exchange reserves. The Government infact took extraordinary measures to overcome these mounting problems. However, the economic crisis reached its peak level in 1990 and the Government of India approached the IMF and the World Bank for additional loans. The request has been accepted with a condition that India should opt for a free market economy. The Government thus has announced the New Economic Policy which intended among other things, to increase considerably the output growth in the economy. It is believed that the output growth would take care of other problems in the economy.

The 1991 economic liberalisation includes the policy changes related to trade openness, fiscal openness, outward orientation and minimal intervention of financial, goods and factor markets[4]. Accordingly, the changes announced for the industrial sector are, the large-scale delicensing, removal of MRTP restriction, removal on expansions, mergers, take overs, raising foreign equity investments upto 51 percent in several industries. The focus has shifted from import substitution to export promotion, and the private sector is expected to play a crucial role in developing the industrial economy of India. As in the words of our Finance Minister, the basic objective of the New Economic Policy is to create a macro-economic environment in which industry speeds ahead with growth rates of 12 or more, generates more jobs and higher levels of wages and incomes through increased productivity level.[5]

A Review of Select Studies

Bhattacharya and Arup Mitra[6], attempted to analyse the employment elasticities for the various sectors of the Indian economy for the year 1991. According to them, employment elasticity has varied widely across the sectors. For the economy as a whole, it was found to be 0.45 and the lowest elasticity was in the manufacturing sector.

In a study Davala[7] concluded that employment in the Indian economy has shifted from organised to unorganised sectors during the last one and a half decades which is found to be a major consequence of the industrial restructuring policies followed during the eighties.

Deshpande and Deshpande[8], while analysing the trends in female employment under the New Economic Policy regime, have argued that the manufacturing employment in India has been sluggish during the 80's. Their results suggest that the structural reforms for the industrial sector would have a limited impact on the overall employment generation in the economy.

While examining the implication of New Economic Policies in various countries, Dutt[9] observed that the structural adjustment programme and the implementation of the exit policy would result in jobless growth in Indian economy in the following decades.

Falloan and Lucas[10] attempted to estimate the trends in employment in 35 Indian Industries using the ASI data for the period 1976 to 1982. The results of their study revealed the long-term decline in the demand for labour as 17.5 percent.

Jose[11] made an attempt to study the earnings, employment and productivity levels in the factory sector industries of India during the 70's and 80's. The comparative analysis of his study indicates a relative stagnation and decline in productivity during the 70's and a sharp acceleration in productivity rates in the 80's. From the estimates he concluded that the deceleration in the rate of growth of employment and increased productivity levels were the outcomes of structural reforms and technological changes which were introduced into the manufacturing industries during the 80's in India.

According to Jain[12], the gravest crisis that Indian economy faces today is the mounting unemployment. Even though the rate of growth of GDP has increased from 3.5 to 5.3 percent, the employment growth has fallen from 2.82 to 1.55 percent during the last two decades.

Mundle[13] in a study on the employment effects of stabilisation programmes in India concluded that much of the reduction in employment would likely to occur in the unorganised sector of the economy. His estimates of open unemployment indicate 3, 8 and 10 millions, under the high growth rate scenario and 4, 5.9 and 6.6 millions, under the low growth conditions for the years, *viz.*, 1991-92, 1992-93 and 1993-94.

Nambiar and Tadas[14] fit a regression model in order to examine the growth of manufacturing value added and employment in India during 1975-76 to 1991-92. The rate of growth in value added and employment were to be 6.8 and 2.3 percent respectively. The study however concludes that the improved performance of the industry has not been secured by the liberalisation policies followed by the Indian Government during the eighties.

In a study, Popola[15] found that the Indian economy is growing at about 6 percent per annum and the estimated employment would be 8 to 8.5 million per year.

While examining the employment growth and social protection for labour in India, Popola[16] has argued that the employment growth has been slower than the increase in labour force in India. Also, the substantial change in the composition of the national output has not been accompanied by a similar change in workforce.

Seema Singh[17] made an attempt to analyse the implication of the New Economic Policy on employment and found that the post-liberalisation policies have not helped in generating employment and equity in the Indian economy. Also, the restructuring package of the IMF-World Bank must be modified for the Indian conditions, so that the vast majority of the people are not alienated from the growth process.

Sethi[18] has worked out the employment projections for the Eighth Plan period based on the observed elasticities of employment during 1983-88. According to the projected estimates, the overall employment elasticity of the economy was found to be 0.53 percent and highest in the construction sector.

Materials and Methods

The study is based on the secondary data compiled from the various issues of *Annual Survey of Industries Reports* and *Economic Survey*. To examine the influence of output growth on the levels of employment in the manufacturing industries, a labour demand model has been fitted. The model is of the following form :

$$LN(L)_t = L + B_1\, LN(Q)_t + B_2 LN(L)_{t-1} + u \ldots \qquad \ldots (1)$$

where

L_t = All employees in the current year.

Q_t = Gross value added (Rs.in lakhs)

L_{t-1} = All employees in the t-1 period.

The B_1, which measures the elasticity of labour demand with respect to output growth is expected to be positive. Generally it is assumed that the long run elasticity is greater than the short run elasticity.

Results and Discussion

Following are the empirical estimates of the labour demand model fitted for the organised Manufacturing Sector of India:

$$LN(L)_t = L + B_1LN(Q)_t + B_2LN(L_t\text{-}1) + u$$
$$= 3.0428 + 0.05568 + 0.1748 \quad R^2 = 0.7862$$
$$(1.9769) + (1.7196) + (0.4155) \quad \text{'F'} = 14.7133$$

The fit model has yielded high R^2 and statistically significant 'F' ratio for the time series data. The coefficient B_1 which measures the output elasticity of employment has not only yielded positive magnitude, but also emerged statistically significant 'F' ratio for the time series data. Thus, we could conclude that labour demand in Indian manufacturing sector is sensitive to variations in output. The positive and significant B_2 value indicates existence of one year lagged impact in the employment adjustment process of the current year employment. A close examination of the lagged labour coefficient further reveals that the speed of adjustment is found to be very low in India.

The estimated long run employment elasticity with respect to output has satisfied the theoretical specification by obtaining magnitude greater than the short run elasticity. The calculated long run elasticity with respect to output was found to be 0.0688. From this estimated elasticity, we could observe that if we try to increase output of the organised manufacturing sector by 10 percent, employment growth would be 0.6 percent in the long run. This implies that employment growth would lag behind the output growth in the Indian manufacturing sector. In order to understand the rate of growth of employment and output during the reference period, we fit two regression models. The estimates of growth are as follows:

B Coefficient for employment	=	0.0049 (9.3240)*
R^2	=	0.8968 (F = 86.9386)*
B Coeffiecient for output	=	0.0619 (22.5769)
R^2	=	(F = 509.6271)

Based on these coefficients, levels of employment were estimated for the following four year as:

1993-94 .... 86.18 (in thousands)
1994-95 .... 86.25
1995-96 .... 86.32
1996-97 .... 86.40

Summary and Conclusion

As mentioned in the previous sections of this article, the basic objective of the New Economic Policy announced during 1991 was to increase the levels of employment in the economy by increasing the levels of output. According to our results, which are based on the pre-liberalisation data lead us to conclude that employment in the organised manufacturing sector has grown at a very low rate and has also lagged behind the output growth.The liberalisation measures announced for the manufacturing sector in order to absorb the growing force, were thus expected to work fruitfully only to a certain extent in the long run elasticity of employment with respect to output and a sluggish growth of manufacturing employment in India. Future growth of the aggregate employment in India would depend on the diversification of investment (employment-oriented) for the output growth from manufacturing to other sectors of the economy.

REFERENCES

1. UNDP (1993), *Human Development Report,* United Nations Development Programme.
2. Government of India (1994), *Economic Survey* 1993-94, Ministry of Finance, Government of India, New Delhi.
3. Nambiar, R.G., and G. Tadas (1994), Is Trade Deindustrialising India. *Economic and Political Weekly,* Vol. xxix, No. 42, October.
4. Deshpande, L.K. (1992) Economic Liberalisation and Labour in India, *Indian Journal of Labour Economics,* Vol. 35, No. 4.
5. Singh, M.M. (1992), *New Economic Policy Poverty and Self Reliance,* Special Lecture, in A.N. Sinha Institute of Social Studies, Patna, November.
6. Bhattacharya, B.B., and Arup Mitra (1993), Employment and Structural Adjustment—A Look at 1991 Cencus Data, *Economic and Political Weekly,* Vol. xxviii, No. 38, September.
7. Davala, Sarath (ed.) (1992), *Employment and Unionisation in Indian Industry,* Friedrich Ebert Foundation, New Delhi.
8. Deshpande, S., and Deshpande L.K. (1992), New Economic Policy and Female Employment, *Economic and Political Weekly,* Vol. xxvii, No. 41, October.
9. Dutt, R. (1994), Jobless Growth—Implication of New Economic Policies, *Indian Journal of Industrial Relations,* Vol. 29, No. 4, April.
10. Fallon, P.R., and E.B. Lucas Robert (1991), The Impact of Changes in Jobs Security Regulations in India and Zimbabwe, *The World Bank Economic Review,* Vol. 5, No. 3, September.
11. Jose, A.V. (1992), Earnings, Employment and Productivity Trends in the Organised Industries in India, *Indian Journal of Industrial Relations,* Vol. 35, No. 3.
12. Jain, L.C. (1992), New Economic Policy—Its Practice and Diabolic Character, *Janatha,* November.
13. Mundle, Sudipto (1992), The Employment Effects of Stabilisation and Related Policy

Changes in India; 1991-92 to 1993-94, *Indian Journal of Labour Economics*, Vol. 35, No. 3.

14. Nambiar, R.G., and G. Tadas (1994), *op.cit.*,
15. Popola, T.S. (1991), *Industry and Employment: Recent Indian Experience*, ISID Foundation Day Lecture, New Delhi.
16. Popola (1992) *The Question of Employment*, in Bismal Jalan (ed.) *Indian Economy : Problems and Prospects*, Viking Penguin, New Delhi.
17. Seema Singh (1993), New Economic Policy in India: Some Implications for Employment and Labour Market, *Indian Journal of Industrial Relations*, Vol. 28, No. 4, April.
18. Sethi, J.D. (1990) Dethroning Growth Rate, *Financial Express*, 9, 10, & 11 May 1990.

17

Liberalisation and Management Education in India

Ranjan Banerjee

A fairly large number of popular magazines and newspapers today are fond of printing 'in' and 'out' columns. These columns are nothing more than a reflector of the things that are being talked about (and that are not).

In today's context the most elementary of surveys would reveal the following inescapable conclusion "Today, management education is 'in' ".

However, the evident boom in the field of management education must not be a cause for unbridled joy among those who are associated with the field. For it must be recognised that the 'management boom' that is seen today has parallels in the 'management boom' that was seen in the US thirty years ago. It must be realized that countries which faced a similar boom not so long ago are today extremely critical and cynical about management education and its products.

It is our responsibility to ensure that in a situation where our management education is largely imitative of the west, we suitably tailor and modify our management education system to keep it relevant and thus benefit from the mistakes made by others by refusing to repeat them.

The History of Management Education

Management education in India came into being to meet the need for managerial manpower which was related to the national strategy of planned development with emphasis on modernisation and self-reliance. The All India Council of Technical Education set up a Board of

Management Studies (BMS) in 1954 to lay down standards of education, coordinate educational facilities and guide Government promotion of relevant institutions.

BMS chose six reputed institutes of higher learning to introduce courses in business management and industrial administration. Some universities were encouraged to begin part-time courses in business management for practising managers, while institutions of science and technology were encouraged to offer programmes in industrial administration. Simultaneously, the Government widened its efforts in management education by promoting institutions like the Administrative Staff College of India and the National Productivity Council for executive training, research and management consultancy.

During the same period, foreign donor agencies began to feel that technical and economic assistance provided by them could bear fruit only if trained managerial resources were available in the recipient country. In 1958, the All India Management Association (AIMA) was established with the aid of the Ford Foundation. The AIMA specialised in short term development programmes in management and the organisation of seminars and conferences which provided forums where professional managers could interact with each other.

The Ford Foundation also played a crucial role in establishing the two Indian Institutes of Management in 1961 to conduct pre-career education, executive development programmes, research and management consultancy. Both the IIM's borrowed ideas and instruments for the content and method of education from leading management schools in America. (IIM Ahmedabad was set up with assistance from Harvard Business School in 1962 and IIM Calcutta was set up with assistance from the Sloan Management School). Even to this day, the orientation and strength of these institutes is reflective of their American associations. IIM Ahmedabad has laid stress on the case study method and is perceived to be more qualitative in its orientation. IIM Calcutta is more quantitative in its orientation with a lot of stress upon statistical techniques.

The charter of the IIMs was designed on the premise that their goal was to participate in the process of professionalisation of management in all segments of economic enterprise. Hence, over a period of time, the range of programmes offered by the IIMs came to include a post-graduate MBA programme, a doctoral programme for teachers and researchers in management, sectorial programmes in priority areas like agriculture, rural development, public sector and faculty development programmes for management teachers/trainers. The IIMs also played a leading role in conducting faculty development programmes for managers in industry and Government. The research and consultancy services of the IIMs have been utilised by a cross section of national and international agencies. Two more IIMs have subsequently been added—IIM Bangalore in the seventies and IIM Lucknow in the eighties. The overall capability of the IIMs in their areas of work is commonly perceived as comparable to the capability of the better American business schools.

Apart from the IIMs, nearly 75 university departments and autonomous institutions conduct full time and part-time programmes in management. The large need for specialised managerial services for sections like rural management, insurance and banking has led to the establishment of institutes like the Institute of Rural Management (IRMA) at Anand, the National Insurance Academy (NIA), Pune and the National Institute of Bank Management, (NIBM), Pune. These institutes have acquired recognition and prestige in their respective fields and are well supported by the organisations which utilise their services.

In recent years, industrial organisations in the private sector and public sector have increasingly invested in management development facilities for their own managers. Some of them (like the Tata Management Centrè) have extended their efforts to serve the need for management development in the wider community.

Thus, Indian management education has evolved to a point where the infrastructure available within the country is quite extensive. Management education is growing increasingly popular and the demand for professional management expertise is felt in all spheres of economic activity. The products of the premièr management institutes are perceived to be comparable with the best in the world. A lot of managers trained in India have grown to be international heads of multinational corporations.

A closer look at the curent stage of management education in India reveals that the plethora of Indian management schools can be sub-divided into the following categories:

(a) Institutes like the IIMs, XLRI, JBIMS which have large full time faculty and the capacity to generate adequate funds for education, research and extension activities.
(b) Sector specific institutes like NIBM, IRMA, NIA, Institute of Forest Management, NICMAR (National Institute of Construction Management and Research) which have adequate faculty and are well supported by the organisations which they serve.
(c) University departments and affiliated institutions which have a relatively small faculty and educational programmes which are well respected.

(d) University departments and affiliated institutions which struggle with inadequate faculty and financial resources and are forced to borrow assistance from various sources.

(e) Commercially oriented management courses with inadequate resources and poor image (An alarming recent trend is the mushrooming of such courses in a bid to cash in on the growing craze for some sort of management qualifications).

While there are many pertinent issues which are suggested by this classification, it must be accepted, in summary, that management education in India has come a long way since independence. However, there has been widespread criticism both within and outside the country of management education in general 5, 6, 7. Further, there has been a lot of criticism within the country of the lack of relevance and orientation of the current management education with its predominant western bias, for a developing country like ours. In order to understand the role that management education should play in the years to come, it is necessary to take a look at the deficiencies in the current management education system.

Management Education in India—Perceived Deficiencies

Deficiencies in any education system can only be identified in relation to the functions which a good system should serve. Previous work in this area has identified the characteristics of a good management education system as :

(i) It should be useful not only for achieving short-term results but also for achieving long-term developmental goals.

(ii) All segments of the community and all regions of the country should be benefited by the system.

(iii) The system must be geared towards the development of complete managers—the system must not only provide training in managerial skills, but must seek to facilitate the total personality development of the individual so as to enable him/her to effectively discharge these skills.

If the existing management system is examined in the light of these criteria, the following conclusions/observations emerge:

1. The cost in the year 1995 in terms of a single year's fees for an MBA at IIM Ahmedabad is of the order of Rs. 45,000. The corresponding figure is Rs. 27,000 for XLRI. It is apparent that those costs are well beyond the reach of the common man. This can only result in the creation and perpetuation of an elite class of managers. (This is further accentuated by the nature of the admission procedure for the premier management

institutes. The written test aims to measure verbal, analytical and quantitative skills, and is patterned on the GRE and GMAT examinations held for admission in the USA). People in the reputed city institutions have greater access to and awareness of such tests. Thus, the very procedure puts students from metros at a distinct advantage. Further, a large number of coaching classes have sprung up, particularly in the cities, which charge fees in excess of a thousand rupees per student and boast fairly high success rates. This again puts students who can access these classes at an advantage.

2. Management education has not lived upto its stated objective of serving all sectors of the economy. The need for professional, managerial skill is acutely felt in the rural, agricultural sector as well as in small and medium scale industries in the unorganised sector. However, management education and its products are neither oriented to, or interested in, the needs of these sectors.

Further, the products of the premier management institutes end up mainly serving large multinationals and Indian corporate houses, like the TATAs, Reliance, etc. The public sector and the growing number of enterpreneurs who are moving from a local (one state) presence to a national presence, are all in need of professional management expertise. These needs go unaddressed, because of the tendency of our management graduates to search for organisations that are both 'professional' and lucrative. (It is a paradox that the 'change agents of tomorrow' see professionalism as something that they should find in readymade form in organisations that they go to, as opposed to something that they should bring with them and input into their organisations).

3. The job preferences of the management graduates veer towards consultancy, finance and marketing/advertising which are both lucrative and glamorous. As a consequence of this, there are two undersirable trends which are emerging:

(a) The top graduates from management schools are reluctant to go into line functions like production and sales. However, in reality, an understanding of the line realities are a must for a successful top manager. Further, there is a great need for professional management capability in these functions, which are the core of any business organisation.

(b) A large percentage (about 60 % in IIM, Ahmedabad and 80 % in IIM, Calcutta) of the students in the management institutes are engineers. A lot of them finally end up marketing consumer non-durables or working for foreign banks and consultancy organisations. Thus, it has been argued by experts, management education tends to shift managerial talents away from productive sectors which need them desperately.

It must be recognised that these trends are also a reflector of a tendency to move into fields where the perceived material rewards are greater and hence the blame cannot be laid completely at the door of management education. It is, however, incumbent upon a good management education system, to attempt to address these imbalances to the extent possible.

4. The management education system has failed in its attempt to develop the complete personality of the manager. Management graduates are perceived as being arrogant, over-ambitious, selfish and lacking in loyalty. In the words of Dipti Bhatnagar, a professor in organisational behaviour at IIM Amhedabad 'The Managers of tomorrow need to factor in ethical considerations in addition to economic criteria while evaluating alternative courses of action'. Students believe that street-smartness and tolerance for corruption are prerequisites for managerial success. This must change. Thus, 'community consciousness' and balance between ends and means which a good management graduate should have seems to be lacking.

5. Management education and training have failed to create adequate faculty for the growth and sustenance of the management education system in the country. A very small fraction of management graduates pursue fellowship studies in India (The management graduates who are interested in research and teaching often end up migrating to greener pastures abroad). Courses taught at management institutes can be broadly classed into two categories:

(i) Core subjects like economics, statistics, psychology which are drawn directly from the mother discipline. The faculty in these areas are normally well qualified functional specialists.

(ii) Applied managerial subjects like marketing, organisational behaviour, MIS etc. In these areas, two types of faculty are typically available:

(a) People with a strong theoretical background in the area with little or no work experience. Typically, the problem here is likely be an inadequate integration of theory and practice.

(b) Experienced and practising industry managers, normally visiting faculty, who teach mainly from their own experience. The problem here tends to be that the faculty tend to indulge mainly in narration of their varied experiences, and do not relate their experience to a broad conceptual framework.

In short, the problem is that barring a few exceptions, the faculty (and consequently the courses), are unable to strike the requisite balance between theory and practical experience.

6. The system has tended largely to borrow its material and concepts from the western world. Preparation of indigenous material has been largely confined to the preparaion of indigenous case studies.

There is a tendency to accept as gospel truth, concepts which are 'the rage' in the western world, and forward them as desirable practices without adaptation or questioning of their relevance to a different environment and culture.

In this connection, we would do well to learn from the method used by Japan. Right from the beginning, Japan recognised that its culture was different, and therefore, management education must be based on its business needs and characteristics. Hence, the Japanese approach has always been to adapt what could and should be taken from western management practice.

In India, our subservience to the 'educational imperialism' of the west is one reason why there is a conspicuous dearth of significant Indian contribution to the body of management thought. (Even today, none of the Indian management journals have acquired a status anywhere near the *Harvard Business Review* or the *Sloan Management Review*).

7. The teaching techniques lay a great stress on the case study method. As pointed out by Livingstone and Mintzberg, the case study method often requires a student to make broad prescriptions within a couple of hour, based on twenty to thirty pages of reading material, on complex organisational problems. Thus, the case study method, if wrongly used, results in tendency to prescribe quickfix solutions on the basis of insufficient knowledge and understanding and thus breeds superficiality.

It is felt that while the case study method is useful way of bringing reality into the classroom, the emphasis should be on analysing and understanding real life situations and problems, rather than prescribing readymade solutions.

8. In terms of the actual programmes taught, it is felt that far too much stress is laid down on complex analytical tools. This has negative consequences in two ways:

(a) In teaching quantitative subjects like statistics or, there is a tendency to emphasise the elegant mathematics in these subjects and underplay aspects like modelling which are critical to the application of these techniques.

(b) The students tend to be overly analytical in their orientation, and do not have enough orientation towards areas like interpersonal skills and intuition, which are felt to be fairly critical in the real world.

Further, in almost any industry, the bulk of a new recruit's job content in the initial years is in the area of logistics management. This is one subject which needs to be addressed in far greater detail by our management institutes.

9. Last, but definitely not the least, institutions of management should themselves be models of ideal management practice. This has not been found to be the case. These institutions are often highly bureaucratic and serve as glaring examples of the disparity between theory and practice.

Having looked at the gaps in the existing management education systems it is necesary to understand liberalisation and the changes it has brought in its wake so as to arrive at future prescriptions for management education.

Impact of Liberalisation

The policy of liberalisation and deregulation, which was ushered in by Dr. Manmohan Singh towards the end of 1991 has impacted significantly upon the management education system in the following ways:

(a) The extent of Government assistance to the management institutes has been frozen at a particular level. This, in turn, has meant that the management institutes have been forced to find alternative means to enhance their funding. This has resulted in:
   (i) an increase in student fees.
   (ii) an effort by the institutes to establish closer ties with industry and explore various ways to enhance industrial support/ sponsorship for various aspects of management education.

(b) The policy of liberalisation has brought about the following changes in the Indian corporate scenario:
   (i) There is a conscious effort to encourage foreign investment in India. NRIs and multinational corporations have been actively encouraged to expand their presence in India. This has resulted in a large number of multinational corporations coming into India. These multinational corporations have all looked to the products of our management institutes to meet their needs for managerial manpower consequently.
      (a) The demand for MBAs has gone up significantly. This increase has been accompanied by a significant hike in

MBA salaries at all levels, as recruiters become more and more aggressive in their efforts to acquire the best talent. MBAs today are in a sellers market. Recognition of the boom in the demand for management education has resulted in increased awareness of the prestige and potential gain attached to an MBA, and a large number of MBA courses have sprung up with varying levels of infrastructure and competence.

(b) There has been significant development in the financial area, and the awareness and interest of the Indian middle class in the share market has grown by leaps and bounds in recent years. The range of services and products offered by banks and financial institutes has gone up significantly, with a proliferation of mutual funds and new schemes being offered to the investor. A large number of finance companies, both multinational and Indian, have entered into the fray. There has been a tremendous hike in pay packets across the financial sector.

(c) Multinational consultancy organisations, like McKinsey, KMPG etc. have expanded their operations in India, and the consultancy and financial sector organisations have emerged as the best paymasters for MBAs. This in turn has led to an increased migration of fresh MBAs to these areas. The increase in demand and the salary boom will also imply that the expectations/pressure to perform will be greater for management graduates. This in turn implies that the management education system will have to make greater efforts to understand the needs of industry through closer contact.

(ii) There is a definite thrust on export through incentives/encouragement/deregulation. Existing companies have been encouraged to step up their export thrust. This implies that the management education system will feel an increased demand for courses on various aspects of export management and will have to orient itself accordingly.

In the light of the deficiencies in the management education systems identified earlier, and the demands that the 'management boom' is placing upon the system the following broad prescriptions can be made for management education in India.

Suggestions

1. While it must be said in all fairness that elitism in management education is not an isolated phenomenon, but is a continuation/culmination of elitism that is present through all levels of our education system. However, the following steps may help to curb the current elitist trend which is being harboured by the management education system:

(a) Sponsored merit-cum-means scholarships should be available to students from lower income groups to enable them to access the management education system.

(b) The entrance examination must be made less patterned and predictable. Perhaps the introduction of essay type questions would help in this regard. Further, as a management degree is a post-graduate qualification what the system is producing is engineer-managers, economist-managers etc. Hence, a paper in the qualifying/graduation subject should ensure a standardized level of proficiency in the graduation subject as a prerequisite for qualification.

(c) The possibility of state/town own minimum quota could be explored as an attempt to correct the domination of a few metro towns.

2. With regard to the lack of attention to the agricultural and small scale sectors, two possible measures could be taken:

(a) More sector specific institutes should be started to cater to the specific demands of these sectors.

(b) The premier management institutes should reserve a fixed number of seats for students who will serve these sectors, *i.e.* the specialisation will be pre-specified at the time of joining. While the first year training may be common with the MBA programme, a separate range of second year electives should be offered for these students. Efforts should be made to collaborate with groups in these sectors to sponsor the students and ensure remunerative placements for them (perhaps institutions like SIDBI could be actively involved in this task).

3. The much touted and published diversion of engineers from the production function could be addressed in two ways:

(a) Institutions like the IITs must be encouraged to start programmes in production/technology management (IIT Bombay has recently taken the initiative in this regard). The premier engineering institutes could also explore the possibility of a five-year integrated masters programme in technology management.

It is critical to the success of these programmes that they be well marketed, both to the student community and industry. Senior industrialists/practicing managers must be involved both at the design and the placement stage. Efforts must be made to ensure that the starting salaries of the products of these programmes are comparable with those offered to IIM MBA's.

(b) It must however, be recognised that the established 'brand image' of institutions like the IIMs and XLRI, will ensure that a fair percentage of engineering graduates will continue to migrate to these institutes. Efforts must be made to strengthen the production management stream at these institutes. This can be done by—

(i) The current situation is a vicious cycle—few students opt for production courses and over a period of time, this means that few quality electives are offered in production management. One way of tackling this is by taking a minimum number of students (say ten) with a specialisation predecided at the entry point itself.

(ii) Faculty and sponsorship should be beefed up. This combined with the minimum batch size pre-specified, should ensure that the number of production management specialisation in subsequent batches will increase.

3. Development of the total personality of the manager is probably the most difficult task the management education system has to face. This is because the largest influences on our value systems are our parents, peers and primary educations, and a post-graduate course is probably too late to address distortions that have not been tackled earlier. However, the following steps are suggested:

(a) Stress on ethics and value considerations through specific courses in these areas.

(b) An understanding of community needs through carefully designed courses on Indian Economic and Political History, Indian Social Structure and Indian Economics/Planning (IIM Calcutta already has courses in these areas). These courses should have a greater project and discussion/seminar content so as to increase student involvement in these areas.

(c) Courses on interpersonal skills, team work etc. should involve high elements of role plays, simulation to orient students to these areas.

(d) The complete professional manager must have an understanding of the complexities of real life. It is recommended that 2-3 years of work experience be specified as a pre-requisite for entry to management institutes. Here, it must be recognised that a good future manager must exhibit his potential at work, and the rating of an MBA aspirant within his organisation should be an important input to the selection process.

4. The faculty requirement of the management education system can be addressed as follows :

(a) Good MBA students with a propensity for teaching should be identified and encouraged to take up teaching through suitable sponsorship. Industry must be actively involved in this process to ensure that a portion of the best talent goes to strengthen the very systems which nurtured it.

(b) Faculty should be encouraged/enabled to take up a significant amount of training and consultancy assignments. This would serve the twin purposes of providing greater integration between theory and practice and making management education a satisfying and paying profession for good teachers.

(c) All faculty must have at least three years of work experience. In case this has not been done at entry point itself, suitable exchange programmes can be worked out with industry whereby faculty and interested middle managers exchange positions for two to three years.

(d) Quality faculty training programmes should be delivered regularly. Responsibility for these programmes should lie with the IIMs, XLRI, Bajaj etc. Perhaps they could be organised by the AIMS with the aid of all these institutes.

(e) Addressing the quantity and quality of faculty would in itself go a long way towards developing indigenous management thought. The AIMS could also take upon itself the task of bringing out an Indian Management Journal with the involvement of senior faculty from the premier institutes. This journal should set high standards for itself right from the outset, and should aim to acquire quality and prestige comparable to *HBR* or the *Wall Street Journal*. It is felt that the existing one brought out by the AIMS does not adequately meet these standards.

5. The steps outlined in 4, should themselves go someway towards changing the faculty orientation and changing the 'analysis paralysis' which MBA students are often accused of. Efforts should be made to have greater emphasis on team projects and assignments in all courses.

Students should be encouraged to stay abreast of the latest trends in management thought, and to criticially question their relevance to the Indian context before accepting them.

Experiments on the line of the German Dual system of education where theory and practice are interspered in bursts of three months each could be tried to integrate theory and practice.

Courses in logistics management, export management should be started. The course package should periodically be discussed with review committees comprising senior managers from industry and suitably tailored keeping in mind the needs of industry. Large sectors like steel, banking, financial services should be encouraged to sponsor sector specific institutes to cater to their requirements of specialised managerial manpower.

Case studies should be used more as examples of real life which can be analysed and assimilated and education should emphasize that broad superficial prescriptions are to be avoided. The need for executive development programmes should be periodically assessed through in-depth industry reviews and the programmes should be designed accordingly. These programmes should ideally be designed by institute faculty in consultation with the participating organisations.

In general, a far greater level of discussion and collaboration between the management education system and industry should be brought about so as to enable both parties to derive greater benefits from each other.

Conclusion

Thus far, this paper has surveyed management education in the emerging environment and made certain broad prescriptions to enhance its relevance and success. These prescriptions would be well supported by research in the following areas :

(a) A realistic projection of the demand for management graduates over the next 50 years.

(b) Study of course content at all the major institutes and the number of times and overall structure has been modified in recent years.

(c) A regular system for student appraisal of all courses. An effort to correlate course feedback with the qualification/experience profile of the instructors.

(d) Extent of awareness of campus recruiters about course content at the institutes.

(e) Work experience profile of institute faculty at various institutes.

(f) Correlation between academic performance at the institute and career success.

It is hoped that these researches, in conjunction with the prescriptions made in this article, will enable our management education system to live upto the high expectations that today's emerging environment is placing upon it and take its appointed place in the global arena.

Impact on Quality of Life

In order to understand the impact of management education in a liberalised environment and its role in enhancing the quality of life it is necessary to state what is meant by enhanced quality of life. Quality of life, as is commonly understood, should be a reflector of

(a) Purchasing power : which is a function of employment/productivity/income.
(b) Availability of goods and services : food, clothing, shelter, infrastructure etc.

An overall enhancement in the quality of life in the Indian context can be said to have occurred if either of two conditions are met:

1. Increase in the quality of life across all classes from a particular base year.
2. Achievement of a subsistence quality of life (in terms of basic needs of food, clothing and shelter being met) across the entire population.

It should be evident that management, which is concerned with the productive allocation and utilisation of resources to achieve economic and societal goals, has an important role to play in enhancing the quality of life. For management to effectively discharge this role, it is essential that the benefits of professional management practice are greatly felt.

If the needs for the enhancement of quality of life are viewed alongside the observations about the impact of management education made earlier in this paper, the following conclusions emerge:

(a) On account of the benefits of management education being concentrated on large corporate houses, foreign banks etc. and not being adequately distributed to sectors like agriculture, the small scale sector and the public sector, management education has not lived upto its potential in terms of enhancing the quality of life of the Indian populace.
(b) Further, the reluctance of top flight management professionals to enter the production stream cannot augur very well for the productivity improvement which is essential for an enhanced quality of life.

(c) This is not to state that efficient management of large corporate houses, foreign banks etc. does not contribute to the overall enhancement of quality of life. It is just that for a developing economy like ours, these are not the immediate priorities for a broad based quality of life.

REFERENCES

1. J Stirling Livingstone, The Myth of the Well Educated Manager, *Harvard Business Review,* January-February, 1971.
2. Hency Mintzberg, Training Managers, not MBAs, Chapter 5 in *'Mintzberg on Management,* The Free Press, 1989.
3. Agarwala A. N., *Business Education in India, Its Past, Present and Future,* Commerce Department, Allahabad Universiy, 1960.
4. N.R. Sheth, *What is Wrong with Management Education, .Economic and Political Weekly,* Vol. 26 No. 48, November 30, 1991.
5. Robert H. Hayes and William J. Abernathy, Managing Your Way to Economic Decline, *Harvard Business Review,* Vol. 58, No. 4, July-August.
6. *Time,* May 4, 1981—Article entitled, The Money Chase—Business Schools May Be a part of the problem?
7. Arabinda Ray (1970), The Indian Manager of the 1980s. *Economic and Political Weekly,* August 1991.
8. R. Bandyopadhyay, Indian Management Education—Need for a Constructive Debate, *Economic & Political Weekly,* Vol. 26, No. 48, November 30, 1991.
9. K.C. Sahu, Reorienting Management Education; *Economic and Political Weekly,* Vol. 26, No. 48, November 30, 1991.
10. Iswar Dayal (1989), Issues in Management Education, in J. Phillip and D. Shanker Narayan (eds), *Management Education in India,* Indian Institute of Management, Bangalore.
11. Cugh, Sampat P., *Excellence in Management Education;* National Institute of Bank Management, Pune, 1988.
12. 'Charting New Courses' (article on MBA careers) *India Today,* May 31, 1995.
13. Kevin Collins (1989), Management Education in Japan, in William Byrt (ed), *Management Education—An International Survey,* Routledge, London.
14. R. Bandyopadhyay, Education for a Enlightened Society; *Economic and Political Weekly,* February 16, 1991.

18

Economic Liberalisation and Management of Education : Importance of Faculty Development

Chandana Goswami

The economic liberalisation is expected to provide lots of new openings, generate employment and of course improve our quality of life. But generation of employment will not assure that all our students will be able to get good jobs in multinational and transnational companies and earn fat salaries. Only those who can prove themselves will be able to do so. It is upto us teachers to equip our students with those knowledge and skills which would be wanted by their future prospective employers. No doubt that only our efforts alone will not help our students get employment, the students too will have to make 100 % efforts in this direction.

Environment Demands

Before we decide the direction of our efforts, we have to analyse what the liberalised economy would look for in Management Graduates. The MBA graduates of tomorrow would have to be globally competitive, so that they can be recruited both by Indian companies as well as multinational companies. These above mentioned companies would be looking for people who have the latest knowledge, are familiar with the state-of-the-art technology and are aware of the global market.

For any academic institution to be able to produce such globally competitive graduates it is essential that its core team—the faculty—be a dedicated bunch of professionals who are familiar with the latest advancements in their fields and aware of emerging trends. Hence it is imperative that the faculty be developed so that their professional skills are enhanced. Only when the façulty is globally competitive, then only can the institute hope to produce globally competitive graduates and thus maintain a reputation for being 'one of the best sources' for producing talented people.

The changing world demands that the faculty be upto date in not only their own specialisations but also keep abreast in other related areas. Today's courses have an inter-disciplinary approach and the faculty having a command in inter-disciplinary areas will be in great demand. The advantage of being a "Jack of all..." is that it enables a teacher to explain the subject matter in wider perspective, relating to a wider frame of reference, better understanding, more interaction with the students and above all it will make the classroom lectures a source of pure joy to the students.

Globally Competitive Teachers

To produce globally competitive students, it becomes imperative that the teacher him/herself is a globally competitive one. The word globally competitive means that the faculty

(i) Is in a position to take up at least 50 % of the papers taught during each academic period;

(ii) Can contribute to designing a courseware that would be of international standards;

(iii) Is most likely to be invited as a guest lecturer by reputed organisations, both within and outside the country;

(iv) Attends seminars and conferences from time to time; and

(v) Has knowledge on a wide field encompassing divergent areas.

The two main contributors to faculty development is the institute and the faculty itself. If one of them lags behind, the development will either not take place or be ineffective.

Contributions expected from the Institute are:

(i) Provide necessary infra-structure, in terms of private study rooms, P.C.s', well-equipped library, clerical assistance, reproduction facilities, conference rooms with audio-visual aids etc.

(ii) Encourage seminars, both by faculty as well as visitors.

(iii) Provide the right environment by balancing between classes, administrative works and free-time.

(iv) Rigidity of working hours should not be emphasised, instead flexitime should be encouraged.

(v) Achievements should be recognised and promptly rewarded. Monetary rewards may or may not be given but rewards as awards and recognition are a must.

(vi) Provision should be kept for an accelerated career path.

(vii) Annual confidential reports must be prepared by the faculty and assessed jointly by the concerned person and the authority. There must be credit points for the faculty who has proven track record of academic performances.

The Faculty is expected to—

(i) Have strong inner motivation.

(ii) Take advantage of the infra-structure provided.

(iii) Strong involvement in classroom lectures as well as administrative matters.

(iv) Contribute regularly to reputed journals of national and inter-national standards.

(v) Be involved in research-oriented works.

(vi) Guide research scholars.

(vii) Take part in seminars, conferences, refresher courses.

(viii) Conduct workshops and seminars.

(ix) Attend part-time classes or faculty devdelopment programmes.

To sustain and retain quality faculty it is imperative that a two-pronged nurture system is adopted.

The Two-Pronged Approach

INSTITUTE

- Good Pay
- Infrastructure
- Clear-Cut programmes
- Adequate HR

- Freedom
- Recognitions
- Involvement
- Flexitime

The Two-Pronged approach provides simultaneously Quantitative and Qualitative incentives (Comparable with Herzberg's Hygiene factors and motivators). The quantitative incentives are the best possible remuneration, adequate physical infra-structure and human resources, clear-cut course programmes, quality syllabus etc. The qualitative incentives include freedom in designing courseware/pattern of examinations, provisions for recognising faculty contributions (classroom teaching, attending seminars/workshops, guiding research scholars, other academic pursuits) etc. Efforts should be made to involve the faculty with institute's activities so that a sense of belonging develops and above all introduce flexitime system and discard away with the suffocating rigid working hours.

New Responsibilities

So far what has been discussed were the traditional responsibilities that a teacher has to fulfil. Slowly, teachers will be viewed as someone more than a teacher—a friend, philosopher and guide. It could also be thought of similar to the ancient days of "gurukul" where the teacher had the entire responsibility of developing a student's mental, physical and spiritual faculties. At this present juncture, where we exist today, few parents would be willing to hand over their child totally to a teacher and allow their child to be moulded. In the present society where both sets of parents are educated and the family has either one or two children, the parents have a definite vision of how they will mould their child's future. Within these constraints, the teacher has to mould the students, the teacher has to :

(i) impart academic training and knowledge.

(ii) instill in the students a sense of values and ethics.

The working environment today is more stiff and competitive than the past. It has become necessary to be always alert so that we can respond to the changing demands of our profession. It is this spirit of flexibility that we should try to inculcate in our students. The more flexible they are in spirit, the more adaptive will they be to the changing scenario. Alongwith flexibility, our students should be imbibed with the spirit of quality—Quality Work, Quality Life, Personal Quality etc.

The future work life will be characterised by the following:

(i) It will operate in a turbulent environment.

(ii) High risk takers will be highly rewarded.

(iii) Entrepreneurial activities of Entrepreneurs will be encouraged.

(iv) Diversity (*i.e.* different people from different cultures and back-grounds) will be a common feature.

(v) Demanding and giving quality service or goods will be routine matter.

(vi) Knowledge of different ethnic cultures would prove to be an asset in rural marketing.

(vii) Knowledge of international cultures would help in international marketing and collaborations.

The concept of quality work, quality life, personal quality etc. has to emancipate from within. A limited amount of consciousness about quality can be developed through training methods. But for the spirit of quality to pervade in our society, we have to instill in each and every batch of our students certain positive traits of ethics and human values. We would prove to be effective in our effort if these students who graduate every year can pass on these new sets of values to a couple of persons who in turn would pass it on, thus radiating out these sets of values and ethics.

In management education, we always stress on how to be efficient and successful managers. We keep on harping that our students are going to be the future managers. This develops in them an inflated ego which sometimes comes in their way. They should be taught to be good employees, since they will begin at the lowest organisational position where no managerial traits are expected of them. In such a situation, it would be traits like honesty, sincerity, intelligence, commitment, loyalty, perseverence, tolerance, hardworking etc. that would be required. Hence inculcating a spirit of values, ethics and quality would not prove to be an useless and frutile exercise.

Challenges for Management

The changing scenario has new expectations from the MBA graduates. The Management of Management Schools must recognise this and make attempt to bridge this gap between expectations from an MBA and the performance of an MBA. The management has to think in the following frames of reference:

(a) An MBA graduate joins an organisation as a trainee or junior executive. At this level he/she is expected to execute decisions. Hence it would be more appropriate to lay stress on developing skills in communication (both verbal and written), comprehension ability to get along with people.
(b) An MBA will not work in isolation. He/she will be a part of a group and hence the administrators keeping this factor in mind should try to build team spirit in the graduates of tomorrow.
(c) Diversity in work force will be a common factor in most organisations. The MBA administrators will have to think of ways to ingrain into the students this concept of diversity, the related problems and to develop in the students a sense of tolerance and respect for different cultures.
(d) Entrepreneurship is one of the keywords today. To enable the MBA graduates to take advantage of this, the management should help in developing entrepreneurial skills, tone up problem identification skills, creativity, negotiation and the thinking and thought process.
(e) The development of courseware should be done by taking regular feedbacks from corporate and business houses. They are the buyers

of the commodity called MBA graduate that management schools have to offer and hence it is imperative that the management of management schools have first hand knowledge of customer needs before giving final shape to the product.

(f) Another point to be considered is whether a student having work exposure will be more suitable for the MBA course instead of fresh graduates.

Conclusion

Change could be for the better or worse. We have to adapt ourselves to the changing world and contribute as much as possible to make it a better place to live in. Management teachers must reorient their ways of thinking in tune with the liberalisation policy. Need based syllabus have to be designed, psychological testing should be included in the MBA entrance exams, stress should be given on industry-institution interactions—these are a few among the many issues that have to be tackled and worked out to make management education more meaningful.

REFERENCES

1. Moller Claus; *EMPLOYEESHIP—Mobilising every one's energy to win,* TMI Publishing A/S 1992.
2. Prof. Balachandran Bala V, *Management Education. National and International Perspectives,* paper presented at the 6th Annual Convention of AIMS, Aug. 1994.
3. Power K.B. Quality Assurance in Higher Education. *Journal of Higher Education* Vol. 17 No. 4, Autumn 1994.
4. Robin Stephen P., *Organizational Behaviour,* Prentice Hall, India 1994.
5. Neelankavil J.P., *Corporate America's Quest for an Ideal MBA, Journal of Management Development,* Vol. 13 No. 5, 1994 MCB University Press.
6. Goswami Chandana, Producing Globally Competitive Teachers, paper presented at the Regional seminar-cum-workshop on Planning and Management of Technical Education in India (sponsored by AICTE) April 1995.

19

Economic Liberalisation and Environmental Management

Suman Kumar Mukerjee

IS SUSTAINABLE DEVELOPMENT A PRACTICAL PROPOSITION FOR LIBERALISED ECONOMIES?

The concept of sustainable development implies balancing environmental protection with the generation of increased opportunities for employment and improved livelihoods. However, the breach between environmentalists and development officials reflects a deep divide over how to implement the rally cry of the World Bank Conference : "Sustainable".

Although there is a widespread agreement on the link between environment and development, it has become clear that one person's vision of development may be another's image of environmental degradation. In fact, just before the Rio de Janeiro conference, a battle was fought over the insistence of developing countries on including of a "right to development" in the Earth Summit summary document—the Rio Declaration.

The USA and other industrialised nations objected to this phrase, fearing that it would provide a basis in international law for developing countries to shirk obligations, including environmental duties by claiming a burden to their economic development. The compromise ultimately was whereas countries had a right to development, this was to be recognised in conjunction with an obligation to make development sustainable.

Sustainable development is something of an oxymoron. The term derives from two verbs—"to sustain" and "to develop"—with almost opposite meanings. Whether one puts the emphasis on "sustaining" or "developing" can lead to quite different policy prescriptions. This, in fact, is one of the reasons the trade and environment debate has received such broad attention.

Most industrialised countries see sustainable development along the lines of the definition developed by World Commission on Environment and Development : The Bruntland Commission which called for development that "meets the need of the present without compromising the ability of future generation to meet their own needs."

Its report noted that poverty is the central cause of ecological stress, but the Commission focussed primary attention on the integration of longer-term and broader policy perspectives into economic and environment decision making. Consequently, issues of inter-generation equity such as resources depletion, bio-diversity and management of the global commons were dealt with. Others seek to address global environmental issues such as climate change.

In contrast developing countries tend to stress the importance of alleviating poverty in discussions on sustainable development and on the ethical dimensions of sustainable development to make them consistent with ecological imperative.

This centres on short-term needs and basic public health amenities. Although the impact of soil erosion, deforestation and other ecological harms can be devastating to their people, officials in many developing countries treat environmental degradation and resources depletion as second-order considerations; global environmental issues are barely a priority at all.

These preferences are not illogical. The World Bank has estimated that every year more than two million people in developing countries die from illness attributable to polluted water and billions of people fall ill from water borne diseases.

Moreover, to people who have life expectancy of 45 to 50 years, the prospectus of getting skin cancer or cataracts when they are 70 from sun exposure exacerbated by depletion of the ozone layer seem very remote indeed. Under these circumstances truly long-term problems such as climate change in 50 to 100 years carry almost no weight. An interesting exception to this principle is the very active participation in the recent climate change negotiations of the island nations are the Pacific and the Caribbean islands as they recognise that their very existence is threatened by sea level rise.

In economists' 'terms' when the daily life is a struggle, people have a high "discount rate" putting greater stock in what happens in the next few days or weeks and having little time to fret about whether their choices today will have a negative impact several years in the future.

With basic survival not an issue, people in more wealthy countries can afford the luxury of worrying about the planet's long-term ecological outlook. Short-term sacrifices to protest future interest become not only possible but rational. The difference in time horizons profoundly shapes risk calculations and environmental spending choices.

The failure of the industrialised nations and their environmentalists to build their policies on the foundation that recognises basic human needs in the developing world is the source of much of the North-South tension over trade and environment.

What is important is to pursue policies that work with not against, the peoples' 'needs and desires'. As Fredric Vester, a systems thinker, observed: "We can only get people to behave in an ecological way—compatible with nature—when we give up the idea of making sacrifices and being ascetic. Egoism is one of the strongest forces in the living world".

While resource conservation and other sustainable development concepts have no resonance with the very poor, the merely poor can and often do make decisions to trade-off short-term gain for longer-term opportunities, particularly if the social structures of their communities, such as land tenure policies give them incentive to do so.

Moreover, how can afforestation policies make sense to the poor who sell firewood to hedge against destitution? In many sections of Africa the current consumption of fuelwood exceeds annual growth in supply by as much as 30 to 200 per cent.

It is now widely accepted that the links between poverty, high population growth and environmental degradation are circular and mutually reinforcing. Investing in people is an urgent moral imperative. This will reduce poverty and population growth and in the long run arrest environmental degradation.

The principle that concern for social and environmental sustainability must permeate all development activity is fundamental to the concept of sustainable development. To promote this principle, it is essential to understand the link between rapid population growth, poor agricultural development and environmental degradation.

New ways must be evolved to examine ways to averaging these links so as to stop and reverse the cycle : which is possible through access to markets : investment in education, health, agricultural services and infrastructural development in the face of rapid population growth, it is all the more relevant to increase per capita agricultural production and income and improve natural resource management. This will ensure economic stability and arrest the spread of both rural and urban poverty.

From a practical perspective interventions that leverage the environment-development news to achieve improvement in human well being and in the health of the environment can be divided into three broad categories.

- ❒ Resource development interventions that seek to improve material well being of the poor.
- ❒ Human development intervention such as those that improve health, nutrition and education to foster efficient utilisation of natural resources, thereby enhancing productivity and physical well being.
- ❒ Social development interventions, which will ensure that the development process touches those who need it most—the poor and needy.
- ❒ To conclude : Environmentally sustainable development is based on two axioms. The first axiom is, that reducing poverty and investing in people are essential for environmental sustainability. The second axiom is, that promoting the efficient use of resources benefits both the environment and the economy. A model of development, based on these axioms, can create a coherent approach that will help to link economic growth to peoples' aspirations.

Objectives

The concept of sustainable development implies balancing environmental protection with the generation of increased opportunities for employment and improved livelihood. This calls for the need to protect and enhance the environment based on a four-fold agenda :

- ❒ Assisting countries in setting priorities, strengthening institutions and implementing programme for environmentally sustainable development.
- ❒ Minimising the potential adverse environment and social impacts of development projects.
- ❒ Building on positive linkages between poverty reduction, economic efficiency and environmental protection.
- ❒ Addressing global environmental challenges.

From Policy to Practice

Liberalised regimes must seek to highlight

- ❒ The need for Governments to strengthen their ministries, agencies and other institutions to deal more effectively with environmental issues.

- Greater integration of environmental concerns into economic and sector work.
- A growing emphasis on the social aspects of sustainable development.

Main Themes for the Future

- Learning from implementation.
- Expanding the scope of environmental assessment.
- Reinforcing the social dimension.
- Mainstreaming global concerns.
- Leveraging private initiative.

Building on the Synergies between Development and the Environment

- Poverty reduction and the environment.
- Efficient resources use and the environment.

Addressing Regional and Global Environmental Challenges

- Regional environmental initiatives.
- Global environmental programmes.

Strengthening the Private Sector Role

- Transforming the soul of business to environmental consciousness.
- Industrial ecology : Issues and approaches.
- "Green" marketing strategies.

The true and the extent of the macro-economic problems, both urban and rural that are now among the most urgent of any confronting the international community must be looked into.

Against that backdrop, the overall objective is two-fold : one is increase the world's awareness of the problems we have cited here, and a second is to awaken it to the potentials of human settlements as important inputs to social progress and economic growth. But this potential can be realised only if we convince the global community that on an urbanised planet we have no choice : our cities, towns and villages must be healthy, safe, just and sustainable. It is time to end the platitudes and cliches. It is time to act.

There are many questions that have to be addressed in developing countries and international countries alike. And the private sector has a major role to play; we urgently need its support if we are to succeed.

PROBLEMS AND CONSEQUENCES OF LIBERALISATION

Problem Statement

As seen in the survey report of NCAER by the author, the main problems relate to resource extraction, deforestation, green revolution, urbanisation and industrialisation.

The most serious challenges that cause environmental degradation are :

Resource Extraction—This arises out of coal, oil and gas production, poor handling of materials, and normal transport activities and major spills.

High Rate of Deforestation—This is endemic to most of the region.

Related to Agriculture—Efforts to ensure food security has led to implementation of high yielding variety package programmes, popularly called the "green revolution". These without a doubt have increased the yield per acre of most Asian and Southeast Asian countries. But, on the down side, the problem arises from a poor use of fertilisers, water logging and the effluents going into the river and waterways creating problems in fisheries and marine life.

Related to Industry—In the textile sector, inappropriate fabric technology is noticed in the use of acids and dyes. In the shoe industry, poor adhesive handling occurs frequently. In other areas, careless use of mercury and lead is observed. In the electronics sector, the disposal of CFC's (carbon-fluro-carbons) add to the problems of urbanisation.

Urbanisation and Industrialisation—Most cities are overcrowded and lacking in adequate infrastructure thus contributing to poor quality of life for all residents. Especially affected are those who are poor and otherwise disenfranchised.

Consequences

These problems have led to a general degradation of the environmental life, high infant mortality from water-born diseases, and waste dumps everywhere.

As consequences of this critical environmental degradation, major problems have surfaced. Some of these are :

The quality of the environmental life is quite low. There is a very high infant mortality rate arising from water-born diseases (*e.g.*, Nestle's problem with its powder milk formula being used with unsafe water).

Invariably waste-dumps seem to show up near the poor.

Centre for Strategic Alliances for Environmental Promotion (SAFE)

A centre should be established to provide a forum and information resource centre for management and training, to provide strategic alliances with key businesses, Government agencies in the States and local and state companies. The centre will be established to address itself toward solving environmental problems that relate to both the "brown" (urban) and the "green" areas of the environment.

The centre probably could be located adjacent to or within a local university or college so that the equipment and staff could be an extension of the local educational system.

The basic problems in the environment will focus first on environmental problems that are in the study community and then expanded into a regional concept to address problems that effect the community from the city, region and state. Some "typical" problems that could be addressed are :

High Rate of Deforestation—Dependency on Firewood

Causes of the problem will be studied as well as effective solution concerning the land that has been deforested to prevent soil erosion and misuse.

Inadequate Water and Sanitation Facilities

Alternative solutions will be examined to provide adequate resources that can be provided from within the community. Solutions in many instances to be self-sustaining by using products of wastes from the community for beneficial purposes (waste for fertiliser etc.)

Local Air Pollution

Air pollution can be caused by sources outside of the region and by many sources within the neighbourhood or community. High density living with small rooms (especially in cooking areas) causes smoke pollution and smoking is especially hazardous in these situations. Reducing the reliance on petroleum use and transportation would also reduce air pollution at a local level.

Solid Waste Accumulation

The organisation of solid waste collection within communities and various forms of "clean-up" is an important first step in the elimination of solid waste. The use of wastes in building structures (straw, rubber, cans etc.) would be another means of reducing waste. Introduction of solid waste systems for use in urban regions would be analysed. The centre would determine the local and regional problems and then coordinate the alternative types of solutions to best answer the problems.

Industrial Environmental Pollution

This type of pollution is the pollution that is caused by factories such as lead in air, chemicals, and the acids and dyes from the textile factories to mention a few. Many poverty areas are located next to these industries and thus have to live adjacent to harmful effluents in the air, soils and water. Even in the electronics sector, the disposal of CFC's (carbon-fluoro-carbons) add to the problems of urbanisation. The centre would serve as a voice for the people affected by this type of pollution as well as being a bridge to businesses to provide solutions in the short and long terms.

Pollution Related to Agriculture

Since agriculture and horticultural production is an important part of the self-sustaining community concept the pollution caused by several "green revolution" practices needs to be examined and use technology that eliminates the poor use of fertilisers, soil erosion and compaction, water logging, and nitrogen pollution of waterways and ground water. Simple crop rotation and tilling can be very beneficial by reducing the build-up of predator insects typical with monocrop production. The use of non-hybrid seeds is another means to encourage "healthy" agriculture with low input costs.

Urbanisation and Industrialisation

Most cities are overcrowded and lacking in adequate infrastructure, thus contributing to poor quality of life for all residents. Especially affected are those who are poor and otherwise disenfranchised. The health of people is an environmental problem. The spread of disease by fleas and rats in just one example.

Local Financial Pollution

People living in poverty in most cases are disenfranchised from financing for improving themselves other than several welfare programmes. In most countries the welfare programmes have to be restructured so that the people are helped by their own efforts or helped by recognition of their problems over which they have no control. The process of "red lining" is a case in point and it prevents people from helping themselves. The processes both political and financial that keep communities in poverty have to be re-examined in the context of a total improvement programme of urban solutions.

Other Pollution Problems

There are many other environmental problems that will be in specific communities and they would be recognised as each project is studied.

The SAFE would be the enter where evaluations of the environmental problems would be studied and providing solutions in conjunction with people in the community.

The Response—SAFE

SAFE would be a centre affiliated with or having strategic alliances with key businesses, Government agencies at home and abroad and the local and country Government agencies as well as professionals and academics. The major alliance would be with the communities so that they can have input into the other alliances.

In response to these problems and their resulting consequences, the centre for Strategic Alliances for Environmental Promotion (SAFE) with support from various regional partnerships. Safe should be involved in technology transfer, economic and business development, environmental studies, joint ventures as well as licensing opportunities with an emphasis on environmental issues.

Most importantly, the proposed centre should explore opportunities for co-operative network among Universities, businesses and Non-Governmental Organisations (NGO's) to address environmental issues. It would also promote efforts of small and middle market companies to demonstrate appropriate environmental technologies that have been developed to meet local needs.

The proposed centre could be associated with a college or university in the foreign countries. Private industry will play a major role in any successful attempt in solving environmental problems. SAFE could plan to address issues such as the relation between environmental protection and economic growth. Private foundations and grass roots advocacy groups play an important role in the United States national debate on and in response to environmental issues. Established International agencies and NGOs could be involved in the project to show the people how private and community foundations are funded to enable private citizens to play an advocacy role on issues of common interests.

SAFE would afford an opportunity for a consortium of business organisations abroad concerned with environmental issues to come together to respond to entrepreneurial needs in any country where the project is located and where environmental degradation is maximum.

The centre should also respond directly to the need for an international centre to monitor environmental issues, promote "green" marketing strategies, strengthen the environmental policies of the Government, business houses and industrial estates. It would also promote technology transfer and strategic alliances as the major intervention to uplift the eastern region of the U.S. We also believe that a centre such as SAFE would also facilitate creation of a bio-diversity conservation network to establish and preserve programmes of judicious sustainable bio-diversity.

Specific Programme

SAFE should be involved in technology transfer, business development, exchange visits, joint ventures and licensing opportunities.

Solutions to environmental problems are inextricably tied to business, the economy and individual rights to clean air and water. Groups of leaders could be exchanged including potential entrepreneurs representing private industry, grassroot organisations, consultants, technical personnel, the Government and the academics in this venture.

Specifically there is need to focus on the eastern region of India. Here are some of the key reasons for our focus :

(a) The State of Orissa has the largest coal deposits in India and therefore coal washing technology is important; other coal mining regions are also in Eastern India;

(b) The State of Assam is India's oil belt and deforestation in the state has caused enormous environmental calamities, *e.g.* Cherapunjee, the world's wettest region two decades ago is now facing drought;

(c) Calcutta and other major metropolitan cities in West Bengal are under severe population density pressure with concomitant issues of urban decay. The backwater from the sewage system could also provide immense business possibilities for U.S. business firms;

(d) The State of Bihar is clearly one of India's poorest states facing problems of deforestation and low standard of living. Yet this is a state which is richly endowed in natural and mineral resources.

All these states have immense business opportunities with an environmental face and environmental problems arising from underdevelopment, lack of (low level) education, poor sanitation, health hazards and poor drinking water. All of them demand an international response to the challenge. It behoves the US and foreign business to aggressively participate in assisting in sustainable development and finding business and commercial opportunities to share and provide guidance in the transfer of technology, sharing of experiences from other similar situations, and sharing of experiences of both from successful as well as unsuccessful practices and implementation in their countries.

In the area of Business Education the purpose will be to serve businesses that are planning to enter into joint venture and trade with the foreign business. The primary objectives include :

(a) Helping local enterprises present themselves as viable joint venture, trade or technology transfer partners to overseas business;
(b) Local expertise for oversight of on-going joint ventures;
(c) Imparting of training for executives and management of local enterprises with overseas partners.

Other recommended services to be provided by SAFE include :

For Local Business

(a) Sponsor educational events and classes for modern management practices and financial management techniques and practices.
(b) Provide training in environmental technology transfer.
(c) Provide consultation for business plan preparation.
(d) Locate possible foreign joint venture partners and serve as a resources centefror local joint ventures.

For Foreign based Business

(a) Screen joint venture projects.
(b) Organise exchange visits.
(c) Manage oversight of joint ventures.
(d) Management improvement of joint ventures.
(e) Location of joint venture candidates in the project region.
(f) Assist with interpretation of unique business practices in the country.
(g) Assist in securing needed supporting services within the local economy.
(h) Development of cost control mechanisms for joint venture companies.
(i) Training in cross-culture practices.

The gamut of issues to be covered by SAFE are seen in the following schematic framework :

STRATEGIC ALLIANCES FOR ENVIRONMENTAL PROMOTION

Monitor Environmental Issues Issues	*Research on "Brown Issues" Urban Environmental Policies and Issues*	*Research on "Green" Marketing Strategies*	*Business Education*
Economic Valuation of Pollution : Prevention and Remediation	Urban Poverty Congestion Urban Planning Health, Nutrition	Waste use and Utilization	For Indian Business for Foreign Business
Strengthen Environmental Policies of Government Business Houses, Industrial Estates	Research on Industrial Ecology Supply Quality Model for Strategic alliances Develop Trade Information Centre Through Internet : Provide MIS to small Business Small Business Environment Management Research to Determine "Excelsior" Award in India	Products for a Healthy Planet Recycling & Green cotton Garments Foxfibre Seventh Generation concepts Research on Technology Transfer	JVCS Location Management Consultation Assist with Interpretation of India Unique Practices Environmental Management Course

ENVIRONMENTAL POLICY FOR BUSINESS : AN AGENDA FOR GROWTH RECOMMENDATIONS GROUPED BY TOPIC

Cost-Benefit Analysis

1. The State should mandate a complete review of current regulations relating to the EPA (Environmental Protection Agency) and all agencies regulating environmental matters to make sure that current science, realistic risk assessments, net health analysis, and cost benefit analysis shall apply in order to reduce, condense or eliminate regulations.

2. The State and the EPA should risk assessment, scientific benefit and cost-benefit analysis before new environmental, safety or health regulations are enhanced, taking into account how they will impact small business, individual property rights and property values. In evaluating impact, costs should meet some such test as percent of gross sales. The regulated community, including small business, should be included in any final cost-benefit studies or reports.

3. Federal and State legislation is needed to force environmental agencies to base their evaluation of proposed regulations on sound scientific criteria and to require the agencies perform risk analysis on all proposed regulations.

4. When the Government passes any regulation requiring specific technology and/or procedures for protecting the environment, it must demonstrate a measurable, quantifiable benefit in proportion to the cost of compliance. In addition, the regulation should include a funding mechanism which will facilitate compliance. Where natural physical conditions warrant, reasonable compliances should be accepted as conforming to the intent of the regulation. In addition, the state must review existing regulations and ensure they adhere to the same standards as new environmental regulations.

5. The Environmental Protection Agency should follow the due process concept of notice and provide assistance for compliance. Risk assessment should weigh the cost versus benefit of regulatory compliance. Any "takings" of private property would require an economic impact study and provide for just compensation.

6. *Risk Assessment/Cost-Benefit:* The State should enact legislation subjecting new and existing environmental regulations to an assessment process to determine if they are scientifically sound; economically cost effective; have regional equity and flexibility; produce tangible environmental results based on valid analysis of statistical data; create

no enforcement duplication; and that no agency levied fines are used for funding the agency.

7. *Economic and Social Impact of Environmental Regulations.* Environmental protections have been legislated, enacted, and enforced with inadequate concern for their economic and social impact on American lives and families. Additionally, the uncertainty and conflict of unclear and conflicting laws, regulations and definitions greatly increases their cost impact because of expensive litigation and the cost of holding unproductive property. There is need to modify such acts as the Resource Conservation and Recovery Act, Clean Water Act, and Clean Air Act, Endangered Species Act, and National Environmental Policy Act to remove these issues from courtroom litigation, and emphasise non-punitive compliance based on incentives, with only mediation and arbitration to be used for settling disputes. Additionally, penalties should only be levied against those who deliberately violate these laws. Finally, all new environmental protections should be held to these same standards.

8. The enforcement system for regulations is inconsistent and does not focus on the needs and constraints of small business. The EPA should modify that system to assure equitable treatment for small business, focussing on constructive enforcement, innovative penalties, alternative dispute resolution, including the naming of small business grievance panels to arbitrate compliance issues, and rewarding exceptional environmental performance.

9. The State should direct the EPA to adhere to the following inspection and enforcement policies;

(a) Voluntary compliance audits to be available with no fines issued.
(b) No fines should be imposed following enforcement inspections if a company is found to be in substantial compliance, considering the company's overall compliance efforts and the potential for significant environmental harm;
(c) Fines should be based on a sliding scale relative to the size of the business;
(d) The EPA should be reviewed to confirm that both consider the real potential for environmental harm.

Property Rights/Takings

10. Any governmental action, law or regulation that deprives a property owner of any value or benefits of his or her private property shall constitute a "TAKING" for which said property owner shall be entitled to full "Fair Market Value" compensation.

11. In order to eliminate significant reductions in property value due to regulatory restriction, the State should shift the burden of proof from land-owners to the Government that land use prohibitions do not constitute regulatory takings.

12. The State should direct the following changes in land wetlands laws and regulations :

(a) To the extent regulations adopted after the date of property acquisition affect a property or its value, the property owner should be compensated by the Government for the loss in value;
(b) The Army Corps of Engineers should be given sole jurisdiction of Section 404;
(c) Differing degrees of regulation should be allowed based on the relative importance of a wetland to the local environment; and
(d) A statutory definition of "wetlands" should be adopted defining a wetland as land that is saturated at the surface during the growing season.

13. The State could learn from the US example which in its fifth amendment to the United States Constitution says "... Nor shall private property be taken for public use without just compensation". The policies of regulator agencies such as the Environmental Protection Agency often result in a "taking" of the value of the assets of small business. The State shall make provision for the compensation at their fair market value of that part of the holdings of the private property owner that is devalued or rendered unusable by excessive federal regulation.

14. The State should analyse the method of evaluation under which private property is taken for environmental protection. Specifically, examine the economic impact before property is taken and prohibit the taking of property without just compensation. Compensation should be granted to those land owners when some or all of their property has been taken by Government through direct actions or negotiation.

15. The State should reform the Superfund programme so that small businesses are not held liable for past legal disposal of regulated substances. Even an expedited *de minimis* settlement process cannot solve the problems of expensive legal fees and contributions nor the financial uncertainty created by the continuing threat of liability. To ensure that small businesses are no longer unfairly burdened by Superfund, the State should repeal retroactive joint and several liability.

16. The State should enact environmental legislation to:

- ❐ Eliminate retroactive liability prior to January 1, 1987.
- ❐ Require good science and realistic risk assessments in assessing hazards from waste sites.

- ❐ Require good science and realistic risk assessments in establishing clean-up standards. This includes a realistic consideration of future uses of the site.
- ❐ Eliminate "re-openers"—re-opening the re-mediation process at a site after it has been closed.
- ❐ Offering alternative funding strategies for site clean-ups.
- ❐ Greater use of *de minimis* or micromis exemptions.

17. Small business should be protected from the exorbitant cost of Superfund litigation by legislation which would apportion clean-up costs based on the business contribution of hazardous to the Superfund site.

18. The State should eliminate "joint and several" liability and replace it with fault based liability and compel the EPA to more actively utilize "*de minimis*" release authorizations for small business. The State should ensure; (a) that prior to enacting proposed regulations or enforcement action the EPA conduct extensive peer reviews of proposed regulations and actions addressing all assumptions, uncertainties, risk assessments and cost-benefit analyses for each proposal; (b) the elimination or retroactive liability.

19. The State should reform the existing Superfund (CERCLA) legislation by eliminating the retroactive and strict liability provision, redrafting "*de minimis*" settlement provisions to compel EPA to settle with minoı contributors and strengthen protection to financial institutions from potential Superfund liability.

20. Current landowners and business can be held liable for a pre-existing environmental problems regardless of fault, which can result in loss of land use and/or the inability to obtain financing. The State should revise the Superfund Act to eliminate the "no-fault liability scheme" and impose a "fault-based liability scheme".

21. The State should enact legislation establishing a self-evaluation privilege under the environmental laws and regulations (Title 40). Specifically, this privilege should create a presumption against the imposition of administrative, civil or criminal penalties for voluntary disclosure so long as the entity making the disclosure initiates appropriate efforts to achieve compliance within a reasonable time frame.

22. The State should enact environmental audit privilege and voluntary disclosure legislation under the environmental laws and regulations. This privilege creates a presumption against impositions of administrative, civil, or criminal penalties for voluntary disclosure so long as the entity naming the disclosure initiates appropriate efforts to achieve compliance within a reasonable time frame.

Other Recommendations

23. The Ståte should enact legislation directing EPA to specify the circumstances under which it would not sue a business that is involved with a State approved site reclamation project. For such "brown field" projects in which clean-up is commensurate with the intended use of the property, the legislation should direct EPA to enter into legally binding agreements (like covenants not to sue) with the parties assuring that no future federal action will be taken.

24. Cost is an effective deterrent to small business investment in pollution control equipment. And loans may not be as available to them as to larger corporations. The State should provide tax incentives to small businesses deductions or credits for equipment purchase, remedial costs and/or pollution prevention/control measures.

25. Flexible approach to waste product disposal. The State should revise the Resource Conservation and Recovery Act to provide for environmentally sound, market-driven solutions to municipal and industrial disposal and recycling, to be accomplished through State agencies.

26. The State should adopt changes in environmental statutes and regulations in order to provide an even playing field across the country in environmental regulation. Specifically the State should have Clean Air Act to eliminate Air Quality Regions and substitute these provisions with a country-wide standard for air pollution abatement requirements. The State should require the EPA to establish and demonstrate substantial fairness in the enforcement of environmental laws and regulations between the EPA regional offiees.

27. The State should pass legislation to encourage continued usage of old industrial sites, and preserve farm land. A Bill should be introduced to include manufacturing plants currently in operation, establishes a process for industrial site clean-up, establishe a framework for setting remediation standards, limit future liability for persons meeting clean up standard, create a loan fund for voluntary clean-up, and provide funding for programme administration. Another bill should provide protection for clean-up liability for lending institutions, and development agencies. The programme would protect the environment and promote economic growth in depressed areas.

28. *Financial Incentive:* The State should create fiscal incentives for small business to fund environmental compliance. Options include; (1) Loans, administered by existing agencies with funds generated from fees and fines, and (2) Tax deductions or credits for cost of remediations,

purchase of pollution abatement equipment, and/or implementation of prevention measures.

SOHO & LIBERALISATION

The Environmental Manager and the Business Community

Many believe that typical US business is a large fortune 500 Corporation with thousands of employees. This has never been true and today large corporations account for an even smaller part of the US economy, than they did 10 years ago.

Just as computers are becoming smaller so are businesses. Businesses have fewer employees because the combination of telecommunications and computers called 'telecomputing' has reduced the need for corporate staff, most of whom are highly educated, talented, and experienced. As corporations shed these knowledge workers many join the growing small office/home office enterprise economy known as the SOHO movement. There are 21 million business enterprises in US today. Only 14,000 have more than 500 employees. The rest are small and mid size businesses. Many are family owned enterprises. These include partnerships, sole proprietorships and unincorporated home business. Small business is increasing at an annual rate of 2 to 3%. The entrepreneurial economy is growing stronger.

- ❐ Today 50% of US exporters are small business with fewer than 100 employees. In some regions less than 80% of exporters have fewer than 100 employees.
- ❐ Small and mid size business with fewer than 500 employees now account for 50% of US exports measured by dollar value.
- ❐ Many of the US' most famous big business—from micro-soft and Apple computer to Ford Motor Company and Disney began as home-based business.

The SOHO movement has important social and demographic implications. It provides a safety value for those caught in turbulance of corporate down sizing. It creates new possibilities for small town and rural economy because so many in the movement want to live there. The SOHO movement will also shape tomorrow's urban areas including how and where people live and how they are connected to home and family and work place colleagues.

The expansion of the SOHO movement is likely but not automatic. It is likely because technology is moving in the direction of smaller units, niche markets and distributed work. But there are also obstacles.

Some are public policy obstacles, like zoning regulations, discriminatory taxation and burden some unnecessary paperwork.

There are also cultural barriers. Many employers and institutions have difficulty shedding old industrial age habits. Other obstacles arise out of business policies and practices in the private sector. These include discriminatory pricing and practices for insurance, telephone professional services that are essential to the SOHO operator.

The lessons are obvious for a liberalised economy, changing old attitudes and reversing bad policies should be a top national priority. India's growing entrepreneurial economy is to be shaped by several key factors:

1. Home based business.
2. Growth of computers and advanced telecommunications, *e.g.* a third of all homes in US have computers, 40% of home computer owners have moderns; more than four million users are linked into on-line services. Americans buy 50,000 computers a day where nearly half of them are equipped with CD-ROM giving home users access to a large volume of multimedia information and huge storage capabilities.

Successful home businesses includes everything from top publishing and accounting firms to pet walking. Every day as many as 8,000 new jobs are created, many of them home-based. Research indicates productivity rises 15-25% when work is done in tele-communicating programmes.

A study of 90,000 managers found that managers in office waste 25% of their time whereas 34% of an employee's day is pressumably frittered away in normal office work. People experience a greater sense of ownership and gain a new feeling of pride when working at home. Also, the cost of living goes down for home workers. If a worker connects 20,000 miles a year on his car commuting to and from a job his mileage may drop to 12,000 if he works at home. That is a saving of 200 dollars a month—that does not include parking.

Other substantial savings include putting in more hours, less need to monitor coffee breaks, lunch breaks and use of office space, the burden on roads is eased.

Working at home can literally clear the air. By far the largest source of air pollution is emissions from automobiles, chiefly from stop-and-go driving during morning and evening rush hours. Home workers help to reduce auto emission by nearly 40%.

Thus small businesses are a driving force in any liberalised economy, providing opportunities for millions to succeed. The ability to respond quickly to rapidly changing market conditions is now the challenge for all businesses, not only the largest corporations.

In a liberalised regime growth will depend increasingly on using technology to meet the three key requirements of today's evolving and accelerating business environment: Controlling costs, cutting cycle time, and improving quality. This can happen if technology meets specific business needs and the environmental manager plays a more important role. Managers must think "environment" today more than ever; knowledge and awareness are keys.

In the developing world about 25 business schools now offer courses that at least touch on environmental issues. According to James Post, Chairman of the Management Department at Boston University's business school, approximately10 or 15 schools will offer elective course, while many others will incorporate "Significant modules" into classes on such functional areas as marketing and accounting. Unfortunately, many business professors find it hard to "teach something that they don't have a good conception of themselves".

For the environmental manager, people with skills representing a managerial look are equally as important as possessing a technical understanding of environmental management.

What distinguishes environmental managers from other manager? The general business school approach stipulates that good managers can manage in any area yet in contemporary corporations most managers, even at the highest levels, are simply "working" managers because of financial cut-backs.

We must constantly evaluate which risks we should be reducing and for what purpose—compliance, criminal or financial liability, community relations, safety concerns, or a combination of all these motivations. The 1991 edition of the *Practical Guide to Environmental Management* for example, will contain approximately 20 additional pages or process hazard management and criminal liability exposure. Senior corporate officials who assumed they were in control or ahead of their environmental issues now find that the cost of these programmes has increased dramatically, which reduces compliances levels. So we managers will need to continually re-examine our programme for the next several years.

Non-compliance will become increasingly likely, since the degree of compliance is subjectively administered and because many of the stipulated requirements have been generalised in the legislation drafted by the State. Moreover staff members with a broad range of environmental help, or safety duties do not have the time to follow new legislation concerning specific technical requirements.

Managers, particularly those who understand legal matters have strongly resisted efforts to "legalised" management programmes. However liability exposure resulting from the new laws and regulations continue to increase. For example, the EPA estimates it will have to promulgate more than 55 regulations in two years under the 1990 Clean Air Act Amendments.

It is important for environmental management to be accepted as an integral part of all levels of management. TQM assumes that integrating the environment aspect of business as part of total quality through-out business will enable environmental management to become a part of Corporate Business Strategy Commitment to quality—both producers and environmental, is essential for firms today.

Environmentalism is not a fact and Corporations must respond correctly. The corporate environmental principles are:

- Boardroom endørsements must be communicated all the way down about the risks; similarly, board members must be receptive to innovative ideas from all employees.
- Make good intentions written policy.
- Do not be afraid to set goals beyond federal and state requirements.
- Take the initiative both in technological innovation and public policy formulation.
- Work closely with public interest groups.
- Work with other companies to use resources effectively and to reflect genuine concern for an industry-wise problem.
- Communicate effectively and credibly with the public.
- Commit to the long haul.

Re-structure the organisation to account for environmental planning, establish liaisons with local and national environmental groups, and higher experienced environmental professionals. The greening of America is not a passing fad. Companies must be willing to make substantial, lasting modification to their operations if they intend to survive even into a next decade. Environmentally aware consumers will demand it and the planners' survival may well depend upon it.

REFERENCES

1. Mukerjee, Suman K. "Is sustainable development a practical proposition"?
2. ESTY, F. "Greening the GATT" 1994.

3. *Products for a Healthy Planet,* The SEVENTH GENERATION 1994.
4. Foundation for a new Century, National Conference Note Book, the White House Conference on small business, Washington Hillton, Sheraton Washington, (June 11 to 15) Washington D.C.
5. Philip M. Burgss & Sarah Edwards, Centre for New West, June 1995.
6. Case, Cohn. (The wonderland economy) *INC. Magazine,* The State of Small Business 1995.
7. Eliason Carol, *The Business Plan for Home Base Business.* US Small Business Administration, 1989.
8. Kamoroff, Bernard., *Small time operator; How to start your own small business, keep your books, pay your taxes, and stay out of trouble.*
9. Eangenden, David. *The Home Office Computing Hand Book,* 1994.
10. Lessinger, Jack M., Making telecommuting happen. Van Nostrand Reinhold.
11. Ross, Mãryline and Tom, *Big ideas for small service business.* How to successfully advertise, publish and maximise your business, or professional practice. Communications Creativity, 1994.
12. Struck Nancy. Working Smarter from Home Your Day Your Way. 1995.
13. Woy, Patricia A. *Small business that grow and grow and grow,* 1989.
14. Friedman, Frank B. The Changing Role of the Environmental Manager. *Business Horizons,* March-April 1994.
15. Friedman F.B. *Practical Guide to Environmental Management.* Environmental Law Institute, 1991.
16. Friedman F.B., Mixing Safety and Risk Issues with Environmental Concerns. *Hazardous Waste and Toxic Law and strategy,* July 1990.
17. Thomas, Lee M. *The Business Community and the Environment—An Important Partnership. Business Horizons,* March-April 1994.

20

Globalisation of Television and Doordarshan: Challenges and Opportunities

Sanjay Kumar

The great revolution of the discovery of the printing press in 1476 followed by Graham Bell's contribution in terms of discovery of telephone and then we have had the radio revolution coming on the turn of the century and then, of course, the space revolution which has totally revolutionsed the communication scenario in this world. And, because of these, the entire world—this blue planet has become a simple small global village where every thing is inter-connected with everything else through the relationship that operates in both the physical, the biological and the social systems of this planet.

Let me come to the audio-visual medium. The first high definition public TV service was started by the BBC in 1936. In India, the service named 'Doordarshan' in Hindi, was inaugurated by Dr. Rajendra Prasad then the President of India in 1959.

A dent in this approach was made when New Delhi hosted the General Conference of UNESCO in 1956 where one of the important decisions of that world body was to make a grant of $20,000 to India to set up a pilot project to study the use of TV as a medium of education, rural uplift and community development. The United States Government provided some essential equipment, and Philips who had demonstrated a close-circuit television at the Industrial Fair in Delhi in 1955 sold the small transmitter at a nominal cost. This helped to clear the initial material and psychological hurdles which had earlier stood in the way of TV's arrival.

Since there were no privately owned TV sets when the experimental service started, the first viewers were those at 21 community centres in middle and lower income group areas in and around Delhi, the receiving sets having been acquired from out of the UNESCO grant. Later 45 more sets were added, the objective then being to have 100 community sets in operation, with viewers organised as 'Tele Clubs'. Each Tele club consisted of 20 to 25 members who, after viewing each day's programme, would record their reactions and send these and their suggestions to the TV centre.

In October 1961, TV took another step forward by launching an Educational Project in Cooperation with Ford Foundation of America and the Directorate of Education, Delhi. 20 lessons each week were broadcast in the morning transmission and repeated in the afternoon. The subjects covered included Chemistry, Physics, Hindi, English, Geography and Social Studies. The findings published later established that TV had proved itself to be a very useful tool for spreading education.

On August 15, 1965, the spacious auditorium built earlier as an Annexe to the Broadcasting House at Delhi for AIR's audience programmes was converted into a television studio utilising the equipment received as a gift from West Germany.

In1972, the Delhi centre was on the air for 37$^1/_2$ hours a week (25 hours of general programmes in the evening and 12$^1/_2$ hours of broadcasts for Higher Secondary Schools during the. day). The transmission hours were 6.30 to 10.30 p.m. on week days, and 6 to 10 p.m. on Sundays. A surveys at Meerut.

Planned Expansion

The Bombay TV Centre, with its studios and transmitter located at the old radio transmitter at Worli, started on October 2, 1972 initially with 2 hours and15 minutes daily from 7.15 to 9.30 p.m. which was increased by 15 minutes from January 14, 1973 and to three hours daily on week days (3 hours 45 min. on Saturdays and Sundays) from April 1, 1973. A two hours morning programme was introduced from June 1, 1974.

After Bombay, the next TV centre to come up was Srinagar which started an experimental service from the Republic Day, January 26, 1973 for one hour (4.30 to 5.30 p.m.) on alternate days, and from 3 to 5.30 p.m. on Sundays. This very rapid escalation in intransmission hours was undertaken to counter the propaganda by Pakistan Television which was received very clearly in the valley, and naturally attracted much attention.

Strategic considerations also led to high priority being given to the setting up of our fourth TV centre at Amritsar on September 29,

1973, beginning with a three hour daily service in Punjabi, Hindi, Urdu and English. Amritsar's main attraction for people across the international border was the Hindi feature films which were immensely popular, and were sometimes characterised in the Pakistan Press as a kind of cultural invasion.

East and South

The TV centre at Calcutta went into operation in August 8, 1975 with a three hours daily programme in Bengali, English and Hindi, with one news bulletin of 10 minutes in each language.

Madras T.V. Centre was inaugurated a week later, *i.e.* on August 15, 1975 with a daily two-hour service from 7 to 9 p.m. in Tamil and English. 60 to 80% of the output was of an educative nature, like programmes for rural areas, industiral workers and the youth. For entertainment there was one play of 20 to 30 minutes each week, and three or four feature films in Tamil and one in another language per month. From December 2, 1975 the service was extended to $2^1/_2$ hours daily (6.30 to 9.30 p.m.) and the telecast of Hindi films increased to four a month.

The seventh TV centre, that at Lucknow, was inaugurated on November 27, 1975 with two hours daily programme on week days, and four hours on Sundays.

A House Divided

The next major development, an organisational one, was the separation of Radio and Television in April, 1976. Mrs. Gandhi, the Prime Minister, spoke over TV on that day to mark the occasion, and her telecast was carried also over all the 2,400 sets in Satellite Instructional Television Experiment (SITE) villages.

On being delinked from Akashvani, the television service got its own Director General and P.V. Krishnamurty was the first to hold this office. The Directorate General was located at Mandi House near the junction of Bhagwan Das Road and Lytton Road opposite Rabindra Bhavan.

This very interesting and exciting project was the first of its kind in this part of the world for transmitting instructional programmes on a large scale. It used a satellite for daily telecast of school, agriculture and social education programmes simultaneously to 2,400 villages located in six states (Rajasthan, Bihar, Orissa, Madhya Pradesh, Andhra Pradesh and Karnataka) for one year from August 1,1975 to July 31, 1976. The Applications Technology Satellite-6 launched in USA on May

30, 1974 was made available to India by NASA (National Aeronautical and Space Administration) for this purpose, and placed in a geophysical stationary orbit. The responsibility for the spacecraft was that of NASA, while the Indian Space Research Organisation (ISRO) had full responsibility for the ground segment.

TV Goes Commercial

Three months before it set up its own separate house, Doordarshan inaugurated its commercial service on January 1,1976 mainly in the form of static picture 'spots', the scope soon afterwards being extended to video and films, and the acceptance of sponsored programmes. Expectedly, feature films and other movie-based programmes like *Chitrahar* attract most advertisements. The revenue from this source was 77 lakh rupees in 1976-77 (for the first three months of the financial year).[1]

In India, mass communication was viewed from the point of view of its social relevance and the national socio-economic objectives. In India, communication is the centre of every human activity in this democratic age when people have begun to matter. That is why we all believed in rapidly extending communication services for rural areas, backward territories and the people. To this end the Government had agreed to also go in for sophisticated technologies like satellite, colour TV and electronic telecommunications.[2] A developing country like India, with subcontinental dimensions and with its multi-lingual and multi-religious character, faces a dual challenge of integrating the various parts of the country in a national network and at the same time ensuring the preservation and expression of regional diversity. There is no technological determinism or inherent technological compulsion for one-sided centralisation or one-sided decentralisation. An integrative, interactive and participatory model of communication which was required by Indian conditions was facilitated by the flexible and dynamic character of modern communication technology. It allowed scope as much for area-specificity and audience sensitivity in programme coverage as for national integration. This idea of evolving an Indian version of the Communication Revolution means being sensitive to socio-cultural requirements of the Indian situation at national, regional and local levels.[3]

By keeping in the mind for the above mentioned feature of the development one of the most spectacular accomplishments of Doordarshan was when it started telecasting in colour since August 1982. It marked the transition from Black & White to Colour TV with a sophisticated technology with video cassettes and tape recorders as its accompaniment. Colour TV made a beginning with the live coverage of the Independence Day celebrations at Red Fort. However the Day for Colour TV came when Doordarshan started covering the 9th Asian Games over 40 transmitters, despite constraints of time and essential equipment.[4]

On 1 April 1984, Doordarshan network comprised eight main kendras, 9 relay centres and 8 post-SITE INSAT centres. During its silver Jubilee year, Doordarshan under a special plan for TV expansion commissioned one transmitter every day for a period of four months, starting 1 July 1984. This plan, unprecedented anywhere in the world, has brought the number of transmitters in India to 172, covering 52 per cent of the population. A major plan for TV expansion in the North Eastern region is also on the anvil. Thus TV has started making a thrust into rural areas in a big way. Practically every State/Union Territory capital besides a great number of villages are now covered by Doordarshan's network. Under a special programme of all-colour transmission, the TV complex expanded to cover 70 per cent of the population, extended over 117 towns with a population of one lakh and their adjoining rural areas.[5]

We find that before 1994, there was a slow pace of development in the area of TV expansion in India. It was the time which is worth to be noted that a number of other TV channels were taking shape and rooting their foot on the Indian soil. So at this juncture the Government of India and particularly Doordarshan was finding that there was a danger of cultural invasion. But it was beyond the means of the Government to stop it. So in the year 1994 we find it seemed to be a repetition of 1984, when Doordarshan had suddenly woken up to the need of expanding its reach and achieved the rate milestone of "a transmitter a day", setting up about 300 transmitters in just one year. The Information and Broadcasting Ministry realised that the only way to "beat them (Satellite channels) is to join them". Apart from increasing the number of its own satellite TV channels to 13, Doordarshan also announced plans to acquire the capacity to have upto 60 channels from the beginning of 1995.

Added to this was the high level study for establishing an information super highway (ISH), and the approval to the Broadcast Engineering Consultants India Ltd., a company under the Ministry's control, for providing engineering and management services to the electronic media within and outside the country. On the Doordarshan front, Independence Day in 1994 dawned with Prime Minister P.V. Narasimha Rao's address from the ramparts of Red Fort being beamed from 13 Doordarshan satellite channels. Later, these channels started beaming regional language programmes. Although Doordarshan already had more than two channels, the major change brought in was the joining of individual kendras the satellite networks. Thus, each channel is uplinked from the individual kendras insteadof from Delhi, except for DD-I (Primary channel). The starting of these channels made it possible for viewers all over the country to see about 25 Indian and foreign satellite channels on their TV sets with the help of dish antennae. The Doordarshan channels now show programmes in more than ten regional languages apart from Hindi and English. The major milestone for Doordarshan during the year was to make the Metro Channel available to various State capitals terrestrially instead of through a dish antennae. Thus, the gradual spread of the DD-II terrestrially will lead to the creation of a second National channel.

The Metro channel is presently available to 20 cities including Delhi, Bombay, Calcutta and Madras. Doordarshan commissioned 109 transmitters during the year, including seven high power transmitters, 81 low power transmitters and 15 very low power transmitters. Of these 21 LPT/VIPT were set up in hilly regions. A total of 267 more transmitters are under implementation, 34 in hilly areas.[6]

Doordarshan Under External and Internal Competition

By seeing on-going changes at the world arena in the field of mass communication, particularly television, the Ministry of Information and Broadcasting has finished drafting the Indian Broadcasting Bill, 1995, which will facilitate the setting up of an independent authority to oversee all matters pertaining to radio and television broadcasting. The draft will be circulated to the Ministries of Finance, Home, Telecommunications and Human Resources Development which will study its copyright implications. The Ministry proposes to constitute an 11-member broadcasting authority, which will issue licenses both for setting up independent radio and television stations, and oversee uplinking facilities. The authority, whose chairperson will enjoy the status of a Supreme Court judge, will look into all aspects of licensing, implementation of the advertisement code and the functioning of cable operators, and provide redressal to aggrieved parties. A two bid tender system from private parties has been worked out. The first round will consists of technical bids providing project details of a venture. Price bids will be entertained in the second round. The draft recommends that those indulging in political and religious activities could not be held eligible for licenses. Even cable operators will not be allowed to run television stations. But it is doubtful if such a directive can be implemented.

The draft does not specify the license fee, the private parties will have to pay to the authority. Setting up these stations will need a multi-crore investment. Not only will it mean setting up state-of-the-art studios and transmission equipment, but also the installation of low or high power transmitters costing crores of rupees. A license will be issued for a 30 KW station in the Ultra High Frequency (UHF) and for one upto 10 KW in the Very High Frequency (VHF) band. On the other hand, an FM radio station will be licensed to cover at most a radius of 60 km.

The broadcasting authority will refer all tenders to the wireless authority, which will recommend the wireless frequency under which the station will operate. The wireless license will continue to be issued under the Indian Telegraph Act of 1885. Licensees will not be allowed to broadcast news and current affairs programmes, and will have to concentrate on sports and cultural events. While providing at least five hours of transmission per day, they will have to indigenously produce 70 per cent of the programming. Only 10 per cent of the transmission time can be slated for foreign programmes and another 10 percent of the transmission kept aside for advertisements. Live broadcasts of programmes from outside India will require prior permission. Programmes inciting communal tension or attacking any religious community will be forbidden, and no radio or TV station can be set up anywhere within 50 km of the international border. The Ministry does not find it economically viable to have more than two or three television stations operating from the same city. "The number will vary from city to city, though the larger metros will obviously attract the largest number of such ventures."[7]

On the other hand US satellite PAS-4 which is being billed as the 'hotbird-to-be' of the Asian skies, was tentatively scheduled to be launched on August 23, 1995 from French Guyana and was expected to become operational by October. The satellite, whose platform is shared by top global broadcasters, is expected to beam 10-12 new channels into India. These channels will offer variety entertainment, both in English and Hindi, and are expected to build up PAS-4 as the new 'Gate-Way' into the Asian market, ending monopoly of Mr. Rupert Murdoch's Star TV platform, which is on Asia Sat-I.

"Among those entertainment giants whose channels will be offered to Indian audiences via PAS-4 are Entertainment and Sports Production Network (ESPN), Walt Disney, Sony Columbia, Time Warner's Home Box Office (HBO), Liberty of Telecommunications Incorporated (TCI) and two channels each from Viacom (MTV and a children's channel by Nickelodeon) and Turner (TNT and CNN)", the regional marketing director of Panam Sat (which owns PAS-4), Mr. Craig L. Moll, told the *Times of India*. Doordarshan also has two transponders on PAS-4, which it expects to use for beaming its international service (DDI) to Europe and the US. That, however, will be possible only towards the end of the year, as the service will need to be coordinated with PAS-I. Mr. Moll said a team from Panam Sat met Indian Government officials on June 1 and 2 to discuss how the satellite could be coordinated with the INSAT satellite systems. "The meetings are required under Geneva based International Telecommunications Union (ITU) regulations, in order to ensure against harmful interference between satellites in geo-stationary orbit. PAS-4 is expected to be located at 68.5 degree east while Intelsat is located at 66.5 degrees", he pointed out. "PAS-4 was originally slated to be launched in June this year, but the launch had to be put off by two months because of the failure of the Arianspace rocket in US on December 1, 1995."[8]

Where is the Way Out?

The recent drive for the modernisation of the communication systems in many countries including India has been characterised by a marked disjunction between hardware and software. The rapid expansion of hardware has proceeded without timely and appropriate planning of software. A developing country is exposed to the danger of erosion of its national cultural identity from such neglect of software planning. For resisting the cultural invasion from outside, restriction of imported programmes is necessary but not sufficient. Positive software planning is the most effective way of strengthening the foundations of cultural independence and of national culture.[9]

Doordarshan can perhaps never acquire an Indian personality unless and until it gives up the identification of India only with the newly emerging Indian middle class and the habit of viewing Indian life through the narrow prism of a middle class outlook. Doordarshan must reflect the changing life pattern and problems of the basic social categories of Indian society—the village-dwelling working peasants, artisans and labourers, the town-dwelling workers, lower middle classes and the intelligentsia, the other 'half' of Indian humanity comprising women, specially those belonging to the villages and small towns with their real problems, conflicts and aspirations; the tribals of different parts of India at different stages of evolution with their colourful heritage but their insecure future; and India's children with their complex problems of growth and development in a changing society looking both backwards and forwards and embodying the hope and promise of India's future. Doordarshan does not even realistically and authentically present the dynamic and productive elements of the middle classes of metropolitan urban centres and dynamic villages. It seems to be getting more and more oriented to the needs of the "New Rich" of the Indian society who are trying to take place of the old aristocracy. They are also aping the affluent elite of the West in their life style. Doordarshan reflects less of the creative, vibrant and growing India of the scientific and industrial age which is replacing yesterday's colonial and semi-feudal India.

Story of the emergence of a new India has yet to be conveyed in words and/or in images. The portrayal of this new India-in-the-making is a creative challenge specially for Doordarshan which is an audio-visual medium and uniquely suited to the visual representation of a dynamic and diverse India. Doordarshan cannot cope with this task alone without opening its windows to winds and currents of fresh ideas and experiments from outside. The producers in Doordarshan must get linked up with all the vital disciplines and the best practitioners of these disciplines in different parts of the country. Any attempt to run Doordarshan as a self-sufficient or a X closed system will lead to ossification of the medium and not to its blossoming. Doordarshan in isolation will not be strong enough to resist the powerful pressures from the commercialised film industry inside and from imported glamourous software from outside.[10]

The challenge today is to put into effect the idea of problem-oriented, development-oriented and entertainment-cum-enrichment-oriented Doordarshan suited to the needs of a developing country like India. In coping with these challenges a creative communicator will generate software which will appeal to professionals for its technical quality and to the people for its beauty and its social message. If this new vision of software has to be realised, the system of management and administration of Doordarshan must be reformed, giving status, power and authority to the creative elements within the broad framework of social accountability. A creative medium requires new rules of the game, not boss-subordinate relations but interactive leadership; not rigid administrative and financial procedure but delegation of administrative and financial powers to creative men with necessary internal checks and balances. Above all, the system needs a new operating culture supporting creativity and not dull uniformity. To identify talented men and women and to allow them to work, experiment, innovate and to grow is the hall mark of a good structure. The procedures and other cadres in Doordarshan must also recognise that not all the constraints on creativity arise from a rigid structure, lack of equipment and lack of incentives. There are also serious constraints which are internal and which can be overcome only by treating communication as service of the people and by cultivating dedication, discipline and team work, and lastly all things will concentrate on the cost effectiveness of TV commercials with quality production because only then anyone can exist in this competitive world.

REFERENCES

1. Luthra H.R., *Indian Broadcasting*, Publication Division, Ministry of I&B, New Delhi. 1986, p. 420.
2. Malhan P.L., *Communication Media*, Publication Division, Ministry of I&B, New Delhi, 1985, pp. 6 & 7.
3. Report of the Working Group on Software for Doordarshan, *An Indian Personality for Television*, Publication Division, Ministry of I&B, New Delhi, 1985, Vol. II, p. 6.
4. Malhan P.L., *Communication Media*, Publication Division, Ministry of I&B, New Delhi, 1985, p. 145.
5. *Ibid*, p. 141.
6. A Year of Awakening for Information Ministry, *The Times of India*, New Delhi, 2.1.1995.
7. New Watchdog body for TV Radio planned, *The Telegraph*, Calcutta 29.5.95.
8. 10 New TV channels via PAS-4 from October, *The Times of India*, New Delhi, 5.6.95.
9. Report of the Working Group on Software for Doordarshan, *An Indian Personality for Television*, Publication Division, Ministry of I&B, New Delhi, p.3.
10. *Ibid*, p. 12.
11. *Ibid*, p. 15.

21

Economic Liberalisation and Rural Development

Tapan K. Panda

Economic liberalisation is the key word in the changing dynamics of Indian social fabric. Trade policy reforms have changed the thrust of the nation, particularly national economy. There has been a lateral shift from protective economy to free market economy. Corresponding to the trade policy reforms, there has been a wider shift in various productive and welfare areas of the country. These liberalisation policies have been widely acclaimed with only one apprehension. That is about its impact on the rural masses. As India lives in villages and almost fifty years of independence and planned economy has not been able to improve the over all rural economy, it is often questioned about the fate of rural development in the changed period of liberalisation.

Rural development is a comprehensive programme of all activities which include agricultural growth, development of economic and social infrastructure, village planning, public health, education, functional literacy and communication. It has two important aspects, *viz.* economic development with a close interaction between different sections of rural society and economic growth specially directed to the rural people.[1] The rural development encompasses both spatial and functional integration of all relevant programmes bearing on increased agricultural production and provision of gainful employment to rural people.

"India lives in villages" was the proclamation of the founder of nation, Mahatma Gandhi. Till date, there has not been substantial shift in the life and psychography of rural masses. A question is often asked as why there is a need for rural development? To answer this one has to go deep into the structural fabric of rural India.

Many of rural settlements cannot sustain themselves on the basic resources like land, water or forest. Over a period of time land has been degraded, water has not been harvested and forests are not protected. As a result there is an exodus from rural areas to urban areas which has led to overcrowding in urban areas, exploitation of unorganised and unskilled labour and lack of development in areas of origin.

The rural folk of India is largely dependent on agriculture and its allied activities. 41.6% of rural population are cultivators and 24.9% are agricultural labours. Agriculture and allied activities contribute around 40% to net domestic product. In reality there is no employment in villages for nine months. Only one crop is harvested during the monsoon season. Resources are not managed, up-graded and conserved for sustainability. Non-farm activities are not introduced or developed along with farm activities. Rural population is caught in the vicious cycle of rural-urban migration on one hand and land degradation due to lack of proper management on the other hand. Hence the sustainability of land is decreasing between urban core and rural periphery.

Rural development is recognised as a *sine quo non* to faster economic development and welfare of the masses. Rural development is not merely development of rural areas but also the development of quality of life of the rural masses into self-reliant and self-sustaining modern communities. Rural development is therefore, development of the rural area in such a way that each component of rural life changes in a desired direction and in sympathy with other components.

Rural development also encompasses structural changes in the socio-economic situation in rural India, so that human welfare, which is the primary goal of all development, is secured at the earliest. "Rural development thus, should embrace all the objectives of enrichment and betterment of the overall quality of rural life through appropriate development of manpower resources, infrastructure facilities and provision of minimum needs and livelihood.[2]

As defined earlier rural development is a complex and multi-dimensional aspect of India's socio-economic development whose components cover agriculture, industry, education, social life, culture and value system. Although there are many rural development programmes but their application and result efficiency are doubtful as they have not much improved the economic standards of small and marginal farmers who constitute a large proportion of the rural mass.

The classical view of public policy assumes that public intervention in economic affairs takes essentially three forms, *viz*; taxes and subsidies, regulation and public production. Besides revenue generation, taxes help in guiding incentives at different levels of economic structure. Subsidies stimulate economic activity considered socially and economically desirable. The Government also intervenes through a law to regulate for stimulating economic activity. The failure of the Indian agricultural and rural development policy is to be explained not so much by inadequate or small allocated investment as by the indifferent performance of the State in devising and deploying all these three sets of instruments of public intervention. There are four common drawbacks which characterise the failure of institutional intervention in rural development:[3]

(a) *Goal confusion*: Most interventions end up trying to achieve more than one and often conflicting goals.
(b) *Mistargeting*: Most fully or partly miss their target groups or objects.
(c) *Redundancy*: Most tend to survive long after they stop serving their original purpose.
(d) *Negative loops*: Most end up in the centre of a new political economy that gets created as the consequence of their implementation with deeply entrenched pressure groups and vested interests.

India's development strategy after independence was largely influenced by (i) the cynicism of policy makers regarding any possible help from the rest of the world by way of investments, transfer of technology and trade; and (ii) reservation regarding the abilities of the marketing force to bring about, of their own, an optimum allocation of resources, thus balancing the country's two main objectives, growth and equity.[4]

Since 1985-86, the Government has embarked upon a series of economic reforms leading to liberalisation and deregulation. The key message from these reforms are the maximisation of growth by allocating funds based on the criteria of highest money rate of return, when prices of goods and factors will reflect their respective scarcity values not only in the domestic but also in the global context. This does not ignore other welfare dimensions of growth and development as it asserts that with a fast growing economy, most welfare needs are automatically satisfied by the so called "trickle down" effect.

The development strategy can be broken down into two phases, *i.e.* a phase of "stabilisation" and a phase of "structural adjustment and growth".[5] The phase of stabilisation is marked by demand management whereas the second by supply adjustment. The recent economic reforms fall broadly under five heads—industrial, fiscal, monetary, financial and trade. The objectives of these reforms are to commit to the pursuit of equity and social justice.

With regard to the impact of economic reforms on social expenditure and poverty alleviation programmes, it is noted that the reasons have affected public expenditure and many of key social service areas like health, sanitation, water supply which largely contribute to the welfare of the poor.

The Eighth Five Year Plan started in April, 1992. The Plan (1992-97) aims at achieving an average growth rate of 5.6% annum in GDP at constant prices over the planning period. Future development issues are related to creation of more employment, generation of larger saving, allocation of sufficient outlay to the infrastructure and social sectors.

New Economic Policy envisages a stabilisation phase and an adjustment programme is aimed at restoring balance on fiscal side. Because of an alarming growth of budgetary deficit which causes inflationary pressure, the ultimate result is the rising prices which affects the rural masses. The two important aspects of stabilisation, *i.e.* curtailment of public expenditure and withdrawal of subsidies have repercussions on the employment and welfare level of rural poor. The subsidies conceal the true social cost of an enterprise or a product.

Subsidies have been extensively used in Indian rural economy as a means to guide incentive and as a means to affect direct or indirect resource transfer to weaker sections. These subsidies include mainly food and fertiliser subsidies. But subsidies always tend to outlive their utility, seldom reach their target groups and are used as an instrument of patronage. But in the present context where a sizeable number of people are suffering from malnutrition, there is less justification for the drastic cut in the food subsidies. The structural adjustment policies involving globalisation and liberalisation through measures like devaluation, reduction of tariffs, removal of price distortions etc. have their impact on distribution and poverty through expenditure switching.

In the liberalised periods, the union budgets have proposed a sizeable increase in allocations for family welfare, women and child development, but for most of the other components of social services notably health, education. The Central Plan outlay on rural development at Rs. 2,610 crores in 1992-93 is somewhat above the revised estimate of Rs 2,356 crores.

The stagflation generated by the adjustment policies is bound to aggravate the poverty levels. The poverty ratio has increased by 0.52 percent in 1991-92, which leads to an increase in number of poors by 10.7 million.

The poverty alleviation programmes undertaken during the liberalised period have two components: (a) the self employment comprising the Integrated Rural Development Programme (IRDP) and its sub programmes like Training of Rural Youth for Self Employment (TRYSEM) and Development of Women and Children in Rural Areas (DWCRA); (b) the Wage Employment Programme like Jawahar Rojgar

Yojna (JRY). The first comprises essentially individual household and poverty group-oriented programmes of income generation through assets and skill development, while the second focusses on supplemental wage employment through public works.

The other rural development programmes include (i) Area Development Programmes for special areas to counter poverty caused by adverse agro-climatic condition and generation of ecosystems. The programmes under this category include Drought Prone Area Programme (DPAP), Desert Development Programme (DDP), Hill Area Development Programme (HADP), Western Ghats Development Programme (WGDP) and Integrated Tribal Development Programme (ITDP); (ii) Minimum Needs Programme which comprises of giving back up support to the poverty groups by providing for social consumption and services. Such programmes aim at improving the quality of life and giving infrastructural support to the programmes of poverty alleviation. These specific programmes include elementary education, rural health, rural electrification, rural water supply, rural roads, housing for landless labourers, environmental improvement of villages and nutrition; (iii) Sectoral programmes which include agriculture and allied sector, irrigation rural industries etc.; and (iv) Structural and institutional reforms which includes land reforms and Panchayati Raj institutions.

There has been a change in the country's economic environment due to liberalisation, there is also a change in the emphasis on approaches on rural development. Initially the emphasis was on the community approach, it was later shifted to target group approach, then to employment approach and finally to the welfare approach which is evident from the following table 21.1.

Table 21.1—Expenditure on Select Social Services by Central Government

(Rs. in Crores)

Sector	*91-92 Budget*	*91-92 Revised estimate*	*1992-93 Budget*	*%age change in 1992-93 Budget over 1991-92*	
				1991-92	*1991-92 revised*
Health	547.6	525.3	560.3	2.3	6.7
Family Welfare	759.4	866.6	1010.4	33.1	16.6
Education	1750.3	1679.0	1725.2	-1.4	2.8
Women and Child Development	439.7	404.7	489.6	11.3	2.1
Welfare	508.1	507.1	559.2	10.1	10.3

Source: Government of India, Budget Paper, 1992-93.

There has been tremendous progress of these rural development programmes even though there is a cut in public expenditure. Under IRDP, ceiling on subsidy has been enhanced by Rs. 1,000 from April, 1993. Nearly 65,50,663 families have been given assistance with an expenditure of Rs. 24,952.2 crores. DWCRA has been extended to all the districts of the country. As a result 26,094 groups have been chosen which bring considerable benefit to about 4,84,382 women. During the said policy under the scheme of TRYSEM, 7,65,569 youth have been trained. JRY is now being implemented in three streams: (i) on the existing pattern with its two sub-schemes, namely Indira Awas Yojna and Million Wells Scheme; (ii) Intensified JRY in 120 backward districts with additional allocation; (iii) Special and Innovative Projects. Under JRY 2,668 million mandays' employment has been generated. In the Eighth Five Year Plan a provision of Rs. 18,400 crores has been made for this purpose. By spending Rs. 1,264.06 crore, a total of about 4.45 lakh wells have been constructed under the Million Wells Scheme. About 5.54 lakh houses have been constructed for the members of SC/STs and freed bonded labourers below the poverty line, free of cost under Indira Awas Yojna.

In 1991-92, an intensive programme has been launched for providing safe drinking water to all the "No source problem" villages, numbering about 5,333. Till 1993-94 nearly 1,78,393 sanitary latrines were provided in the villages in addition to 5,52,883 sanitary latrines constructed under the state sector Minimum Needs Programmes. A new Employment Assurance Scheme (EAS) for providing assured employment to the rural poor residing in 1778 Revamped Public Distribution System Blocks of 261 districts was implemented from October 2, 1993. The objective of the scheme is to provide about 100 days of assured casual manual labour employment during the lean agriculture season at the statutory minimum wages. Under EAS, more than 4.30 million persons have been registered and more than 4.81 mandays have been generated. The central plan outlay on major social services has increased slightly from 3.4 percentage of GDP in 1990-91 to 4.4% of GDP in 1993-94. Revised estimates for 1993-94 show that the share 4.3 percent of is lower than the estimates of 1993-94.

The thrust of the liberalisation has been that of adopting macro policies which are expansionary with a view to sustain levels of output, investment and satisfaction of human needs over the adjustment periods which gradually moves towards accelerating rural development. The policies of liberalisation are designed in such a way as to fulfil priorities in meeting the needs of vulnerable and rural mass. They aim at devising compensatory programmes to protect the basic living standards, health and nutrition of the low income group.

Table 21.2—Central Government Plan Outlays on Select Social Services

(Rs. in crores)

Item	*1990-91 (Actual)*	*1991-92 (Actual)*	*1992-93 (Actual)*	*1993-94 (BE)*	*1993-94 (RE)*	*1994-95 (BE)*
Education art and Culture	965	993 (2.90)	1175 (18.33)	1489 (26.72)	1512 (1.54)	1749 (15.67)
Health & Family Welfare	1037	1101 (6.17)	1531 (39.06)	1753 (14.50)	1780 (1.54)	2008 (12.81)
Water Supply, Sanitation & Housing	718	845 (17.69)	690 (-18.34)	1043 (51.16)	1060 (1.63)	1305 (23.11)
Information and Broadcasting	154	112 (-27.27)	51 (-54.46)	75 (47.06)	64 (-14.67)	61 (-4.69)
Welfare of SC/ST and OBC	344	414 (20.35)	479 (15.70)	558 (16.49)	589 (5.56)	632 (7.30)
Labour and Labour Welfare	20	69 (2.45)	63 (-8.70)	160 (153.97)	65 (-59.38)	126 (93.85)
Social Welfare and Nutrition	359	413 (15.04)	605 (46.49)	652 (7.77)	661 (1.38)	735 (11.20)
Total	3597 (3.4)	3947 (3.5)	4594 (3.7)	5730 (4.4)	5731 (4)	6616 (4.3)

Notes:
1. Figures is parentheses under items 2 to 7 indicate percentage change over previous year.
2. Figures in parentheses under item 8 indicate percentage to GDP.

Source: Government of India, Expenditure Budget Volume I for respective years.

Even though the structural adjustment and maintenance of economic growth are the key components of liberalisation, but this process is not on the specific economic criteria rather there is an ample evidence that the Government is concerned for the rural poor. May be the fact that a majority of population have a rural base, the Constitution and administrative mechanism of the country are guided by the solid principles laid down by Gandhiji and Nehru or for political advantage. the Government has tried to, at least honestly trying out a formula of their own rather than in copying any socio-economic model of Western World.

One of the vulnerable and neglected areas during the planning period is rural education. While the direct action programmes in rural development have been the betterment of the standard of living but sufficient effort has not been taken for improving the standard of rural education. With a very high drop-out rate during primary education, the thinkers have taken a quantitative outlook in establishing more number of so-called schools rather than creating an environment for motivating the people and the pupil to take interest in school. In the liberalised period, the Government is giving a different look towards rural education by developing value education and is often critisised for running various popular programmes like mid-day meal in rural schools for attracting students to schools, to gain political advantage, but it should be looked upon beyond the horizon of political maladjustment.

In last few years, India has undergone a manifold change in the field of communication. Communication is one of the important tools in taking the plans and programmes of Government towards the public. The Jawahar Rojgar Yojna and programmes alike have created additional man hours which have been utilised for constructing, modifying and connecting the rural road networks. As the Government is giving a major boost to the export, this road communication improvement will smoothen the rural-urban transaction and traffic. There has also been a telecommunication revolution in the liberalised period. The Panchayati Raj system has been revitalised and each Panchayat is taken as a core unit for dissemination of efforts on rural development. Many of these Panchayats and villages are not well connected by STD facilities for faster movement of information in rural India. The television in the form of the Doordarshan and cable television due to satellite uplink have invaded the rural sky of India. These patent media have changed the overall dimension of rural socio fabric. The weather forecast for the farmer, the forecast for catching fish for the coastal fisherman and various programmes related to agriculture, education, sanitation and childcare can now be taken with ease to the rural masses by television which has a broader and stronger impact on rural masses in bringing a change in their life style.

To match up the process of liberalistion, the Government has also brought out various changes in rural banking sector so that the much enlightened rural man does not have to depend on either the informal money lenders or the ill-grown co-operatives for obtaining loan.

Recently three policy changes have been introduced by Government of India and Reserve Bank of India for rural banking operations for the commercial banks. These are :

1. Continuation of minimum interest rates on loans upto Rs. 2 lakhs but lowering them by 1% point for loans above Rs. 2 lakhs.
2. Lowering of maximum interest rates by 1% point of fixed deposits.
3. Permission to close loss making rural branches.

These policy changes have been entirely prompted by the concern for improving the profitability of banks. There are two other objectives for promoting rural banking. These are to encourage (i) private investment for agricultural development, and (ii) financial deepening to the rural sector.

Diversifying lending and deposit portfolios with commensurate interest rates and non-price policy support change has a potential to transfer funds from deposits for promoting agriculture and rural development.

The minimum interest rates in loans upto Rs. 2 lakhs should also be lowered by one percentage to enable rural borrowers to benefit from lower inflation rate. This would encourage growth in rural loan demand and thereby enlarge volume of loan business leading to scale economics in transaction costs of rural banks. The rural masses will be encouraged to substitute loan demand from informal lenders. These provide a large loan business potential from APS (Agricultural Production Sub-system) and other rural households. The agricultural technology breakthrough due to liberalised economy also increases loans from entrepreneurs engaged in selling agricultural inputs termed as Agricultural Input Sub-system (AIS) and in marketing and processing of agricultural produce terms as Agro Marketing and Processing Sub-system loans (AMPS). So in the changing period lending may be viewed in a system framework, wherein three sub-systems are interdependent.

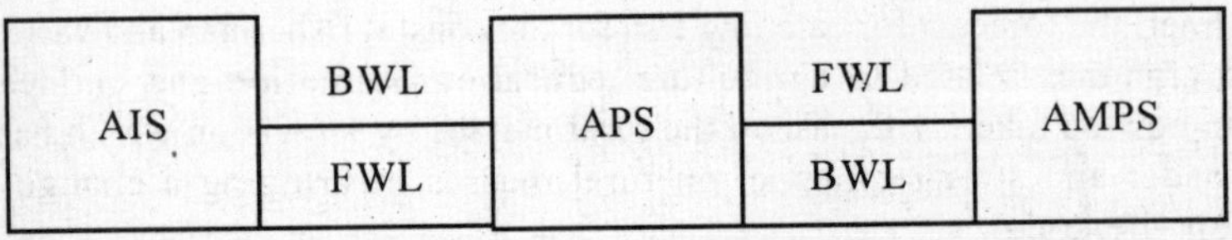

Loans to APS generate demands for farm inputs, assets and services. Loans to AIS and AMPS generate supply of these resources. Extending loan to all the three sub-systems would lead to more balanced demand and supply forces and thereby avert inflationary implications for Credit. It would also encourage backward (BWL) and forward (FWL) linkages among the three sub-systems which will increase agricultural productivity, production and value added.

In the liberalised period, the policy of direct rural credit for working capital is to be changed. Presently it covered only loans for crops but it should cover dairy, animals, sheep rearing, cottage industries, loans for soil and moisture improvement works, land reclamation and levelling and simple soil turning operations.

Liberalisation has also initiated a process of regional balanced development. Industrial lisation were a political decision in the past because of various pressure groups at Centre. But this new process has brought about a radical change in the outlook for balanced development. The Centre as well as State Governments are offering various packages to domestic and foreign industrialists to establish industries in backward areas in bringing them to match with national standards. The industrial houses are considering factors like proximity to raw materials, availability of power and cheap labour as the deciding criteria rather than to succumb to political pressure. This healthy process will bring a greater change in rural India.

Rural economy is never treated in isolation to national economy. The structure of the rural economy is largely agricultural even though there is a small percentage of artisan, cottage industry contributing to the rural economy. The major changes in agricultural sector due to liberalisation are positive in character. Since the importance is being given for value based and economic surplus generation, the agricultural sector will not lag behind, rather it will march to adopt the process of technology transfer. The small farmers will get a better reward for their crop due to strengthening of rural banking sector and boosting up of agro-based exports by Government. The cut in subsidies will definitely affect the rural farmer particularly small time farmer but in a larger interest of nation, they can be motivated, although with difficulty, to give importance in adopting modern technology. Patience and its effect on rural India will be a time tested axiom.

The most important is the cottage and small scale sector which is going to be affected adversely by the liberalisation. These sectors, though of primary importance for rural development, have categorically become parasytic under a protective economy. The subsidies, Government's bearing of loan as well as loss due to under-production have taken aback the purpose for which these industries were promoted. In the liberalised period, Multinationals (MNC's) are entering into Indian market with a larger capital base, more business attitude and flair for risk bearing. So suddenly there is going to be a huge cry in political area about the exposure and potential threat generated by MNCs for these sectors. These small and cottage industry sectors' contribution to the national economy is not that significant, so they will go down in the changing period, only to come up with a more positive attitude for providing better to the masses. They have to come up within a short period and contribute to a larger extent to rural development as these MNCs need some time to settle down their voice to the tone of rural India.

Another important phenomenon in the pre-liberalisation period is the failure of co-operatives. Co-operative movements have become a failure due to many reasons. The entry of MNCs to Indian market, the promotion of self-sustenance of rural masses by Government for rural development and strengthening of rural banks will bring a drastic change in the performance of co-operatives. Either they will contribute for what they were originally thought of or they will perish in the post-liberalisation period.

Patent has become a controversial issue after GATT agreement and Government should try to protect the interest of the rural farmer in the case of patent against fertilisers, seeds and neem plants. The objective of liberalisation should be bifold. On one hand, it should try to bring the economy into world order and on the other it should protect the interest of the rural poor. Rural health is also going to be affected by liberalisation. In the pre-liberalised period, we have seen a sad condition of high mortality rates of children, malnutrition, iron and calcium deficiency in the rural health sector. The rural health sector is yet to be formalised and become adaptive to changing medical and technological developments. The blind belief, the quacks, the Indian system of naturopathy do come often as hindrances to the adoption of modern medical technology in rural India. Liberalisation will bring foreign investors and inventions which will be more life saving and helpful in healing the pain of the rural masses.

The liberalised period is going to see a revolutionary change in the rural demography. The advent of television and cable network to the rural skies and the importance given by the MNCs on rural marketing will make the rural mass much aware about various products and brands available on domestic market. The survey conducted by NCAER (National Council of Applied Economic Research) confirms that the rural market is going to be flooded with various brands and products in near future in bringing change in the quality of life of the people. Corresponding to the change in preference and brand choice, there is going to be a broader social impact by which the gap between the rural and urban will be narrowed and greater social justice will work out in bringing a positive change in the life of the rural people.

It has to be kept in view that while decentralisation of economy is necessary to develop the potential of a region, the region has also to be integrated with the national economy if national integration is to have any meaning. In terms of priority, thus the rural development should address itself to the following objectives:

1. The improvements of human resources through inputs of education, health care, sanitation and hygiene, ensured supply of potable water

and other facilities.

2. Development of infrastructure through roads, means of transport and communication power etc.
3. Development of production potential:
   (a) The most important sector of production is naturally agriculture. There is still vast potential in it through such improvement as levelling of land, proper water management, crop rotation, better seeds, organic pesticides and manures. The example of Israel is before use. Through the application of scientific methods they have converted barren lands into lush fields and orchards.
   (b) Forests give us a rich variety of their products which can be systematically exploited for the benefit of rural people.
   (c) Development of orchards and vegetable gardening can provide both income and employment to the youth of the villages.
   (d) Dairy and poultry farming have great scope of development. These should be located in villages in preference to towns.
   (c) Other productive activities which can be beneficial to the villages are : flower and plant nurseries, bee-keeping, fisheries, village arts, to name a few.
   (f) Villages are best places for agro-based industries and food products. With a little training and the provision of the necessary technology, various food products can be produced in villages and marketed in towns. These should rather be made exclusive domain of the rural sector.
   (g) There are various other products which are exclusively produced in villages for the use of villagers, such as leather goods, earthen utensils, carpentry works. With a little help, these goods can find market even in towns and cities.

   An enquiry and survey can locate several other spheres of economic activities which are more suited to rural conditions.
4. *Marketing research and facilities for marketing:* So many projects have failed because proper marketing research has not been done before starting a production unit. With proper marketing research the products can find a steady market in near and even far away places.
5. The villagers must be assured of first claim over the resources of their area. To give an example, Tendu leaves of the forest are auctioned to the highest bider. The village labourer earns only such wages as the contractor chooses to pay. If the village co-operatives ran the business the villagers can earn much better profits. At present the profits go to a few pockets only.

6. *A really integrated approach in rural development*: At present, there is a multiplicity of agencies which usually work at cross purposes. Instead, there should be an integrated agency which will not only aid the villager but also monitor the utilisation. It should help in storage and marketing of products so that the villagers get fair returns for their labour. Technical and operational advice should be made available to the rural artisans by the same agencies.

There are several areas where action is to be taken if the rural poor has to participate in the growth process initiated by the New Economic Policy. Some of them are :

1. Greater investment in infrastructure to facilitate the spread effect of economic growth and generate productive employment.
2. Devising adequate and timely social security measures for rural poor.
3. Strengthening a well directed public distribution system catering to the basic needs of the poor.
4. Greater investment in human resources development to strengthen the recipient system and improve its social status.
5. Greater emphasis on programmes like IRDP, TRYSEM and JRY provide an asset and skill boost to poor.

This development will linger beyond the time frames envisaged by the thinkers. The results of liberalisation will be the goal directed to bring a new outlook towards rural development. An integrative approach of liberalisation and development will be the demand of time to provide not only a better standard of living present but also a greater tomorrow for mankind.

REFERENCES

1. Jha, Kumudnath, *Economics and Impact of Technology Transfer to Rural Areas.*
2. Verma, Dr. S.K., Rural Development through Co-operative Marketing, *Kurukshetra* Nov. 1994.
3. Shah, Tushar, Agriculture and Rural Development in 1990's and Beyond, Re-designing Relations between State and Institutions of Development, *Economic and Political Weekly,* Vol. XXVIII, No. 39, Sept. 25, 1993.

4 & 5. Gupta, Dr. S.P., Recent Economic Reforms and Their Impact *Liberalisation and its Impact on the Indian economy.*

6. Prabhu, Seeta K., The Budget and Structural Adjustment with a Human Face, *Economic and Political Weekly*. Vol. XXIX No. 16 & 17, April 16-23, 1994.
7. Desai Bhupat, M., Rural Banking : Misdirected Policy Changes, *Economic and Political Weekly,* Vol. XXVIII No. 52, Dec. 25, 1993.
8. Lahiry, Amitav, The Concept of Rural Development—An Overview, *Kurukshetra* Vol. XLIII, No. 4, January, 1995.

22

Agribusiness in a Liberalised Rural Environment

A. Shiv Kumar

India is an agro-rural economy with seventy percent of the population belonging to the rural areas and sixty-five percent of people dependent on agriculture as a vocation.[1] Agriculture being one of the oldest and traditional professions forms an integral part of life in the rural areas. Economic development of rural areas therefore greatly depends on the gains of developments in agriculture.

Agriculture possesses unique features which distinguish it from the industry. The biological basis of production system and the dependence on nature for the operation of the production system enhance the risk and uncertainty of agriculture. Decision making process is therefore made complex unlike the industry.

Scientific pursuit in the form of research and development in the field of agriculture resulted in reducing the element of risk and uncertainty and paved the way for efficient utilisation of inputs in order to produce outputs in excess of consumption. The conversion of traditional agriculture based on self-sustaining or subsistence principle into commercial agriculture, on an economically viable basis was an aftermath of this development. Green revolution and the rapid strides made in Indian Agricultural Research have made this possible in India.

Rural environment is no longer exposed and influenced only by the regional forces. The two major events namely economic liberalisation at the national level and trade liberalisation at the international level have started exerting their profound influence, thus transforming rural sector into a liberalised set up (Fig. 1). Rural activities thus have been presented with the opportunity of operating in a liberalised environment which would enable rural people to translate their entrepreneurial abilities into action.

Commercial agriculture has transformed into Agribusiness which encompasses all players in agriculture from seed and genetic stock producers to the consumers of raw and processed agricultural products. Agribusiness in the liberalised rural environment would represent its different sectors without protection and that are able to generate their own internal resources in maintaining their sustenance.

The very purpose of this paper is to visualise the various implications of economic liberalisation on the different sectors of Agribusiness and to suggest measures for employment and equitable wealth distribution in a liberalised Agribusiness setup.

The whole gamut of Agribusiness can be conceptualised into four sectors, namely Agro input business, Agro production business, Agro processing business and Agro exports business. Each of these sectors have their specific requirement for Research and Development and services like finance and marketing. The study of each of these sectors in detail would give immense insight into the implications on the nature of development of these sectors in the future.

Agro-Inputs Business

Land is the major fixed input for production in Agribusiness. Land has been subjected to extreme pressure due to competing non-agricultural activities. Land reforms are therefore an absolute necessity to provide an incentive environment for land to be utilised for agricultural purposes.

Subsidies have been one of the prominent factors supporting the use of variable inputs in Agribusiness like fertiliser, irrigation and pesticides. This has resulted in the indiscriminate use of these inputs in areas well endowed for agricultural production.

Budgetary constraints have been mounting a heavy pressure on the subsidies being provided on most of these inputs. This might entail the wiping out of direct subsidies for fertilisers and subsidy in the form of free or nominal electricity and water charges for irrigation in the future.

Capital is another important input in Agribusiness. Agricultural credit through the schemes of priority sector lending and differential rates of interest through commercial banks and other rural financial institutions might be phased out in the future as they are being considered as a drain on the economic viability of the banks. Banks have also been squeezed for funds due to poor recovery of agricultural loans and populist waiver of loans by the State Governments.

The real pricing of factor inputs in future would result in judicious use of scarce resources like water in the production system thus increasing the total factor productivity and productivity of Agribusiness in turn. Seed industry which would also include biotechnological products and factor saving device manufacturers like drip irrigation system manufacturers would get a big boost in the Agri-inputs business.

Agro-Production Business

India endowed with geographical, climatological and biological diversity is one of the important countries favourably placed in the production of good quality seeds of commercial crops which would not only be a paying proposition in the domestic market but in the overseas market too.

Botanical entrepreneurship can be expressed by individual Agropreuneurs in going in for industrial crops. Industrial crops are plants and their derivative materials that serve as substitute for existing inputs or as new inputs in the manufacturing of non-food and non-feed goods.[2] These crops used as industrial feed stock represent an economic opportunity to entrepreneurs in rural areas. Biological and chemical properties of the crop are enhanced to create potential economic value. This would result in considerably greater income generation by the Agropreneur than the ordinary farmer because of the fact that an industry's dependence on a raw material would make the supplier at a relatively better bargaining position.

Agro-Processing Business

India loses substantial portion of its agricultural produce due to the absence of adequate agro-processing facilities. The establishment of local agro-processing facilities would greatly benefit the farmer in obtaining a forward linkage after his production process. Agro-processing involves value addition of agricultural produce thus being able to thrive as a business activity in a self-sustaining manner.

Agro-processing creates additional opportunities for employment by providing jobs in this expanding sector with a special emphasis being given to develop this sector after the formation of an exclusive Ministry of Food Processing.

Agro-Export Business

The comparative advantage India possesses in the economical production of various crops, gives it a distinct edge in the post-GATT scenario of world agricultural trade to export significant quantities of agricultural produce, resulting in the realisation of international prices benefitting the farmers. APEDA has the task of decentralising its activity in order to locate specific rural areas for production of crops suitable to these areas for the purpose of exports so that the marketing channel link of production and export is shortened, thus ensuring the maximum share of the consumer's price to the producer.

Market reforms in the form of allowing free movement of agricultural produce within the country and the discontinuance of monopsonistic procurement would make agribusiness really vibrant in the rural environment. Development of rural infrastructure, rural information network providing domestic and international commodity market intelligence and a planned and effective rural transport system would make Agribusiness in a liberalised environment more meaningful.

The fears of loss in employment in future due to capital intensive agriculture, inequity, environment damaging and unsustainable nature of agricultural production are sought to be allayed by the establishment of the Small Farmers Agribusiness consortium.

Small Farmers Agribusiness consortium has been one of the pioneering efforts of the Central Government to extend the advantages of Agribusiness to small farmers. The benefits have been sought to be provided to resource poor farmers by the establishment of an autonomous corporate entity owned by participating rural families and management by these primary stake holders. This would be backed up by public and private sector institutions providing centralised services and transferring the economies of scale and marketing to the primary stake holders. Economic benefits accrue due to selection of market driven enterprises and integrated attention to technology, techno-infrastructure, training and producer-centered trade.[3]

The International Commission on Peace and Food has estimated that intensive development of value added cash crops can generate more than 40 million additional year round jobs in the country. Expanding the capacity of agro-industry and agri-business service units to process, pack, store and distribute fresh farm produce, fish and poultry, to mill the sugar and grain and to convert the cotton and silk into yarn, fabric and garments can generate an additional 13 million direct jobs. The stimulating effect of these jobs on the demand for consumer goods, housing, transport, entertainment, health, education and countless personal and industrial services would be sufficient to raise total employment by 100 million or more.[4]

Studies reveal that non-farm income is greater than farm-based income in the rural areas. This gap tends to get reduced with the commercial nature of agriculture as in Agribusiness. The scope for non-farm income linked to Agribusiness exists in the establishment of an agro-industrial township which would act as a conduit for import and export of goods from the catchment rural areas similar to a watershed approach. The formation of an agro-industrial estate would cater to the establishment of agro-industrial village enterprises that would foster better development of rural areas.

Agro-processing enterprises on a scale that would ensure their maximum capacity utilisation can be set up. The conversion of raw agricultural produce into value-added forms would help reap greater benefits for agroprenerus by the sale of the value-added products in the domestic or export market.

Agro-industrial village enterprises involved in production of inputs that are feasible on a small scale like fortified compost, enriched biogas slurry, neem coated urea, fertiliser mixtures and botano-chemical based pesticides would ensure efficient use of local resources. Machinery manufacture suited to local needs would replace the need for huge capital investment on farm machinery.

Conclusion

Agriculture is one of the prime occupations in a rural set up. However, it is a vocation of only a seasonal nature specially with the dependence on monsoon by the majority of agricultural lands. Agribusiness therefore requires the utilisation of the various opportunities provided by the components of agriculture like Animal Husbandry in order to ensure maximum number of productive mandays in a year.

Strategic mix of low cost production, product differentiation and market awareness and focus should be one of the prime aims of agricultural production in a liberalised rural set up.

Customer centered approach, which is the hallmark of business strategy in the present day world would entail orientation of Agribusiness activities to be tailored to the needs of the changing tastes of the customer to survive and prosper in a liberalised environment.

REFERENCES

1. Jacobs Garry, "Generating Jobs for All", [illegible] *Hindu,* Weekly Edition, 2.,30 April, 1995, p.V.
2. Wilson N. Paul, James C. Wade and Julie P. Leones, "The Economics of Commercialising New Industrial Crops", *Agribusiness,* Vol. II, No. 1 (1995) p. 45.
3. Jacobs Garry, *op. cit;*
4. Swaminathan M.S. and Vineeta Hoon, "*Sustainable Strategies for Job Led Growth*", Working paper, I, M.S. Swaminathan Research Foundation.

23

Management of Foodgrains Production in India

P. Narain

The increased foodgrains production and improved productivity are the most important means to accelerate economic growth and improve the living standards of the population engaged in agriculture and a very large proportion of total consumer spending is on food products. Increased foodgrains production contributes to capital accumulation within and outside the agricultural sectors. This provides the basis for further production expansion in these sectors leading to the acceleration of the demand for factors of production and providing oportunities for increased employment and higher wages. Because of increased income of those possessing resources, this production expansion also results in the increased demand for consumption goods. The economic growth thus achieved is self-sustaining. In our country, however, the foundation for such a self-sustaining economic growth is yet to be established. Low productivity level for land and labour has, in the past, limited agricultural production and contributed to low incomes and limited capital accumulation in the agriculture sector. The immediate consequences have been a limited purchasing power and low standards of living for those depending directly on agriculture. The distribution of personal incomes and resources has become very skewed. A large proportion of the population now suffers from lack of even the basic needs of life while a minority enjoys standards of living far exceeding those found in rich countries. The agricultural development strategy has, therefore, to be based on an equitable distribution of economic benefits resulting from increased foodgrains production and productivity. This calls for a greater role of the distribution management issues in agricutural planning.

Increased food production can result from area expansion as well as vertical growth in terms of enhanced yield per unit area. Their relative importance has however undergone change in the recent times. Prior to 1960s, both of them contributed about one-half of the production increase but since the advent of green revolution, the relative importance of area expansion has fallen to about one-third. Very little scope for increased production from area expansion is possible in the future. In fact, according to a study of the FAO (1979), the expansion of agricultural land will only account for about 28 percent of output growth upto the year 2,000 A.D. The modern agriculture has, therefore, to concentrate on producing more and more output from the same unit of land and per unit of time. Agricultural scientists in this country have demonstrated that this can be achieved by adopting "seed-irrigation-fertiliser-pesticides" technology. As a result of this as well as due to the adoption of better management practices by majority of farmers, the total foodgrains production went up considerably to as much as 151 million tonnes in the year 1985-86 but for the recent agricultural drought. Despite unfavourable weather, the production has now acquired a greater degree of resilience due to the modern biological and chemical technology. However, simultaneous with the increased production in the country, there has occurred a tremendous amount of regional disparity. In some states like Punjab, the rate of growth of foodgrains production (5.92 percent) is considerably higher than the corresponding growth rate (2.15 percent) in the population whereas in some other states like Bihar, the reverse is true, the foodgrains production growth being 1.25 percent against population growth rate of 2.18 percent. The strategies for increasing goodgrains production using biological and chemical technology should, therefore, have different emphasis from one region to another. This requires a detailed examination of the dynamics of foodgrains production on regional basis.

The provision of food for the masses is the foremost responsibility of the Government. It becomes, therefore, important to estimate reliable supply and demand projections which form the basis for planning long, term policies and strategies for meeting the future foodgrains needs of the people in the country. The supply projections of foodgrains in conjunction with demand projections and the existing production levels indicate the directions in which further efforts should be made to augment the suply of foodgrains and to expand or further modernise the existing production system. The perspective for foodgrains production in future is primarily therefore, a race between the population and income growth on the one hand and growth in production and reduction of absolute poverty on the other hand. While there is some reason to believe that the population growth rate will be reduced significantly within next 15 to 20 years, the foodgrains production, for some time to come, will have to be increased at a rate which can maintain the per capita foodgrains production at the desired nutritional level. In a study of IFPRI (1977), it has been estimated that growth in population and incomes together will cause an increase in food demand in the developing countries of 4 and $4^1/_2$ percent annual between 1982 and 1990. If the past trends for food production continue, this would lead to increased food shortages in many developing countries. According to this study, India is expected to have the food deficit of about 17 to 22 million tonnes by 1990. It is, therefore, important to examine how far the supply projections of foodgrains at a future date, say 2000 A.D., is going to match the demand projections and how much increases in the significant inputs over their predicted use levels in 2000 A.D. should be there so as to match the demand by the said date. For this purpose, the methodology of production function adopted in Narain et. al. (1982, 1984, 1985) could be used.

Agricultural development is a long-term process over time effecting economic development. The dynamics of such a process involves two aspects, the growth and instability in production over the period under study. Both are essential for rapid economic development, the latter for ensuring the food security in the region as well as for taking care of the risk associated with the growth process. Sen (1967) indicated, for the first time, that increase in the rate of growth of production is accompanied by an increase in instability especially if the growth comes about mainly as a result of extension of acreage and increase of inputs like fertiliser rather than improvement in skill, unless sufficient corrective action is taken simultaneously. His observations clearly emphasised the role of management technology in the strategy for agricultural development. The growth associated with risk factors like weather, particularly rainfall, tends to introduce greater variability in the production and yield of major food crops over time. Mehra (1981) and subsequently Hazell (1982) found that recent growth in India and U.S. cereal production was accompanied by a more than proportional increase in the standard deviation of production over time. The increased instability in production was due to synchronised movements in area, yield and cropping pattern of the crops forming the cereals group. Jain et al. (1985) however, concluded, based on the trends in cereal production of India over a 35 year period, that the modernisation process of agriculture should ultimately emerge as a major source of food security and also greater stability of agricultural production and productivity. Ray (1983, 1987) argued that comparing fluctuations between periods before and after the introduction of new technology may hide the fluctuations in the measure of instability itself. Sen (1987) recently indicated that agricultural growth does not always take place along an unbroken upward rising curve or on the same plane. Over the last 40 years, agricultural growth seems to have taken place in a succession of undulating plateaus, sometimes marked by one or two serious falls but ending up in a very sharp rise to another new and much higher undulating plateau as it were. The increased instability in agricultural growth therefore, calls for a much greater role of management in production as well as distribution. Increased growth rate involves better management of the inputs. Equitable distribution of economic benefits of the increased growth rate calls for better distribution management. But when such agricultural growth is accompanied by some degree of instability, the management factors need to be tuned to a much finer degree than when the growth process is a stable one. It is, therefore, of interest to analyse the trends in instability in foodgrains production by following a moving period approach as indicated by Mahendra Dev (1987) recently.

Trends in Foodgrains Production

For the purpose of examining the foodgrains production over the five year plans, the whole country is divided into five regions *viz.*, northern, eastern, western, central and southern, consisting of the several states as shown in *Table 23.1*.

Table 23.1—Demarcation of States into Regions

Region	*States*
Northern	Haryana
	Himachal Pradesh
	Jammu and Kashmir
	Punjab
Eastern	Assam
	Bihar
	Orissa
	West Bengal
Western	Gujarat
	Maharashtra
	Rajasthan
Central	Madhya Pradesh
	Uttar Pradesh
Southern	Andhra Pradesh
	Karnataka
	Kerala
	Tamil Nadu

The plan-wise area levels for total foodgrains for the various regions as well as over All-India show that by and large the increases in acreage under total foodgrains were not very significant in all the regions excepting for the western region where there appears to be a significant increase in the acreage from First to Second Five Year Plan. The plan-wise yield productivity level for total foodgrains production indicates that after the Third Plan, the northern region went far ahead in increasing productivity levels compared to all the other regions. The lowest productivity levels were found to be in the western region. As a result, the All-India level also got averaged with productivity levels being of the order of about one tonne per hectare. The plan-wise yield productivity levels for total rice, wheat, coarse cereals and total pulses reveal significant features. The same story of regional disparity is repeated in the case of rice and wheat, the northern region taking off quite rapidly over the other regions, particularly after the mid-1960's. This clearly brings out the impact of high yielding variety programme (HYVP) resulting in what is popularly known as Green Revolution. In respect of other regions, the levels of production have increased mostly for the wheat crop but to a differential extent. In the case of coarse cereals and total pulses, yield productivity levels show rather irregular pattern for different regions. However, at the All-India level, coarse cereals did show a significant increase from about 600 kg per hectare to about 750 kg per hectare between the First and the Sixth Five Year Plans. In regard to total pulses, the productivity level even seems to have decreased during the later Five Year Plans and stands at around 500 kg per hectare at the All-India level.

Despite our best efforts to extend irrigation facilities to as large area as possible, only about 30 percent of cultivated area is irrigated. The rest of 70 percent of the cropped area still remains rainfed and therefore, subject to the vagaries of weather. As a result of large weather induced fluctuations, foodgrains production in India has been marked not only by peaks but by troughs successively. The peaks and troughs experienced since the mid-sixties when HYVP was introduced, however, reveal a very interesting pattern as may be seen in Table 23.2.

Thus, in the 20-year period 1966-85, we have had 7 peak points and an equal number of troughs, *i.e.* we had a peak and a trough about once in 3 years. Also, the peaks and troughs are progressively of increasing order with the only exception of peak 1973-74. Another notable observation is that the troughs were always higher than the peak of about 90 million tonnes obtained prior to 1966-67 which clearly brings out the inherent strength of Indian agriculture, *viz.* that even under duress, the adverse performance has an element of improvement in it.

Table 23.2—Foodgrains Production Fluctuation During 1967-68 to 1984-85

Year	*Peak*	*Trough*
1967-68	95.1	
1968-69		94.0
1970-71	108.4	
1972-73		97.0
1973-74	104.7	
1974-75		99.8
1975-76	121.0	
1976-77		111.2
1978-79	131.9	
1979-80		109.7
1981-82	133.3	
1982-83		129.5
1983-84	152.3	
1984-85		145.5

All-India Growth Rates of Different Crops

A quantitative indication of the growth rates in the productivity as well as production for several cereal crops and pulses is shown in Table 23.3.

Table 23.3—All India Growth Rates in Different Crops (1966-67 to 1982-83)

Crop	*Productivity*	*Production*
Rice	1.74*	2.37**
Wheat	3.25**	6.38**
Jowar	2.74**	1.84*
Bajra	1.11	0.16
Maize	0.51	0.87
Pulses	0.12	0.50
Foodgrains	2.30**	2.72**

* Significant at 5% level.

** Significant at 1% level.

For the total foodgrains as a whole, a highly significant growth rate in productivity of the order of 2.3 percent is obtained for the period 1966-67 to 1982-83. The highest and significant growth rate in productivity is found to be for wheat and the lowest but insignificant for the pulses. The total foodgrains production during this period has increased at a highly significant growth rate of 2.72 percent which is higher than the population growth rate of 2.24 percent. It is important to note that the production of wheat increased at a much significant growth rate of about 6.38 percent.

Methodology of Determining Perspectives for the Future

In the first instance, country's demand projections at a future date are determined on the basis of assumptions of the growth in national income or gross domestic product (GDP) and initial production projections linked to demand. Intermediate demand of seed, feed and waste is also determined. For projecting supply of foodgrains, state-wise production functions relating the foodgrains production with the inputs are estimated. Such production functions enable projections of the foodgrains production, state by state, at a future date by first projecting the corresponding input themselves on the basis of their growth rates and then substituting them in these functions. Using state-wise projected productions, the total foodgrains production is projected by summing over them. The projected levels of production are then checked up with the demand projections. If the demand exceeds the supply, the input levels are so adjusted that a match between the two is brought about.

Future Demand for Foodgrains

The demand projections for foodgrains production would need data on relative prices, growth in income, population levels, degree of self-sufficiency for the states and trading policies between the states. Similarly, intermediate demand of items such as seeds, feed, wastage and other industrial uses would also have to be determined state-wise.

Theoretically, the domestic demand function on per capita basis can be written in the following form

$$D_i = f(P_i, P_s, I, T)$$

where

D_i = per capita demand for ith crop,
P_i = price of the ith crop,
P_s = price of substitute crop/crops,
I = per capita income,
T = trend factor.

The trend factor is primarily included to capture the effects of factors such as changes in consumers' preference, degree of urbanisation, etc. Such demand functions require specification of the function which could be linear or log-linear etc. These have to be estimated separately for rural as well as for urban areas since the minimum nutritional requirements are different for the two areas. The income elasticities of demand for each of the crops has also to be determined. Data on consumers' expenditure such as those collected by the National Sample Survey Organisation (NSSO) could be one of the sources of data for determining the income elasticities of demands for various crops. The aggregate demand for the state would be obtained by taking into consideration the projected population of the state.

The total demand for foodgrains in 2000 A.D. using the above procedure was estimated as 205 to 225 million tonnes by the National Commission on Agriculture (1976). Sanderson and Roy (1980) however, obtained a figure of 221 million tonnes. The total demand included demand for direct human consumption and requirements due to seed, feed and waste.

Resource Use Pattern

For higher productivity, crop production in the coming years will have to depend on the resource availability, and use of modern biological and chemical inputs such as improved seeds, irrigation water, fertilisers and pesticides. This biological and chemical technology, which is labour, land and fuel energy saving, has got to be appropriately matched with the mechanical and management technology. For the present study, compound growth rates of three crucial input factors, *viz.* gross irrigated area, area under high yielding varieties, and total nutrient consumption have been estimated for the years 1970 to 1984. The results are presented in Table 23.4.

Estimation of Production Functions

The foodgrains production functions for different states have been estimated by regressing to production on the four input factors as explanatory variables. The proportion of actual to normal rainfall has been included as the fifth variable. The linear model fitted is

$$Y_j = a + b_1X_{1j} + b_2X_{2j} + b_3X_{3j} + b_4X_{4j} + b_5X_{5j} + e_j$$

where

Y_j = total foodgrains production in the jth state ('000 tones),

X_{1j} = unirrigated area under foodgrains in the jth state ('000 hectares),

X_{2j} = irrigated area under foodgrains in the jth state ('000 hectares),

X_{3j} = area under high yielding varieties in the jth state ('000 hectares),

Table 23.4—State-wise Compound Growth Rates (per centage) of Selected Input Variables (1970-71 to 1984-85)

State	*Gross Irrigated Area*	*Area under HYV*	*Total Nutrient Consumption*
Assam	—	14.16**	4.47
Bihar	2.33**	7.97**	8.42**
Orissa	0.51	17.33**	7.40**
West Bengal	0.42	7.92**	12.38**
Gujarat	4.74**	7.63**	9.17**
Maharashtra	3.99**	12.10**	7.25**
Rajasthan	2.61**	10.64**	10.46**
Madhya Pradesh	4.66**	13.37**	9.24**
Uttar Pradesh	3.18**	8.82**	11.71**
Haryana	3.59**	7.15**	12.82**
Himachal Pradesh	0.22	7.03**	6.68**
Jammu and Kashmir	1.34**	8.14**	13.21**
Punjab	3.80**	6.93**	12.56**
Andhra Pradesh	1.00**	11.71**	9.85**
Karnataka	1.13*	11.17**	9.12**
Kerala	-5.11**	6.63**	5.29**
Tamil Nadu	-1.37	0.79	6.41
All-India	2.31**	8.64**	10.25**

* Significant at 5% level.
** Significant at 1% level.

X_{4j} = total nutrient consumption (N + P + K) in the jth state ('000 tonnes),

X_{5j} = proportion of actual to normal rainfall in the jth state, and

e_j = random disturbance term.

The various estimated production functions are based on time-series data for the 15-year period from 1970-71 to 1984-85. The estimated functions are presented in Table 23.5.

Estimated Future Resource Use

Assuming the continuance of the present trends in the linear form for the future, the use of various inputs factors for the selected regions comprising various states has been predicted for 2,000 A.D. It is observed from past data that the remaining States/Union Territories of the country were contributing about two percent to the total input use at the national level. Assuming this to continue in future also, the input use at All-

Table 23.4—Estimated Foodgrains Production Functions for Different States and Associated Input Factors (1970-71 to 1984-85)

State	Intercept	Partial Regression Coefficients					
	(a)	X_1	X_2	X_3	X_4	X_5	R^2
Assam	—1500.93	2.003*	—	—0.553*	56.476**	—	0.845**
Bihar	—14970.61	2.560*	—	1.730**	—	19.700*	0.811**
Orissa	—4554.40	0.982	0.950	0.418	—4.208	37.464	0.545*
West Bengal	—17334.13	2.218**	7.673**	—	4.016*	23.820**	0.860**
Gujarat	—6020.96	1.936**	—	0.574	5.751**	—	0.886**
Maharashtra	—12343.17	1.235**	3.180**	0.510**	—	—	0.953**
Rajasthan	—7073.75	0.814	—	—	15.552**	22.01	0.499*
Madhya Pradesh	1646.83	—	—	—	14.919	73.900	0.735**
Uttar Pradesh	—24856.38	2.697	0.342	0.555	9.432	1.020	0.773**
Haryana	1694.89	—	—	—	10.510**	16.520**	0.862**
Punjab	—1954.87	—	2.746*	—	3.956	—	0.981**
Andhra Pradesh	—885.86	—	2.150*	0.810**	—	—	0.823**
Karnataka	—3673.71	1.638**	—	0.359	—	—	0.868
Kerala	1313.74	—	—	—	—1.533	1.465*	0.525**
Tamil Nadu	—3368.87	1.163	2.407*	—0.009	1.883	3.580	0.796*

*Significant at 5% level.

** Significant at 1% level.

India level has been estimated by upward adjustment to the same extent. This has been termed as alternative I and the results, region-wise as well as All-India, are presented in Table 23.6. Two other alternative levels of input use (alternative II and alternative III) obtained by increasing the level of selected inputs by 10 and 20 percent respectively above the predicted levels have been computed and are presented in Tables 23.7 and 23.8 respectively for the regions as well as All-India.

Table 23.6—Projected Input Use and Foodgrains Output in 2000 A.D. (Alternative I)

Regions	*Gross cropped area (m. h.)*	*Gross irrigated area (m. h.)*	*Gross area under HYV (m. h.)*	*Total nutrient consumption (m. t.)*	*Foodgrains production (m. t.)*
Eastern	25.13	7.57	18.63	1.36	30.87
Western	37.10	7.22	19.17	2.09	35.02
Central	41.70	17.47	26.57	3.55	56.95
Northern	11.01	10.69	11.01	2.55	34.32
Southern	20.29	8.02	14.70	3.64	28.82
All-India	138.34	52.09	92.42	13.59	191.56

Table 23.7—Projected Input Use and Foodgrains Output in 2000 A.D. (Alternative II)

Regions	*Gross cropped area (m. h.)*	*Gross irrigated area (m. h.)*	*Gross area under HYV (m. h.)*	*Total nutrient consumption (m. t.)*	*Foodgrains production (m. t.)*
Eastern	25.94	8.34	20.49	1.50	33.70
Western	37.83	7.95	21.08	2.30	37.47
Central	43.44	19.20	29.23	3.90	62.10
Northern	12.08	11.75	11.70	2.80	37.64
Southern	21.07	8.80	16.16	4.00	30.86
All-India	143.59	57.33	101.21	14.88	207.82

(i) Gross Cropped Area

Assuming that the possibility of bringing area under the plough is limited, some expansion in the crop acreage would take place due to higher intensity of cropping. Table 23.6 reveals that the total gross cropped area under foodgrains would be 138.0 million hectares. The gross cropped area may increase further to 149.2 million hectares provided the irigation facilities are extended to larger areas (*Table 23.8*).

Table 23.8—Projected Input Use and Foodgrains Output in 2000 A.D. (Alternative III)

Regions	*Gross cropped area (m. h.)*	*Gross irrigated area (m. h.)*	*Gross area under HYV (m. h.)*	*Total nutrient consumption (m. t.)*	*Foodgrains production (m. t.)*
Eastern	26.76	9.09	23.36	1.64	36.72
Western	38.55	8.66	23.00	2.50	39.93
Central	45.18	20.95	31.89	4.26	67.23
Northern	13.55	13.22	12.79	3.05	40.96
Southern	21.84	9.58	17.64	4.37	33.11
All-India	149.23	62.91	110.48	16.23	224.59

(ii) Area under High Yielding Varieties

Based on the current growth rates, the area under high yielding varieties during 2000 A.D. has been estimated around 92.4 million hectares at the national level. The area under HYV would expand to 110 million hectares with the increased availability of HYV seeds and irrigation facilities by the turn of century (Table 23.8).

(iii) Gross Irrigated Area

The predicted irrigated area under foodgrains in the country, assuming the curent growth rates in different states would be 52 million hectares (Table 23.6). About 38 percent of the area under foodgrains would be under irrigation. The irrigated area would be 62.9 million hectares, if the irrigation facilities are expanded by 20 percent over the predicted level (Table 23.8).

(iv) Consumption of Fertilisers

Based on the current growth rates, the total consumption of nutrients would be 13.6 million tonnes in 2000 A.D. Assuming the higher level of selected inputs in certain states (Table 23.8), the total nutrients consumption would reach to 16.2 million tonnes.

Projected Foodgrains Production

Using the fitted production function equation for each state as discussed earlier, the production levels for different states were projected for 2000 A.D. In the projection of the production level of different states, it is assumed that the present structure of equations would remain the same in future. Moreover, the input levels are assumed to increase at the rate prevailing during the years 1970-71 to 1984-85. As already indicated, two other alternative production levels have also been estimated by assuming 10 percent and 20 percent increases in the predicted input use. The region-wise results under different alternatives are presented in Tables 23.6, 23.7 and 23.8 respectively. It is observed that the selected states included in the analysis contributed about 97 percent to the total foodgrains production. On this assumption, All-India foodgrains production level has been estimated by upward adjustment of the total over states to the same extent.

The total output originating from the selected states at alternatives I, II and III would be 186.0, 201.8 and 218.0 million tonnes respectively. Assuming that other States/Union Territories not included in the study would continue to contribute 3 percent to the total output, the total foodgrains productions at the national level have been estimated at 191.6, 207.8 and 224.6 million tonnes at input use alternatives I, II and III respectively.

It is observed that the foodgrains production level of 191.6 million tonnes obtained using inputs specified in alternative I would not be sufficient to meet the total demand of 205 to 225 million tonnes as projected by the National Commission on Agriculture (1976) as well as 221 million tonnes as projected by Sanderson and Roy (1980). It is apparent from Table 23.7 that by increasing the crucial inputs by 10 percent each, the total foodgrains production increases to 208 million tonnes which just meets the total demand of 205 to 225 million tonnes as projected by the National Commission on Agriculture. It is further observed that by increasing the fertiliser consumption, irrigation facilities and area under high yielding varieties by 20 percent each, the foodgrains production at 2000 A.D. goes upto 225 million tonnes which just matches the total demand projected by both the sources referred to above. We may, therefore, choose the levels of inputs given under alternative III (Table 23.8) as the desired input requirements for meeting the domestic demand projected at 2000 A.D.

The output level of 225 million tonnes by the turn of this century could thus be produced by bringing the gross cropped area to 149 million hectares, area under HYVP to 110 million hectares, gross irrigated area to 62 million hectares and total nutrient consumption to 16 million tonnes.

Instability in Foodgrains Production

The usual way to measure instsability in foodgrains production is to compute standard deviation in year-to-year changes in production for fixed periods. The data are first transformed to the logarithmic scale and then first differences are taken. Next, standard deviation in these year-to-year changes is estimated. The results obtained by Mahendra

Dev (1987) using this approach, indicated their dependence on the period chosen for the computation. At the All-India level, the instability in production increased from 8.9 percent for the period 1949-50 to 1964-65 to 10.1 percent for the period 1967-68 to 1984-85. These two periods correspond to those before and after the introduction of new agricultural technology. However, if one bad year, in terms of weather, such as 1979-80 is omitted, the instability in production declined to 8.5 percent in the latter period. Because of this limitation, a moving period approach was adopted by Mahendra Dev (1987) as discussed below.

A nine yearly moving standard deviation (SD) in year-to-year changes in production of various crops was estimated for the period 1960-61 to 1984-85. Nine years' instead of 3 to 5 years' moving period was used to provide more stable estimates. A semi-log function was fitted to the 9 yearly moving standard deviations in order to obtain trends in instability of foodgrains production. These estimated trends for rice, wheat, coarse cereals, pulses and foodgrains are given in Table 23.9. The table reveals that instability in total foodgrains production varied from a high declining trend in Punjab to a high increasing trend in Tamil Nadu. While the foograins production in the States of Haryana, Jammu and Kashmir, Kerala, Bihar and Rajasthan also showed a statistically significant downward trend, the States of Assam, Karnataka, Orissa and West Bengal noticed a statistically significant rising trend in instability. At the All-India level, however, there was an upward but insignificant trend.

Looking at the trends across the crops in various States, we find that the rice showed an increasing significant trend in instability in majority of the States except for Kerala, Bihar, Rajasthan and Jammu and Kashmir in which the instability had a declining trend. The instability had a declining trend. The instability for wheat output declined in all the States with the exception of Himachal Pradesh. Contrary to the usually held belief, pulses witnessed declining trend in instability in all the States except for Karnataka, Kerala and Tamil Nadu in which increasing and statistically significant trends of value 9.35 percent, 10.58 percent and 8.98 percent respectively were found. In case of coarse cereals, instability showed an increasing trend in all the States barring few States of Orissa, Punjab and Jammu and Kashmir wherein the instability had declined. At the All-India level, however, instability significantly increased for rice and declined for wheat while coarse cereals and pulses recorded insignificant decline. The pattern of trends in instability in the crops in the various States as well as at the All-India level reveals the importance of irrigation in stabilising production. For crops, mostly grown under unirrigated conditions or on marginal lands, instability is expected to show increasing trends whereas crops grown under mostly irrigated conditions are expected to show declining trends.

Table 23.9—Trends in Production Instability (1960-61 to 1984-85)

(Percentages)

States	*Rice*	*Wheat*	*Coarse cereals*	*Pulses*	*Total foodgrains*
Andhra Pradesh	1.79*	-0.69	0.01	0.46	0.98
Assam	2.30*	-0.83	-0.32	-1.67	2.17*
Bihar	-6.00*	-5.60*	-2.07	-3.57*	-5.07*
Gujarat	-0.11	-2.60	1.90	1.56	0.31
Haryana	0.25	-3.27*	3.01*	-0.97	-4.28*
Himachal Pradesh	1.98*	2.43*	2.29*	-6.94*	1.61
Jammu & Kashmir	-3.20*	-5.90*	-3.53*	-3.43	-6.36*
Karnataka	2.80*	-7.52	5.97*	9.35*	5.67*
Kerala	-6.70*	—	6.12*	10.58*	-7.23*
Madhya Pradesh	2.46*	-0.88	0.39	-1.56*	1.52
Maharashtra	-0.82	1.11	-2.1	2.07	-3.43
Orissa	6.28*	-1.01	-4.15*	-0.13	6.02*
Punjab	0.92	-11.03*	-3.58*	-3.98*	-0.04*
Rajasthan	-4.27*	-5.59*	-0.13	-0.43	-3.25*
Tamil Nadu	9.53*	-5.81*	8.25*	8.98*	8.90*
Uttar Pradesh	4.18*	-2.40*	2.04*	-1.88*	1.15
West Bengal	4.00*	-4.89*	-0.86*	-0.58	4.15*
All-India	3.07*	-4.99*	-1.34*	-1.16	0.18

* Significant at 5 per cent or lower levels.

Management Issues in Agricultural Production

The projected foodgrains production by the year 2000 A.D. would be about 225 million tonnes under the input strategies stipulated under alternative III as already discussed. This level of production would require the necessary resources and their management on about 89 million land holdings covering 163 million hectares of land area in the country. The expansion in foodgrains production depends on technological advance as well as institutional development. The management of the provision of the input levels stipulated above to the holdings which are spread over in far-flung villages is a stupendous task. With the modernisation of agriculture, production is more dependent on purchased inputs. The management involved in the production, procurement and distribution of these inputs to the cultivators is very complex and requires great degree of specialisation. The Departments of Agriculture at the Centre and in the States are therefore, greatly concerned with the management of these inputs.

The advent of Green Revolution has increased crop production and some of the foodgrains have witnessed instability in production as already discussed. Three major groups of factors influence stability of production—weather, pest epidemics and public policies. Pest epidemics can be kept under control through proper pest surveillance and plant protection measures. Public policies relating to land reforms, pricing and marketing can further stimulate agricultural production. To minimise the effect of bad weather, it is necessary that contingency plans are developed for the areas which are prone to drought and floods.

The foundation of self-sustaining economic growth, as already mentioned, ultimately depends on the advances in the technology used at the farm level. These technological advances are based on the system of agricultural research. This system is managed through a network of central research institutes, agricultural universities, project directorates, All-India coordinated research projects, and national agricultural research centres of the ICAR. A national grid of such cooperative research has been established in our country in which the role of central institutes, and state agricultural universities, as equal partners, has been well defined and recognised.

Besides the timely availability of fertilisers and manures, improved seeds, plant protection chemicals, irrigation and modern implements and machinery, a proper extension support for guiding the farmers in the appropriate use of resources and technology is very necessary for achieving a high and stable growth rate in agriculture. Land is the primary resource on which agriculture is based. Proper land reforms are necessary for adoption of technology by the tenants and share croppers. In the past, the agricultural administration for this purpose had not received adequate attention in most of the States. Things are now improving in the recent years and it is hoped that administrators and management specialists will rise to the occasion.

For expanding production base and modernisation of production, adequate credit is extremely necessary, particularly for bulk of small and marginal farmers. Linked with the credit is an important measure—the crop insurance. A comprehensive Crop Insurance Scheme has recently been introduced by the Government of India from Kharif 1985 season. The scheme is being implenented by the General Insurance Corporation of India in collaboration with the State Governments as co-insurers in the ratios of 2:1. The scheme is based on homogeneous area approach so that the premium rates paid and indemnities received are uniform for all the farmers of the notified areas. The role of proper management cannot be over-emphasised in the administration of rural credit and crop insurance schemes.

With the availability of increasing marketable surplus in agriculture, inadequancy of storage is a serious problem of post-harvest management. A national programme of storage with a view to develop a well spreadout storage grid right from the farm to the national level is therefore, required.

Prices play a major role in motivating producers to produce more. A marketing system which protects the interest of both, the producers and the consumers, is the back-bone of agriculture. The provision of remunerative prices to cultivators is therefore, very important for improving productivity and production.

Indian agriculture is by and large dependent on the mercy of weather. Natural calamities in the form of floods, droughts, cyclones, etc. not only damage crops but cause untold havoc to the human and animal population. The current serious drought of the century has upset our calculations and planning. It has raised immediate problems, of the supply of food, water and fodder to the seriously affected areas of Gujarat and Rajasthan on a war-footing. These are administrative issues to be dealt with a certain degree of urgency with diversion of funds from programmes which can wait. Independent India has faired well in terms of averting the consequences of famines due to general awareness, democratic institutions and responsiveness of top administration. At a macro level, Governments—both at the Centre and the States—are doing their utmost to divert funds to drought relief measures by curbing non-productive expenditure and unnecessary consumption. Indian society has, in fact, responded to the needs of the hour with necesary sacrifices. In the long run, however, we need to develop a strategy for the management of natural disasters like the present one. This needs to be incorporated urgently in our agricultural planning system.

REFERENCES

Food and Agriculture Organization (1979), *Agriculture: Toward 2000.* Rome, Italy.

Hazell, Peter B.R. (1982), *Instability in Indian Foodgrain Production,* IFPRI Research Report 30, Washington D.C.

International Food Policy Research Institute (1977), *Food Needs of Developing Countries: Projections of Production and Consumption to 1990,* IFPRI Research Report No. 3, Washington D.C.

Jain, H.K., Dagg, M. and Taylor, T.A. (1985), *New Agricultural Technology for Improved*

Food Security and Stability, Paper presented at the IFPRI-DSE Workshop on Sources of Change in the Variability of Cereal Yields', Feldafing, Federal Republic of Germany, November 26-29.

Mahendra Dev, S. (1987), *Growth and Instability in Foodgrains Production in India—An Inter-State Analysis,* Paper presented at National Symposium on 'Growth and Instability in Agriculture' IASRI, New Delhi, August, 19-21.

Mehra, S. (1981), *Instability in Indian Agriculture in the Context of the New Technology,* IFPRI Research Report 25, Washington, D.C.

Narain, P., Pandey, R.K. and Sarup, S. (1982), Perspective Plan for Foodgrains, *Commerce,* 145 (3713).

Narain, P., Pandey, R.K. and Sarup, S. (1984), Perspective for Foodgrains in 2000 A.D., *Commerce,* 148 (3813).

Narain, P., Pandey, R.K. and Sarup, S., (1985), On Foodgrains Production Projections, *Agricultural Situation in India,* 11(5).

National Commission on Agriculture (1976), *Report Part III.*

Ray, S.K. (1983), *Growth and Instability in Indian Agriculture,* Institute of Economic Growth, Delhi.

Ray, S.K. (1987), *Instability in Indian Agriculture Revisited,* Special Lecture delivered at National Symposium on 'Growth and Instability in Agriculture', IASRI, New Delhi, August 19-21.

Sanderson, F.H. and Roy, S. (1980), *Food Trends and Prospects in India,* Allied Publications Private Limited.

Sen, S.R. (1967), Growth and Instability in Indian Agriculture, *Journal of Indian Society of Agricultural Statistics,* 19(1).

Sen, S.R. (1987), *Growth and Instability in Agriculture,* Key.note Address delivered at National Symposium on'Growth and Instability in Agriculture'. IASRI, New Delhi, August 19-21.

24

Irrigation Management for Agricultural Development in India

Neelmani P. Verma

Principal Ingredients

The primary goal of irrigation management is to secure and sustain the optimum feasible net benefits in order to enhance agricultural growth and bring equity. It may also be said that better irrigation will lead to a fall in the cost of production. If irrigation management is not proper, it will impair the economy through waterlogging, growth of salinity, environment pollution and so on. Irigation increases stability in production. This is possible when irrigation management is efficient and the efficient management involves both management and non-management factors. If it is efficient then there will be reduction in farmers' uncertainty. It will bring greater predictability and homogeneity in croping patterns which in turn, will help farmers to make a forward planning and following a timetable. As a consequence, it will be easier for agricultural staff to properly respond to farmers' need under irrigated condition. The staff and farmers especially in the case of surface water, will have to be acquainted with the farm-level water management for efficient use of irrigation. Thus the first prerequisite of irrigation management is to ensure timely delivery of water to farmers in required magnitude. The second preprequisite of irrigation management is related to the distribution of water. If supply of irrigation water is less than demand, rationing of water should start. The rationing can be performed well if management skills both technical and non-technical, have been fully developed. This will also require proper coordination among farmers, engineers and administrators. In case they collaborate closely, planning and implementation of water distribution is expected to be maximised. Lastly, the large-scale irrigation projects, once they have started should be supplied with all the required inputs in time up to the completion stage. From the equity side, either inter-farm equity or spatial equity. It is equally essential to see that the delivery of irigation water is matching to these equities or not. If it is not, then inequitous distribution of water will lead to several spin off economic effects in the long-run like what Hirchsman told, unbalanced growth in production and income. Thus proper water management at the macro level requires both farm level and spatial level planning.

Besides, there are some institutional factors such as public investment, inducement for private investment, etc. that help in management. The non-management factors can be classified in three categories : (a) natural factors, (b) technical factors, (c) infrastructural and institutional factors.

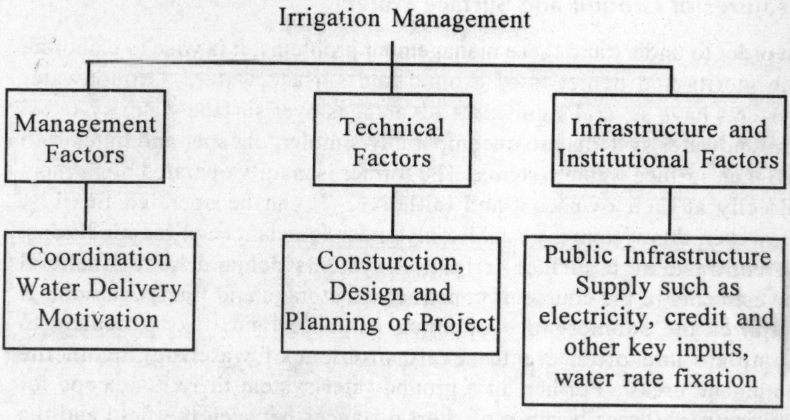

If some natural calamities disturb irrigation management then it is the technical factors which should overcome the natural disturbances.

Thus, broadly, there are three factors which determine proper irrigation management. However, these three factors do not have substitutability characteristics. It means in order to enhance sound irrigation management in a situation where one factor is damaging it, we can compensate it through concentrating on other factors. All these factors are distinct and hence of equal significance.

It may be further noticed that there are some basic differences in the management of surface irrigation and groundwater. In a country like India, irrigation is a state subject. Surface irrigation is mainly under public and groundwater is under both public and private control. Surface irrigation has to be primarily managed by the public authorities and it is also true in the case of public operated groundwater as well. In contrast in the case of privately operated groundwater the irrigation is mainly operated by the farmers. Further, surface irrigation being the major project and groundwater mainly the minor project, this difference in irrigation management is but natural. Therefore, irrigation management is influenced by size and ownership of the irrigation projects. The bigger the irrigation, the bigger will be the command as well as the management problem. On the other hand, if an irrigation project is small (minor), the management problem is less. It implies that the responsibility of management is mainly on the shoulders of the public authorities, because private irrigation in India commands much less area in comparison to the major projects. It means institutional factors of management are quite significant.

Features of Ground and Surface Water

In order to understand these management problems, it is wise to elaborate the merits and demerits of ground and surface water. Groundwater systems have several significant advantages over surface water systems. Groundwater systems are uncomparably simpler, cheaper and quicker to tap than surface water systems. The former is mainly operated by farmers directly at their own cost and initiative. It can be operated flexibly. However, this system is possible only under abundant acquifer conditions. In contrast, high surface irrigation systems demand huge financial investments in the course of construction, storage and transportation. It requires the submergence of much valuable land, take a decade to complete and often create severe problem of waterlogging in the command areas. Further, in a groundwater system there is a scope for lower water losses because of short distances between the field and the system of location. In the surface irrigation systems, however, there are serious losses of water due to long distance between the field and the location of the system. As a result, water losses take place because of evaporation and seepage. In order to reduce such run-off losses of precious water the management authorities will have to restore permanent vegetation in denuded non-cultivable lands on an entire mini catchment basis. Thus in the groundwater system the typical management problems do not crop up as is the case in the major surface systems.

Spatial Dimension of Irrigation Management

The management problem also differs in different geographical situations. The management of either groundwater or surface water in planes hardly copares with the management of the same in hard rock regions or hills. In hilly areas, lifting of water from low lying rivers/rivulets has become a popular device of irrigation. This requires different types of technical management and know how. Even in plains water is lifted but the distance of lifting is quite low in plains as compared to the hills. Similarly, in the hard rock regions construction of surface irrigation systems and their operations are quite different to that of plains. In the hard rock regions evaporation is much larger in comparison to plains, which requires very costly vegetation management. In the case of groundwater also, there is need of a separate conveyance management system. These conveyance managements are much simpler in plains than rocky regions. Another difference is that acquifer conditions in plains are quite different from that of the hard rock or hilly regions. In plains water layer is much above than the rocky regions. Even in plains there is slight difference in water table depending on distance between river bed and location of a groundwater system. These regional factors which are nothing but natural factors need special and distinct management in plains and hilly areas. The technical aspect of management can resolve these problems to a greater extent.

Complexities in India

In a mixed economy like India irrigation is both publicly and privately owned. How choices should be made between public and private ownership and among technologies depends largely on the following factors (Bottrall 1981: 228) :

(a) groundwater depth,
(b) abundance or scarcity of groundwater supplies,
(c) the need for drainage (against waterlogging),
(d) water quality,
(e) oportunities for conjunctive use with surface water,
(f) size of land-holdings,
(g) density of water course,
(h) social structure of the farming community, and
(i) the quality of public sector management.

Further, in the groundwater category also there is need of a choice, *i.e.* which source of groundwater is preferable for a particular region. For instance, in some areas dugwells and in some areas shallow tubewells can be preferable in installation. All these choices depend on the acquifer condition. If the water table is quite high, dugwell may be preferable to shallow tubewells or shallow tubewells may be preferable to deep tubewells. The technical aspect of management will have to look into this natural gift. Similarly, a technique of choice will have to be applied for opting a particular surface irrigation system. If the public authorities further feel that there is a lack of financial resources for development of surface water or groundwater in a particular region, then again the problem regarding choice of development occurs. In this situation the Government (management) can mobilize resources from farmers in advance for developing public sources of irrigation—surface or ground. But this seems a hypothetical case because farmers may not be so resourceful to contribute in advance. Then the only choice is to develop groundwater in the private sector. Surface water development by private sector is hardly a feasible solution because it needs large resources. Even then some farmers may need credit for developing groundwater. Thus the management can partly meet the required financial resources in terms of extending credit to farmers. If private groundwater systems are developed then the only problem is to bring equity in irrigation. Since all farmers cannot install groundwater schemes because of lack of resources, the commercialisation of irrigation water will start. Big farmers will install such irrigation systems and will sell to the smaller farmers at a certain price which may be exorbitant, if the seller monopolises or duopolises the region and the situation. Thus from equity viewpoint publicly owned groundwater systems are preferable. In a situation when the management is resourceful financially, then it can think to develop surface irrigation scheme if the objective is also to bring equity in irrigation and through irigation.

To recapitulate, irrigation management is a very complex issue. It is determined by management related as well as non-management related factors. The non-management related factors are basically natural, regional, technical, institutional and economic. But, broadly, in our analysis, these factors have been classified as technical and institutional factors of management. Thus there are several options open before the management. The management can be either Government or a private person, but the responsibility is mainly on the former in a welfare state. Thus the Government will have to decide

(a) development of groundwater or surface water or both,
(b) type of groundwater according to source and ownership,
(c) regional factors and choice of technology,
(d) institutional management structure, *i.e.* credit and other key inputs management, and
(e) fixation of water rate in both the publicly and privately owned systems.

Thus, in this process of irrigation, the role of the Government as well as farmers is important. However, the role of the former seems bigger because of being a welfare wisher. The farmers can respond to the Government property if the management is sound. Indian economy has seen transformation in irrigation management. In the ancient India irrigation management was not like that of medieval or modern India.

Water Management in Drought Prone Area

There are 99 drought prone districts in India, which comprise 723 talukas and 10,81,500 sq. km. of area. This identification of areas and districts is based on a study of the Drought Prone Area Study and Investigation Organisation set up in the Central Water Commission in 1975. This department combined the two lists of drought prone areas identified by the National Commission on Agriculture in 1976. This selection of drought prone districts was based on a criterion. According to this criterion drought is a situation occurring in an area when the annual rainfall is less than 75% of the normal in 20% of the year examined. If anywhere it has occurred in more than 40% of the years the area is identified as chronic drought area. Besides, any taluka or equivalent unit, where 30% or more of cultivated area is irrigated is considered to have reached a stage which enables it to sustain a reasonably stable agriculture and to be reasonably protected from drought. The preliminary studies show that out of a total area of about 109 million hectares covering 99 districts, only about 51 million hectares spread over 74 districts can be considered as drought prone areas (CWC, 1988). Further, it is seen that in 75 districts the water available at 75% dependability is more than the requirements. In the remaining 24 districts, however, the water available at 75% dependability falls short of the assessed requirements.

Since in drought prone areas level of irrigation is low and rainfall is also less than normal in most of the cases, management of irrigation water is quite important for the area. In drought prone districts water table is also very low, so groundwater technique of irrigation has not been able to grow. Even big surface water system could not flourish because of its capital intensiveness. Thus, the other option before the cultivators is to preserve rain water which can be used at the time of need of the crop. Although in almost all the key states there are a few drought prone districts, however, the management of rain water could flourish intensively in a few talukas of Pune of Maharashtra State. More than 25,000 farmers in the chronically drought prone areas have benefited by a new way of distributing scarce water. The new technique was devised by Vilas Salunke. In this system a charitable trust called Gram Gourav Pratishtan (GGP) was established initially to provide relief to farmers of Purandar taluka of Pune. A bund or earthen wall across a nullah or a gully which becomes a seasonal stream during the monsoon was constructed. Then lift irrigation technique was also adopted.

The GGP had stored one million cft of water in a percolation tank and it was sufficient to irrigate 2.4 hectares during Kharif, 8.20 hectares during Rabi and 0.5 hectares in the summer. The productivity aspect, as a result, could become very sound in this system of water and irrigation management. This system became more appreciable day-by-day because of growth in employment in the region. As a result, a series of construction of bund and community minor lift irrigation schemes started. Under this system it was preferred to allocate water to a large number of small farmers rather than to a small number of big farmers to bring down the level of income skewness. The cropping pattern was such that could absorb less water. As a result, cultivation of sugarcane and other commerical crops was discouraged. For operational management GGP established a series of `Panl Panchayats' (Water Councils) wherein all the families participating in a particular scheme took part. The manager selected in each scheme is preferably from a neighbouring village or another person who is not directly involved in the scheme itself. The manager is a monthly paid person who is responsible for day-to-day operation of the scheme Insuring fair allocation of water to all participants. The average cost of irrigation varied from Rs. 6,250 to Rs. 8,750 per hectare with a participating partnership of about 30 to 40 households. With a gestation period of two to three years, the increase in the annual income of a family had been from Rs.1,500 to Rs. 8,000. The farmers are paying community water tax regularly and also return the loans regularly. All these economic benefits from small but manageable lift irrigation schemes have been possible by utilizing rainwater which was being wasted in the past due to lack of professional and technological guidance. Thus an attempt ought to the made to disseminate this system probably in all the talukas of the drought prone districts of various States.

Ground *vs* Surface Water Management

The development of groundwater has registered a phenomenal growth during the last few decades. According to the Seventh Plan groundwater accounted for, at the end of the Sixth Plan, as much as 26.1 million hectares in terms of gross area irrigated. This figure is marginally in excess of the area served by big irrigation projects, which stood at 25.3 million hectares. It is also of even greater importance that groundwater irrigation is more productive than that of the big canal systems. The reason is, unlike the latter, it ensures the farmer to apply water to his land in time and also as per the need of the crop. Further, according to a study the productivity of groundwater irrigation is around 100 % above that of canal irrigation. So it is useless to think only in terms of big dams and canals, rather we should appreciate the true field value of groundwater as a source which is comparably easier, economical and quicker to install and use than surface water and that too at the farmer's own cost and initiative. In fact, big surface water projects are capital intensive and thus need huge public investments during the construction, storage and transportation periods. They also require the submergence of much valuable land, take years and often decades to complete, suffer from serious conveyance losses of water through evaporation and seepage and often create acute problems of waterlogging in command areas. There are numerous empirical results showing how such losses can be reduced through restoring permanent vegetal cover to denuded non-agricultural land and through terracing and bunding agricultural lands on an entire mini catchment basis. Experiments carried out at the different soil and water conservation centres of the ICAR as well as in other countries have demonstrated that such treatments reduce run off losses and soil losses up to 100 % depending upon local slopes and rainfall and land use patterns, etc (Dhawan, 1987). For example, in a small watershed of 8.4 hectares near Agra, the yearly run off out of a total precipitation of 624 mm in 1962 was 54 mm which amounts to 8.7 %. This watershed which is situated in the ravines of the Yamuna and is under agriculture to the extent of 80 % was treated for soil and water conservation by appropriate physical and biological measures in the early sixties. Observations made in 1981 showed that, of a total of 863 mm of precipitation in that year, the run off calculated was only 8.5 mm, which accounts for about 1 %. It may be noted further that out of 330 mm or so of effective precipitation that we receive per annum around 150 mm enter the soil, around 20 mm are impounded, mostly in big reservoirs, and 160 mm reach the sea through river flows. There is a need to reduce these losses which may be possible with more afforestation and better land management. Thus groundwater is superior to surface water and has proved itself valuable in a labour surplus and resource constraint economy like India. So groundwater needs more management oriented attention during its construction and operation periods in comparison to the surface water. However, the importance of surface water cannot be undermined everywhere especially where water-table is very low. Thus in exceptional cases or for the purpose of diverting/lifting flood or river water we may think of canal/surface irrigation but generally we should not go for surface water.

Management of Conjunctive Use

So far the management aspects of ground and surface water have been discussed separately. Ground and surface water belong to the same hydrological cycle and are interdependent. That is to say, surface water becomes groundwater and groundwater becomes surface water in the hydrological cycle. Hence it is imperative and desirable to consider the management of these two sources together for meeting the demand to supply.

A conjunctive management of the two sources is advantageous in the following ways :

(a) Efficient conjunctive use and management will discourage the decline in the level of groundwater.

(b) Conjunctive management will help and reduce the deficiency in water supply at the tail end of a canal command area through pumping from tubewells and the like.

(c) Since for some areas groundwater is more yield giving and less capital intensive and for some areas surface irrigation is suitable a combined management will lead to an optimum efficiency and maximum yield.

(d) Waterlogging is an evil phenomenon which arises due to rise in water table by overuse of surface irrigation. A conjunctive management will reclaim the waterlogged areas through enhancing gradual fall in groundwater levels by controlled pumping.

(e) At some places where quality of either of the water is not usable, a blending of the two waters may improve the quality and may be usable. For instace, brackish groundwater in arid and semi-arid lands may be usable after blending the surface water. Even control of salt water intrusion in coastal and deltaic tracts may be possible.

But the conjunctive management of the two sources is a very complex one. Their use and management face several constraints. For example:

(a) There are different water rates for both the sources. These differential rates jeopardise conjnctive management because surface water is normally cheaper than groundwater for farmers.

(b) There is no bar on the use of groundwater. However, there is a law regarding the use of surface water, so conjunctive management becomes very difficult for efficient use.

(c) Lack of power supply at different places at the time of

requirement is observed in India. It hinders the management of conjunctive use.

Thus management of integrated use of ground and surface water aims at economical and efficient development of the two sources in a complementary framework. It also aims to benefit wider area. So the management has to answer three questions :

(i) Where, when and how to use surface water more than groundwater?

(ii) Where, when and how to use groundwater more than surface water? and

(iii) Where, when and how to adopt a mixed policy?

All these three questions may be answered in the light of the national plan objectives, *i.e.* eradication of unemployment and poverty in a short span and financial resource as a constraint. However, normally in areas which may be irrigated by surface water and where groundwater potential is also substantial, irrigation should be planned in the light of regional and national plan goals and also examined in the light of cost-benefit analysis. However, in India management of proper conjunctive use has been a distant dream so far.

25

Privatisation of PSUs in India : Post Liberalisation Scenario

Atmanand

Public enterprises were expected to achieve certain socio-economic goals. The country had decided to create a sector where it would be able to develop an industrial base which being free from exploitation, achieved faster growth and acquired a "commanding height in the economy". It was not only to generate resources for developoment but, promote redistribution of income and wealth, create employment opportunities and promote balanced regional development. However, for long it has been felt that these objectives are being largely unfulfilled. It is no secret that we have not been able to provide productive employment to an overwhelming majority of employable people and disparities in income have perhaps further increased.

In terms of performance to be judged by indicators such as capacity utilisation, profitability and productivity, public sector units have almost always lagged behind the corresponding private sector units. And this has led to the resume that public sector units be ereturned to private enterprises so as to achieve higher standards of efficiency. "Privatisation" of public units has become a new topic of discussion in the area of public enterprise management.

1. Growth of the Public Sector in India

A large public sector dominating the basic industries and key infrastructure—public sector control of the "commanding heights" of the economy—was an integral part of India's development strategy for about four decades from the year 1950 to 1990. Both the industrial policy statements of 1948 and 1956 articulated this approach and massive investments were made under the successive Five Year Plans during this period to build up a public sector with a dominating presence in the Indian economy. The Central and State Governments together established nearly 1,000 public sector enterprises in a wide range of activities—some 250 Central Government public sector enterprises and more than 800 State public sector enterprises.

Table 25.1 gives data on the evolution of the basic parameters of CPSEs over the past few decades.

Table 25.1 Evolution of CPSEs from 1960-61 to 1992-93

	1960-61	*1970-71*	*1980-81*	*1992-93*
Number of CPSEs	32	87	171	245
Total CPSE employment	NA	660	1,505	2,204
Total investment—equity + loan (Rs. in million)	9.53	39.00	211.02	1,469.71
Value of sales (Rs. in millions)	2.13	33.09	286.30	1,467.13
After tax profit (Rs. in millions)	NA	0.03	1.82	33.96
Dividends paid (Rs. in millions)	NA	0.14	0.83	7.92
Retained earnings (Rs. in millions)	NA	1.81	7.15	26.04

Source : BPE Reports; *India : Review of Public Enterprises,* The World Bank (October 1988); *Public Sector in the Indian Economy,* May 1991 CMIE, Bombay.

The total investment of Rs. 1,469.71 millions in CPSEs (1992-93) represents nearly one-fourth of the value of the country's GDP. The enterprises are also engaged in a variety of activities; of those in operation in 1992-93 as many as 129 were in manufacturing, 26 in energy, 13 in minerals and metals and the remaining 72 in services. Apart from their significant share in the output and employment of the organised sector, the CPSEs provide the rest of the economy with important raw materials and intermediate products like oil, power, coal and steel.

When the commercial public sector enterprises were set up in various areas their founders had high hopes about their future. It was believed that the "state-ownership" of management would imbue the management and labour with a sense of public good, that productivity and efficiency would increase and that wage, demand and price increases would be moderated. Therefore, over the years liberal financial, legal and administrative support has been extended to the CPSEs even within a highly regulated and restrictive economic system.

In practice, however, the performance of the CPSEs like their counterparts elsewhere in the world has been generally considered disappointing. Though it is very well clear that profitability should not be the sole criterion to evaluate the performance of public sector undertakings, however, it is very important to consider financial profitability as an yardstick to measure the returns to the public enterprises over which huge amounts of money have been incurred at the cost of the public exchequer. Profitability can be judged by taking the following indicators into consideration:(a) Gross profit before interest and tax, (b) net profit after payment of tax, (c) percentage of gross profit to capital employed, (d) total turnover, (e) internal resources generated. Gross profit before interest and tax rose from Rs.559 crores in1974-75 to Rs.18,438 crores in 1993-94. As far as net profit after tax is concerned the position was unsatisfactory for a number of years. For instance, starting from 1977-78 net profit after tax was negative in 1977-78, 1978-79, 1979-80 and 1980-81. However, situation changed thereafter and public sector recorded impressive profits. In 1981-82 the net profit after tax was Rs. 445 crores which went upto Rs. 1,769 crores in1986-87 and Rs. 3,782 crores in 1989-90 and Rs. 4,435 crores in 1993-94. It may be noted that the gross profit as percentage to capital employed ranged betweeen 11 and 12 % since 1981-82.

Table 25.2 Profitability Profile of Central PSEs

	1981-82	*1990-91*	*1991-92*	*1992-93*	*1993-94*
1. Operating enterprises	188	238	237	239	240
i) Profitable enterprises	104	123	133	131	120
ii) Loss-making enterprises	83	111	102	106	117
			(Rs. Crores)		
2. Capital employed	21,935	1,02,083	1,17,991	1,40,110	1,50,307
3. Gross Margin	4,012	18,212	22,223	25,227	27,600
4. Gross Profit	2,654	11,102	13,675	15,957	18,438
5. Net Profit	445	2,272	2,355	3,271	4,435
6. Profit of Profit-making enterprises	1,293	5,394	6,079	7,384	9,722
7. Losses of Loss-making enterprises	848	3,122	3,723	4,113	5,287
			(Percent)		
8. Ratio of Gross Margin to Capital Employed	18.29	17.94	18.83	18.01	17.83
9. Percentage of Gross Profit to Capital Employed	12.10	10.88	11.59	11.39	11-12
10. Ratio of Net Profit to Captial Employed	2.03	2.23	2.00	2.33	2

Though there is no dispute regarding the role of the public sector undertakings in the country's economic development yet the feeling widely prevalent is that the rate of profit in these undertakings is either too low or is negative. The return on capital employed has been low (around 2%), their record on prices, productivity and manpower costs has been disappointing and constant criticism has been voiced about the low level of customer service which they provide. Over-manning and the resultant high labour costs due to salaries and wages not being commensurate with producitivity improvements, actively high capital investment costs in projects due to time and costs overruns combined with low capacity utilisation, obsolescence of products and fixed assets, high financial charges attributed in part to excessive inventories and substantial working capital needs and operational inefficiency illustrated by excessive consumption of raw materials in a number of manufacturing enterprises have been both the cause and reflection of the poor financial and commercial performance of public sector enterprises, particularly in the non-petroleum sector. All these also add up to a larger economic problem in that the manufacturing CPSEs produce high cost products in important sub-sectors which has its effects throughout the economy. This affects the competitiveness of Indian industry adversely and makes it difficult to meet import competition at home and export competition on the world market.

Like the CPSEs, the State Land Public Enterprises (SLPEs) are also in deep crisis. There has been a massive growth in the number of SLPEs. From a mere 51 in the 1951-60 decade, the number of SLPEs set up shot upto 135 during 1961-70. The number of SLPEs established in 1971-80 hovered around 300. During 1981-86, the number of new SLPEs established was estimated to be 350. In terms of numbers they are approxiately three-fold of the CPSEs. The major expansion of CPSEs took place during 1955-65. The growth was most marked in the SLPEs during 1971-80. During 1980-86, on an average an increase of one PE at the central level was followed by an increase of two in the number of SLPEs. The State Governments have set up the SLPEs as a policy with an intention to use them as an instrument of public policy to quicken the pace of development.

The investment in SLPEs account for about 35% of the total investment in the public sector. The figures speak for themselves. The total investment in the public sector stood at Rs. 1,30,000 crores on March 31, 1989 and SLPEs gobbled up a substantial Rs.46,000 crores out of that.

The range of activities that SLPEs concern themselves with is very wide, but using a broad brush they can be grouped into three basic categories : commerical, developmental/promotional and welfare related. Out of the 754 SLPEs existing on March 31,1987, 371 were commercial enterprises, 290 developmental and promotional and the rest 93 welfare enterprises. If one excludes State Electricity Boards and State Road Transport Corporations, the investment in these enterprises hovered around Rs. 2,860 corres in March 1977 and Rs.13,000 crores in March1987. The growth rate in investments during this decade was 45% a year in the case of the SLPEs against 30% in the case of CPSEs. The debt-equity ratio turned heavily in favour of the equity component, though in a Few states like Kerala and West Bengal, the debt component assumed higher proportions mainly because of accumulated losses which were funded by incurring debt.

So far as the financial performance of the SLPEs is concerned, an Institute of Public Enterprises Study (Hyderabad) shows an encouraging trend but a discouraging performance, the rate of return in the case of commercial enterprises improved, but only from 0.53 % in 1981-82 to 0.37 % in 1982-83. It increased to 3.90 % in 1986-87. The scenario is not much different in the case of promotional SLPEs. The rate of return fluctuated between low of 2.64% in 1982-83 and a high of 9.13% in 1986-87. Welfare enterprises have a different story to tell. Their rate of return turned minus in1982-83 (it was 2.42% in 1981-82) and could never turn positive thereafter.

Thus, the above analysis of the financial performance of the SLPEs also indicates that they have become a burden on the States exchequer and are not making any return on the investments already made by the State Governments.

An overview of the current scenario now reveals that there is a wide gap between the conceptual merits and actual performance of Government enterprises, public concern for the relatively poor performance of the public sector enterprises has been growning since the early 1980s. For there is not only a micro-economic aspect of their failure in terms of economic and financial inefficiency, there is also a macro-economic dimension to the problem of low profitability. The failure to give adequate return on the huge public sector investment has been a major contributing factor towards the recent fiscal and foreign exchange crisis which has put severe strains on the Indian economy. The urge for better performance has also grown due to tight budgetary constraints, a growing and powerful cadre of professional enterprise managers and a gradual increase in policies with more emphasis on market forces and less on centrally directed economic planning.

A number of official committees have examined various aspects of public sector performance emphasising the need for better incentives and greater autonomy and accountability for the management of the public sector enterprises. The Committee to Review Policy for Public Enterprise, known as the Arjun Sen Gupta Committee (1984) in particular recommended the holding company structure and the performance contract or Memorandum of Understanding (MOU) System with a view to ensuring an "arm's length" relationship between the Government and the CPSEs. Its other recomendations included decontrol of the prices of products of the public sector, abolition of price preferences, closure of chronically sick units and giving primacy to financial and technological upgradation.

In July 1991 the Government initiated programmes of economic stabilisation and structural reform which aim at creating a competitive and market driven economic environment in India.

2. Public Sector Reform Measures

The major elements of the reform of 1991 towards public sector are :

- changes in the financing pattern of the capital investments of public sector enterprises,
- the holding company and the performance contract or MOU system,
- partial divertment of shares in selected Public Sector Enterprises, and
- reference of chronically sick public sector enterprises to the BIFR for rehabilitation/closure.

The most important reform of 1991 in the area of the public sector relates to ownership stucture. For the first time the long-held principle that "once a public enterprise always a public enterprise at any cost" has been given up. There are three steps indicated in this direction, *viz.* review, referral to BIFR or BIFR type of mechanism and disinvestment of ownership.

Change in the Financing Pattern of the Capital Investments of PSEs

During the period from 1960-61 to 1985-86 for example the gross capital formation of the non-departmental non-financial public sector enterprises, ranged between 9% and 27%. This meant that a major portion of their capital formation (63% - 81%) was financed by outside sources, mostly by budgetary support from the Government.

The budgetary support for the plan schemes of the CPSEs is provided in the form of loans and equity. Loans carry an interest obligation whereas dividends are payable if profits are made. In practice, however, there are very relaxed requirements for both these obligations.

Due to the constraints on resources, partly as a result of the poor return from huge investments made in the public sector enterprises, the relative contribution of the Government's budgetary support for financing the plan outlay of the CPSEs has been declining since 1985-86. Table 25.3 gives the figures for a few selected years.

Table 25.3 Financing of Central Public Enterprises : Plan Outlay

(*Rs. in Crores*)

Revised Estimates	*Total Plan Outlay*	*Budget Support*	*Internal Resources*	*Other Borrowings*
1984-85	122.64 (100)	6.5 (53)	45.18 (39.3)	9.46 (7.7)
1985-90 (Seventh Plan)	963.47 (100)	385.1514 (40)	334.7977 (34.7)	243.5209 (25.3)
1991-92	294.2122 (100)	69.2026 (73.5)	120.07 (40.8)	104.9396 (35.7)
1992-93	366.6131 (100)	65.7647 (17.9)	161.2875 (44)	139.5009 (38.1)
1993-94	438.921 (100)	74.507 (16.97)	188.5252 (42.96)	175.8879 (40.07)
1994-95	500.6633 (100)	72.0092 (14.38)	229.3078 (45.80)	199.3263 (39.82)

(Figures in brackets indicate percentages).

Source : Government of India, Expenditure Budget, Vol. 1, Various issues

The data presented in Table 25.3 also shows that the CPSEs are increasingly resorting to commercial borrowing to finance their plan outlay. The process has been somewhat facilitated by the Government's decision to permit (since the year 1985-86) a few selected public sector enterprises to raise resources from the market through taxable and tax free bonds/debentures. In the year 1992-93 however, public sector enterprises were only able to raise a sum of 10.62 million rupees as against the target of 62.91 million rupees and the preceding year's realisation of 52.11 million rupees (Table 25.4). The developments in the bond market following the securities irregularities could be a major reason for the shortfall.

The Holding Company and the Performance Contract or MOU System

The Arjun Sen Gupta Committee (1984) recommended the formation of holding companies in the areas where a number of PSEs were functioning in similar fields of activities and coordination could be brought about in their business and commercial operation through common top-level arrangement. The holding company would also deal with the Government and pass on the decisions taken to the subsidiary units, which could be insulated from Government interference in their business operations.

Table 25.4 Issues of Bonds by Central PSEs (1985-1995)

(*Rs. in millions*)

Year	*Amount Budgeted*	*Amount Raised*
1995-86	N.A	3.5370
1986-87	13.6408(RE)	16.7410
1987-88	15.0002 (21.0842)	26.8420
1988-89	20.3928 (24.7528)	24.9770
1989-90	31.1466 (44.9362)	37.2900
1990-91	39.4201 (49.3298)	54.6300
1991-92	58.6912 (57.2169)	52.1080
1992-93	60.5810 (62.9064)	10.6250
1993-94	68.8220 (62.3716)	N.A
1994-95	74.6402	

Note : Figures in parenthesis indicate revised estimates.

Source : RBI Annual Report 1992-93 and Expenditure Budget, Vol. 1.

The financial performance of all the holding companies in the public sector, except that of SAIL has been poor and most of them have incurred losses for many years.

Thus it can be safely stated that apart from facilitating operation, the formation of holding companies has not made any significant difference to the operational results of the concerned companies.

The MOU System

The MOU system is presently the centrepiece of public sector reform in India and the New Industrial Policy of July 1991 seeks to make it an effective mechanism for performance improvement by providing greater management autonomy to public sector enterprises and at the same time making them accountable by various means which include placing the MOUs signed between the Government and the CPSEs in the Parliament.

An MOU is an instrument which defines the relationship of the public enterprise with the "Government and clarifies their respective roles in order to achieve better performance. The emphasis is on achieving the negotiated and agreed targets/objectives rather than interfering in the day-today affairs. Each MOU spells out the corporate mission, objectives and annual targets of the enterprise. In addition, an MOU imposes certain obligations on both sides for progressive performance improvement—financial, fiscal and qualitative. High level committees have been constituted for evaluating the MOUs as well as the performance of the public sector enterprises.

The MOU system started in the year 1987-88 when four CPSEs signed performance contracts; by the end of the year 1992-93 the number of such enterprises had gone upto 98. Of these 97 enterprises (which signed MOUs with their administrative ministerials) were evaluated; 34 were rated "excellent" and 35 as very good.

The MOU system has been further strengthened. During 1993-94, 101 PSEs signed MOUs as against 98 in the preceding year. Based on their audited accounts, performance of 100 PSEs was evaluated, out of which 46 were rated excellent (46%), 29 as very good (29%), 12 as good and 10 fair. In 1994-95, 106 PSEs have signed MOUs which is five percent higher than last year.

An evaluation of the impact of the MOU system has shown that there is hardly any congruence between the MOU scores and the financial performance of the CPSEs as indicated by the useful financial ratios. It has also been commented that the overall financial performance of the PSEs is not due to the effectiveness or otherwise of the MOU system. The MOU system is not designed to and cannot address to other issues which impinge public sector enterprise operations and make efficient behaviour on the part of the PSEs virtually impossible. Therefore, at best, an MOU can be another performance evaluation tool alongwith the existing instruments like budgetary control and performance budgeting, corporate planning, the management information and control system, project approval and monitoring and the like. To consider it as a substitute for more fundamental reforms in the public sector would be a great mistake.

Divestment of Shares in selected Public Sector Enterprises

Partial divestment of Government shareholding in selected Public Sector enterprises has been another element of the public sector reform programmes. During 1991-92 equity varying between 5 and 20 percent of the total capital in the selected PSEs (31) was divested in two phases in December 1991 and February 1992. The total realisation from the divestment during the year was 30.38 million rupees.

Table 25.5—Divestment of PSE Shares

Year	*No. of shares sold (millions)*	*Total realisaion (Rs. in millions)*	*Average realisation (Rs. in millions)*
1991-92			
1st Tranche	0.5162	14.27	27.65
2nd Tranche	0.3559	16.11	45.25
1992-93			
1st Tranche	0.1287	6.82	53.00
2nd Tranche	0.3106	11.84	38.10

Source : Reserve Bank of India, *Annual Report,* 1992-93.

For the year 1994-95 the budget estimates provide a target of 40.00 million rupees on this account but given the unsatisfactory performance in the past its realisation remained a matter of doubt. The Table 25.6 indicates changes in Central Government equities in 35 selected public sector enterprises where it approved disinvestments until the end of December 1994.

Table 25.6—Year-wise/PSU-wise Details of Shares Disinvested Since 1991-92

Sl. No.	*Name of the PSE*	*% of Central Govt. Holding*				
		1.791	*31.3.92*	*31.3.93*	*31.3.94*	*31.12.94*
1	*2*	*3*	*4*	*5*	*6*	*7*
1.	Andrew Yule	71.30	62.60	62.80	62.80	62.80
2.	Bharat Earthmovers Ltd.[1]	100.00	80.00	80.00	80.00	80.00
3.	Bharat Electronics Ltd.	100.00	80.00	80.00	80.00	75.80
4.	Bharat Heavy Electricals Ltd.	100.00	80.00	79.54	79.45	68.46
5.	Bharat Petroleum Corpn. Ltd.	100.00	80.00	70.80	49.62	69.62
6.	Bongaigaon Refineries & Petro. Ltd.	100.00	80.00	74.60	74.59	74.59
7.	CMC Ltd.	100.00	83.31	83.31	83.31	83.31
8.	Cochin Refineries Ltd.	61.16	55.04	55.04	55.04	55.04
9.	Dredging Corpn. Ltd.	100.00	98.56	98.56	98.56	98.56
10.	Fert. & Chem. (Travancore) Ltd.	98.99	97.46	97.35	97.35	97.35
11.	HMT Ltd.	100.00	95.14	90.32	90.32	90.32
12.	Hindustan Cables Ltd.	100.00	96.36	97.97	97.97	97.97
13.	Hindustan Copper Ltd.	100.00	100.00	98.88	98.88	98.88

1	2	3	4	5	6	7
14.	Hindustan Organic Chemicals Ltd.[1]	100.00	80.00	80.00	80.00	56.90
15.	Hindustan Petroleum Corpn. Ltd.	100.00	80.00	70.00	69.72	69.72
16.	Hindustan Photofilms Mfg. Co. Ltd.	100.00	87.47	87.47	87.47	87.47
17.	Hindustan Zinc. Ltd.	100.00	80.04	75.93	75.93	75.93
18.	Indian Petrochemicals Corpn. Ltd.[2]	100.00	80.00	60.97	62.40	62.40
19.	Indian Railway Const. Co. Ltd.	100.00	99.74	99.74	99.74	99.74
20.	Indian Telephone Industries Ltd.	99.65	79.72	77.79	77.67	77.67
21.	Madras Refineries Ltd.	84.62	67.70	67.70	51.80	51.80
22.	Mahanagar Telephone Nigam Ltd.	100.00	80.00	80.00	80.00	67.18
23.	Minerals & Metals Trading Corpn.	100.00	99.33	99.33	99.33	99.33
24.	National Aluminium Co. Ltd.	100.00	97.28	87.20	87.19	87.19
25.	National Fertilizers Ltd.	100.00	97.72	97.66	97.66	97.85
26.	National Mineral Dev. Corpn. Ltd.	100.00	100.00	98.38	98.38	98.38
27.	Neyveli Lignite Corpn.[2]	100.00	95.42	93.86	94.19	94.19
28.	Rashtiya Chem. & Fert.	100.00	94.36	92.50	92.50	92.50
29.	Shipping Corpn. of India	100.00	81.49	81.49	81.49	80.12
30.	State Trading Corpn.	100.00	92.02	91.02	91.02	91.02
31.	Steel Auth. of India Ltd.	100.00	95.02	89.49	89.45	89.36
32.	Videsh Sanchar Nigam Ltd.	100.00	85.00	85.00	85.00	85.00
33.	Container Corpn. of India	100.00	100.00	100.00	100.00	80.00
34.	Indian Oil Corporation	99.88	99.88	99.88	99.88	88.17
35.	Oil & Natural Gas Corpn.	100.00	100.00	100.00	100.00	98.00

1. Recently the company had come out with public issue.

   DPE don't have the latest details of Govt. holding after completion of public issue. The above information is based on approval given by the Government.

2. Due to further release of equity by Govt.

Source : The Economic Times, 15.3.95

Partial divestment of the equity in public sector enterprises fails to address the efficiency problem particularly because divestment can be made only upto 49 % of the total capital and has no impact on ownership, control and management of the enterprises. It has been used more as a fiscal tool in order to raise cash to finance the Government deficit rather than improve the efficiency of the enterprise operations which should be the overriding goal of public sector reform. There is also the danger that such an approach can be a temptation to privatize badly and to postpone the more difficult but much needed longer term fiscal reforms.

Reference of Chronically Sick PSEs to the BIFR

In December 1991 the provisions of the Sick Industrial Companies (Special Provisions) Act, 1985 (SICA) were extended to public sector enterprises permitting the reference of the chronically sick Public Sector Enterprises to the BIFR for rationalisation/rehabilitation/closure. Manufacturing Public Sector Enterprises which satisfy the conditions of SICA, namely seven years of incorporation, complete erosion of the net worth and two years of continuous cash losses could be referred to the BIFR.

As on 30 November 1993, as many as 106 industrial companies in the public sector — 47 CPSEs and 59 State level PSEs — had been referred to the Board which declared 80 of these undertakings (45 CPSEs and 35 SPSEs) sick. So far the BIFR has issued winding-up notices in respect of three CPSEs and four SPSEs.

For public sector enterprises there is also a Voluntary Retirement Scheme (VRS) for employees who have put in at least ten years of service. The National Renewal Fund (NRF), established in February 1992, provides funds for meeting the requirement of CPSEs under the VRS and also covers the cost of retraining and reemployment arising as a result of modernisation and technology upgradation and also provides a social safety net to workers affected by industrial restructuring/closure or partial closure. However, in the absence of a policy and legislative framework which will facilitate the exit of unviable firms and enable the management of the public sector enterprises to adjust their work force to their requirement or close unviable units, these piecemeal measures (like VRS and NRF) have limited value.

Few Examples

Apart from general reform measures, there have been a few individual cases of divestiture or privatisation in respect of a few public sector enterprises. One is the case of Maruti Udyog Limited, an automobile joint venture with Suzuki Motor Corporation of Japan, where Suzuki has been allowed to increase its shareholding to 50 percent by the purchase of fresh equity and also to acquire greater management control. Some public enterprises like Indian Petro-Chemicals Limited have been permitted to go for a fresh issue of equity in the capital market in order to finance their expansion plans.

3. Assessment of the Reform Measures

Next we assess the impact of the public sector reform measures in terms of increases in the efficiency (or profitability) of the public sector enterprises, improvements in their contribution to public savings and reductions in their contribution to India's pulic sector (fiscal) deficit. This will indicate if these measures have at all been effective in achieving the main objectives of public sector reforms.

The overall financial performançe of operating central public sector enterprises during the last six years was as given in Table 25.7.

These data show that there has been some decline in overall PSE financial performance although reform measures like the MOU system have been in operation. The overall performance no doubt marks different trends in profitability in different segments of the CPSEs. The enterprises in the petroleum sector, for example, earn the highest return (about 20 %) in respect of gross profits to capital employed and 9 % in terms of net profit to capital employed. But these are in the nature of petro-profits not in any way related to the reform measures. The rates of return for both non-sick and non-petroleum manufacturing companies are low and the sick companies depress the profitability of the central public sector enterprises to a great extent. In any case the reform measures seem to have had no effect on the profitability (or efficiency) of the public sector enterprises.

Table 25.7—Overall Financial Performance of CPSEs (1987-93)

Year	*Investment (Rs. in Net milliards)*	*Profit (Rs. in milliards)*	*%age of gross profit to capital employed*	*% age of net profit to capital employed*
1987-88	556.17	20.30	12.48	3.65
1988-89	676.29	29.94	12.68	4.43
1989-90	847.60	37.89	12.53	4.47
1990-91	1,020.84	22.72	10.88	2.23
1991-92	1,179.91	23.55	11.59	2.00
1992-93	1,399.33	33.96	11.42	2.43

Source : *Public Enterprises Survey, 1992-93,* Department of Public Enterprises, Governemnt of India, New Delhi.

There has also not been any improvement in the public sector enterprises' contribution to public savings as a result of the implementation of the reform measures. Throughout the period from 1985-86 to 1991-92, the gross savings of the public sector enterprises (Government companies plus statutory corporations) were about 3.5% of the gross domestic product at factor cost (Table 25.8). The share of these savings in the gross domestic savings in fact declined from about 15% in 1985-86 to 12% in 1991-92.

Table 25.8—Share of PSE Savings in GDP and Total Savings

(Rs. in milliards-current prices)

Year	*GDP at factor cost*	*Gross domestic savings*	*Public enterprises savings (gross)*	*Percentage*	
				PSE savings to GDP	*PSE savings to gross savings*
1985-86	2,337.99	496.55	75.12	3.21	15.13
1986-87	2,600.30	570.48	89.08	3.43	15.61
1987-88	2,948.51	717.12	105.30	3.57	14.68
1988-89	3,535.17	866.65	133.30	3.77	15.38
1989-90	4,058.27	1,115.25	160.07	3.94	14.35
1990-91	4,726.60	1,251.09	165.41	3.50	13.22
1991-92	5,418.88	1,480.39	175.40	3.24	11.85

Source : *National Accounts Statistics 1993,* Central Statistical Organisation, Government of India.

In order to assess the public sector enterprises' contribution to the reduction of India's public sector or Government (fiscal) deficit, we have examined the share of CPSEs' contribution in the form of dividends, corporate taxes, excises, customs and other duties to the total receipts in the Government budgets for the period from 1985-86 to 1994-95 with actual or realised figures being given for the three years 1990-91 to 1992-93 (Table 25.7). It can be seen that the Central Government fiscal deficit as a percentage of the GDP after coming down to about 6.5% during the years 1991-92 and 1992-93 from a high of 9.4 % in 1990-91, again climbed up to around 8 % in 1993-94. During this entire period, however, the CPSEs' contribution to the total receipts remained at around 30%, in fact, during the two years (1991-92 and 1992-93) when the fiscal deficit was relatively low, there was some decline in this share. The percentage of the CPSEs' dividend contribution to the non-tax revenue receipts (where it is included) also averaged around 3.5% to 4.5%. These figures show that during this period the contribution of the CPSEs to the reduction in the Government deficit was negligible.

4. Privatisation Option

Our analysis thus shows that although public sector reform is an important component of the structural reforms programme it has not made much headway. The main reason seems to be that the reform measures introduced so far have failed to address the key issues of public sector reform.

There are a number of reasons for the poor performance of the pubic sector enterprises but in most cases these can be traced to the system or the structural framework within which the enterprises operate. There are mainly three elements of this system — the external policy environment, the close relationship with the Government and internal management practices of the enterprises (including the incentive framework) — which to a considerable degree have been influenced by the close Government-enterprise interface. Since liberalisation of the economic policies, there have been significant changes in the external policy environment although problems related to management's ability to adjust the work force to its requirements and the exit of unviable firms still remain. The other two elements of the strucutural framework have hardly changed and the reform measures so far introduced have not been able to address these problems. The public sector enterprises are still open to political and bureaucratic interference—both formal and informal—and conflicting social and commerical objectives have been placed on them to the detriment of both. Although the share of Government budgetary support in the financing of the public sector enterprises' capital investment has declined, it has not been completely phased out and the system of capital restructuring (and "turned around" stragtegies) and the financing of the time and cost overruns of the PSEs' capital investment projects give the signal that success and good financial performance are not necessary for them to survive. Simultaneously, a complex framework of administrative and parliamentary control has been built comprising elaborate investment approval system, the procedure for top-level appointments, scrutiny and allocation of the plan outlays, fixation, monitoring and evaluation of production and financial targets (*a la* MOU) and examination of public enterprise performance by the Parliament and its committees. Though not stated explicitly, the intention seems to have been to create a set of external mechanisms that would provide pressures similar to those provided by the market. If so, the attempt has been singularly unsuccessful for the simple reason that no bureaucratically designed and operated market can every be as effective as the real market when it come to stimulating efficiency.

Table 25.9—Share of CPSEs' Contribution to Receipts of the Government Budget

(Percentage)

Year	*Contribution to total receipts*	*Dividend contribution to non-tax revenue*	*Fiscal deficit of the GDP*
1985-86	30.05	3.07	8.71
1986-87	32.24	3.08	8.78
1987-88	35.60	3.27	8.02
1988-89	34.21	3.61	7.94
1989-90	31.91	2.38	7.45
1990-91	32.18	3.45	9.39
1991-92	26.56	4.09	6.59
1992-93	26.79	3.67	6.40
1993-94	29.40	4.50	8.09
1994-95	29.43	4.40	6.59

The basic issue in public sector reform, therefore, is to change or replace the system, not merely tinker with it. The objective has to be to distance, as far as possible, the Government and its agencies from commercial (public sector) enterprises. Although in theory, the efficiency of an enterprise is not a function of ownership, in practice governmental owners tend to interfere, often in non-economic ways, thereby distorting efficiency. Public sector reform, therefore, should aim at changing both the form and content of the Government-public sector enterprise relationship so that the enterprise can function independently as a commercial enterprise in the market place. The difficulty with the holding company and the MOU system is that these were mere attempts at changing only the form of the relationship, not the substance.

Basic changes are also needed in the context of the new economic environment which the structural reforms seek to create. The changes brought about in the economic policy framework since July 1991 are increasingly exposing Indian companies (both in the public and private sectors) to internal and external competition and the global market. They are under pressure to restructure and reorganise their production facilities and technological parameters in order to survive and prosper in a highly competitive market. The major player in the new business environment is the "company" or "corporation", not the Government. Competitive advantage in specific industries has to be built by the efforts of individual companies which must relentlessly improve productivity, raise product quality, improve production technology and boost production efficiency. They have to continuously scan both internal and external markets and access these for capital, technology, goods and services. In order to be able to do all these, a company (or public sector enterprise) should be in a position to take quick decisions, face the consequences of its actions and exhibit flexibility in operations. Presently this is not possible in the structural framework in which the public sector enterprises operate—a system which makes decision-making slow, diffident and promotes the habit of playing it safe. The framework needs to be replaced by an arrangement which would enable these enterprises to function independently as Board-managed professional companies, subject to the rigorus of the market place and the discipline of the shareholders. This implies deregulation, marketisation, privatisation and distancing the Government from commerical public sector enterprises through a fundamental reorientation in their relationship so that this change occurs both in form and in substance. This is very much a practical necessity not dictated by any ideological consideration.

India, therefore, should have an explicit policy of privatisation which involves transfer of ownership, management and financing of the state-owned enterprises to the private sector in order to tackle effectively the efficiency question in the context of an emerging competitive, market-driven economy. The focus should be more on improving the performance of the public sector enterprises through increased efficiency, greater responsiveness to consumers and relief from the public sector financial and administrative constraints and less on raising cash through the sale of enterprises or assets to meet the Government deficit.

It would, however, be counter-productive if we ignored the ground realities while designing the privatisation policy and programme. In India the public sector has come to be treated as a "sacred cow" and there is often opposition to the concept of privatisation on ideological grounds. It would require considerable tact, time and effort to establish that privatisation in the present circumstances is a practical necesity, not related to any ideological motivation. A strong and long-term political will and a broad enough consensus have to be built for the privatisation programme to succeed. Besides, there is a wide variety in the nature, function and performance of the public sector enterprises, all of which may not be amenable to privatisation in the short-term. It would be necessary to be flexible and adopt different approaches depending on the circumstances of each enterprise or group of enterprises.

It would, therefore, be desirable to initiate a structured and systematic programme of commercialisation (or marketisation) which includes privatisation as its most visible form. The major elements of the programme could be the following :

- An overall commercialisation policy statement should be formulated outlining among other things, the place of privatisation in the Government policies for the liberalisation of the economy, the rationale and objectives of the commercialisation programme, the modality, criteria and evaluation procedures and the relative roles of foreign investors, employees and the general public in the privatisation process.
- A thorough review of the laws, regulations, guidelines, procedures and practices that govern public sector operations and the Government-public sector enterprise relations should be made with a view to changing these provisions and arrangements conform to market principles.
- All public sector enterprises should be subjected to a thorough scrutiny with a view to categorising them into four broad groups; (1) enterprises which would be retained in the public sector for strategic or public interest considerations; (2) enterprises which are profitable and viable and can be privatised; (3) companies where the performance is not good but which can be turned around through reorganisation and preparatory measures for eventual privatisation; and (4) PSEs which are loss-making and terminally unviable and therefore should be closed. An appropriate privatisation programme over a 10-15 year period may be prepared based on this categorisation.
- Finally, suitable institutional arrangements will need to be made in order to design the policies and programmes and implement these in a focussed and systematic manner. A Governmental agency has to be identified and will have to be given strong political and administrative support for its work. A high-level advisory body comprising professionals from relevant fields may have to be associated with the agency in order to advise on all matters related to the commercialisation (including privatisation) programme.

5. Conclustions

1. Massive public investments have been made since 1950 to build a public sector which has a commanding presence in the Indian economy. The public sector enterprises function in a variety of fields and have made significant contributions to industrialisation, the achievement of self-reliance and the creation of employment opportunities. However, their financial performance has been poor and the low return on capital employed has been a contributing cause for macro-economic imbalances. Their record on productivity,

manpower costs and responsiveness to the consumer has been disappointing. The recent liberalisation of the economic policies has put additional pressures on them, necessitating basic changes in their mode of functioning.

2. Since the mid-1980s, more particularly since July 1991, a few public sector enterprise reform measures have been introduced as part of the structural reform programme. Changing the method of financing the capital investments of PSEs, the MOU system, the partial divestment of Government shareholding in selected PSEs and reference of the chronically sick PSEs to the BIFR are the major components of the partial reform programmes. These have not been effective in improving the operational efficiency of the PSEs, which should be the main objective of public sector reform. These also do not address the key issue of public sector reform which is to change the system in which the PSEs operate and distance the Government from the enterprises.
3. In these circumstances privatisation of PSEs becomes a practical necessity. However, given the socio-political milieu in India a careful, structured and systematic programme of commercialisation (including privatisation) will have to be formulated and implemented in a focussed manner. Appropriate institutional arrangements and a long-term and strong political will be necessary for the programme's success.

26

Learning by Doing : An Experiment with Case Writing as an Experimental Learning Tool

Krishna Kumar

1. Introduction

Management education is peculiar as compared to most other fields of study in that it draws very heavily from several different disciplines such as economices, psychology, accounting, engineering etc, which demand higher level of multidisciplinary orientation and integrative skills. The ability to draw upon inputs from different areas to solve managerial problems, each one of which is in a unique organisation setting, also require a very high degree of application skills. The application skills require a very high level of internationalisation of conceptual input, so that various issues/dimensions of a problem and relevant concepts, tools and techniques of analysis and problem solving 'occur' to a person, when faced with a managerial problem.

Management schools, therefore, use a mix of pedagogical tools, instead of banking on traditional lecture method alone that is typically used in many other fields of study. Lecture method is a very efficient mode for transmitting the knowledge inputs, but it falls short of the requirements of 'assimilation' and 'internalisation', so important for enhancing one's application skills, and hence less effective in terms of end use, *i.e.,* the ability to use the inputs for addressing managerial problems. More time consuming and demanding pedagogical tools like discussions, exercises, case analysis, project work are, therefore, used at times at the cost of efficiency of "knowledge imparting" associated with lecture method.

The discussion mode of teaching and training improves the clarity in the knowledge imparting process. However, it also falls short in fulfilling the objective of developing application skills. Exercises are very effective in establishing a point, illustrating concepts, and to some extent in highlighting multi-dimensionality of organisational issues. The case analysis method considerably improves knowledge assimilation process and enhances application and integrative skills, by making the participants come face to face with complex managerial situation of a real life organisation[1]. It is learning by doing in a simulated situation. The case becomes laboratory material on which one applies concepts, tools and techniques taught. The case method is exceptionally useful pedagogy for structuring problems, improving analytical process and solution development, particularly if the problem situation demands drawing of inputs from diferent disciplines or functional areas in courses like Stratgegic Management.[2]

2. Case writing as a Pedagogical Tool for Experiential Voluntary Learning Tool

Case writing is generally looked at only as an activity undertaken to produce course material, which is necesary for using case method in teaching and training[3]. Case writing often emanates from case research and consultancy assignments involving in-depth analysis of an organisation's functioning. Both the case research as well as the consultancy assignments provide very good opportunity for learning new things through exploration. What is often not realised is that case writing besides enabling learning new things, also provides more clarity about management concepts, tools, techniques and processes as well as develops conviction in them by seeing them in use. Case writing, if done properly, takes one a step further in enhancement of clarity and conviction in concepts that can be reached through case discussion, project etc., as transcription of an experience ensures the logical flow of issues and ideas.

Although case research too helps in improving the clarity to some extent, but unlike case writing the main focus of case research is exploration of new, unknown facets of management, rather than enhancing clarity and conviction. The case writing is done with a purpose of illustrating some specific concept, tool or technique of management to enable learning through case analysis. It requires all the relevant data to be made available in the case, which is not possible to identify and collect, unless one is very clear about different aspects of case situations, the decision and action points involved, various alternative courses available and so on. Case writing thus pushes one to scan and collect relevant concepts, tools and techniques from the existing knowledge base to interpret the case situation (rather than focusing on enhancing knowledge base). The process of case writing, therefore, forces one to have familiarity with and clarity about the existing knowledge base. All in all while case research focusses on exploration of new knowledge with the fringe benefit of enhancing the clarity and understanding of existing knowledge, the benefits from case writing are in the reverse mix. While the benefits of case research are well established, the tremendous learning value associated with case writing does not seem to have been realised at least in India as borne out by the quantity and quality of referred case material produced in various management schools of the country.

Once the learning value associated with case writing is realised, it can be considered as a pedagogical tool also in the management education programmes. Since learning process in case writing is slow and less structured than what is demanded by the 'programmed learning' (typically prescribed in management schools and marked with rigid, time bound, discrete evaluation system) the case writing may not exactly fit as a standard pedagogical tool in the management education programme. However, it can perhaps be used as a gradual, experiential learning process even in a programme with highly structured evaluation system, as borne out by an experiment underway in a management institute in India. In the following pages this experiment is described.

Case writing by the students of MBA programme is not a new thing. There have been plenty of cases written by MBA students in Harvard Business School and elsewhere.[4] Attempts have also been made for case writing through case writing competition.[5] However, such instances are few and mostly in the U.S. Organised efforts with the purpose of internalisation of knowledge imparted through case writing are rare, especially in the South East Asian countries.

The Experiment of Learning Through Case Writing

The experiment being conducted comes very close to the Live Case Approach and contextual learning reported by Amelia Klein[6] with some differences. First, the focus in the current experiment is not so much on action problem solving as on enhancing the understanding and the assimilation of concepts. The emphasis here is on improving clarity and enhancing the comprehension, the integrative and the problem structuring skills. Secondly, the efforts here are directed on increasing the students' understanding of the subject using case writing as one of integral component of pedagogy for a regular programme (employing a mix of pedagogical tools), rather than as an independent, stand alone pedagogical tool for learning. The third difference lies in the focus of the exercise which is to examine the feasibility of case writing as a pedagogical tool in a highly stressful, highly structured, time bound educational programme.

(i) The Experimental Setting

West Coast Management School (WCMS), established in 1985 had, *inter-alia,* a two years master's level course in management. WCMS was one of the four leading national level management institutes of the country. Each of the institutes was highly rated by the client group as reflected by campus placement performance. The academic performance level of students admitted was quite high. The students also, had keen desire to learn that was fuelled by the expectations of better career opportunities. The students were keen to undergo high order of rigour especially if inspired by faculty to do so.

The 2-year post-graduate programme of the school included two courses on Strategic Management, focussing on strategy formulation and implementation aspects respectively. The faculty of the institute had laid special emphasis, on the following aspects, in the basic design of the programme.

- The Programme be designed as an integrated whole, (thus, synthesis, symbiosis and synergy among its components were to be ensured).
- The internalisation of knowledge, rather than its mere acquisition be emphasised.
- Development of capability of 'learning to learn' be given a high priority.

Accordingly, a combination of instructional methodologies were employed in various courses depending upon the nature of the course. The basket of teaching methods included lectures, case analysis, exercises, seminars, role plays management games, project work and computer based learning methods.

Although efforts were made in each of the courses to enhance integrative skills, the expectations of achieving integrative skills were more from the strategic management courses. The integrative skills demanded much higher level of clarity and quick recall of points from different fields, as determined by the case situation, hence higher level of internalisation of inputs was necessary. An instructor of the Strategic Management had been teaching the courses for over six years. He had been observing that although case method was helping the students in appreciating and understanding the inputs, the students faced the following problems:

(a) The students were, at times, bewildered with the vastness of data and the number of issues to be considered.

(b) The students were able to understand the issues when discussed in the class. However, when faced with a new case situation, it looked unique, as the prescribed reading at times was felt inadequate for the purpose, because case analysis repeatedly called recollecing/ drawing inputs from other courses covered in earlier terms.

(c) Despite availability of extremely powerful and simple conceptual framework, the students found it difficult to realise the issues involved and apply the tools and techniques available.

(d) The course was heavily oriented towards case method and was supported with project work. The project work required submission of the reports towards the end of the course. In the project work, the students faced 'blocked by openness' phenomena, associated with strategic management, with multitude of options available on account of freedom to decide 'what to do' at the broad level of objectives and strategies which was typical of a functional area course that operated within boundaries of objectives and strategies.

(e) There was some kind of 'automatic erosion' effect. When students moved from one topic to the next, they tended to slip some significant points that they seemed to have understood well earlier. Once pointed out, they were able to recall it well. Thus, the problem did not seem to be with regard to understanding and appreciating the inputs, but of internalisation.

(f) The problem of comprehension and visualisation increased as the students moved from strategy formulation to implementation stage and reverted back to complete the alternatives for strategy formulation purpose, *i.e.*, visualising strategy implementation issues while formulating the strategy. Indeed, the problems of missing links increased as the students grappled with implementation issues, *e.g.* if they proposed new strategy, they considered technology and financial issues but missed skill development, structure and system issues, or when they suggested change in the structure, the system, the style and the organisation culture issues did not 'occur' to them.

(ii) Use of Modified Project Work

As mentioned earlier, the project work was an integral part of the Strategic Management course. The students worked in groups to analyse corporate strategy of different organisations. This field oriented project work did help them in appreciating the concepts and techniques of analysis and synthesis, by seeing their use/non-use in the organisational setting, reporting and sharing with the instructor their bewildering experiences, as to why things did not happen as expected, pointing out the inadequacy of literature (mostly American) and impressing upon the need of indegenous course material. The difference in contextual setting of organisation described in the cases (U.S.A. being a free market economy and India comparatively highly protected and regulated one) were real ones, especially when one was analysing the State Government enterprises. The project work was more of evaluation exercise, testing the level of clarity and application skills achieved by the students towards the end of the course rather than enhancing it.

Three years later the project work was slightly modified by the instructor. The students were asked to submit the project reports two weeks ahead, rather than at the end of the academic session. The instructor perused the reports and returned them to the students, pointing out the deficiencies, data gaps etc. Students were also required to make presentation and attendance in the project presentation was made compulsory for all the students of the class.

When the project presentations were made, the instructor and the class closely examined the analysis and recommendations made by the group. The data inadequacies, missing linkages and conceptual mistakes that emerged during the discussions helped the students realise the concepts better. It was further buttressed by sharing of each other's experiences.

A further modification was introduced next year in that the instructor started indicating the data inadequacies, analytical and other deficiencies before the project presentations were made. The students were allowed to incorporate additional data and improve the analysis for presentation and also revise the project report if they so desired and resubmit them before the end of the academic term as earlier, and thus improve their grade. The project groups, more often than not, improved upon their initial analysis and report.

Another variation was incorporated in the following year by assigning the students a variety of organisations, especially not-for-profit organisations such as developmental agencies, scientific laboratories, educational institutions and the like. These experiments further bolstered students' confidence and belief in the soundness and power of conceptual frameworks developed elsewhere for application to different types of business and non-business organisations.

(iii) Use of Case Writing as an Experiential Learning Tool

The instructor had in the past been wondering about the use of project works done by students for case writing. The time and efforts spent by them were going waste as project reports collected dust or were disposed off. Once it occurred to him to make use of the same, with the help of three project reports he thought of devleoping a case. The school did not have much of case writing, and the students' project reports had not been used by the faculty thus far. The instructor developed the case material and used it in two of the School's "Management Development Programme" and found it very effective. He was quite happy with the insights he got about the industry and clarity of concepts applicable in analysing and solving the problem and was convinced of the soundness of concepts.

Another experience further buttressed the belief in learning through case writing. While developing a case material on the invitation of a company executive he gave the draft to a faculty in Personnel Management area. The reviewer's feedback was that the work ought to be dropped straight into dust bin. He was, however, kind enough to give his detailed comments on the lack of data, impressionistic information and certain editorial deficiencies. The instructor took it as a challenge and while incorporating the changes he also developed a teaching note, and submitted to the same faculty colleague to review it again. To his utter surprise, this time the reviewer was full of praise, thanking the instructor to enable him understand a bit of strategic management as a subject. The instructor was astonished. He was reminded of the celebrated article "clear writing means clear thinking"[8] and convinced about the immense power of case writing, especially if the teaching note also accompanied the case.

The instructor then thought to use case writing itself as a learning exericse in the courses on Strategic Management. His prior experience in case writing had given him a lot of insights and clarity on the functioning of organisation. He had however, apprehensions about the feasibility for several reasons. For example, the school's master level programme was highly structured with extremely rigid time-frame for the completion of requirements of every course, which was difficult to conform to if case writing was used. The issue of evaluation was yet another question. Besides, each course was having certain prescribed hours of students' involvement and it could not be exceeded without approval of the faculty council.

There were some favourable points also. The instructor was able to develop a reasonable interest in students in the subject. Many students were highly enthusiastic persons and were keen to try out new things even if that stretched them. The school on the whole had very close teacher-student relationship. However, the instructor was not confident whether he could make case writing happen. He had, however, realised that the students' efforts had to be purely voluntary to start with.

An opportunity soon came by. In the next year, the instructor gave the project work on "Analyse and Develop the Corporate Strategy of..........." to a number of groups. While evaluating the project reports he made comments on some of the reports indicating that there was a good potential to convert the project reports into case material for teaching/training if some additional efforts were put in. He also enquired whether the groups were inclined to do the job. Most groups consented, but many of them could not finally do so, as they got caught in some other activities at the same time. One group almost prepared the draft, but nothing came out finally.

(iv) Renewed Efforts for Case Writing

The next year provided another opportunity to the instructor as he was teaching both the Strategic Management course to the entire batch of the MBA students, spread over two terms. In addition, he also had to teach another course in the Strategic Management area, in the third of the final year, which was subscribed by almost 40% of the batch of students purely as an additional course, *i.e.*, beyond the requirements for the award of Master Degree. This meant that the instructor had an opportunity to interact with the entire batch over two terms of academic year and further one term of the academic year with almost 40 % of the batch. It was also an indication of interest and voluntariness on the part of students to stretch out if need be for academic pursuit, which was rare in earlier days.

The instructor considered it a rare opportunity to try out, although case writing required guidance beyond the usual course work. It also required the students to involve in a task which was not a prerequisite for the award of degree. The task of seeking voluntary involvement was not easy as the Programme workload was almost highest among the management schools in the country. The instructor explored the possibility of case writing during initial sessions of Strategic Management Course. Luckily, the students community, had in the previous years been complaining about use of dated and non-Indian cases. The instructor took the opportunity to share the past year's experience and seek the students' involvement as a way to solve the problem, even if partially. The call of the instructor made some impact, especially when the instructor highlighted that the exercise would help in improving visibility of the institute though contribution to management education. The students too were keen and were trying to improve visibility of the institute in several ways. The overall class response was quite positive.

The instructor, therefore, gave the assignment "Analyse and Development of Corporate Strategy of ...." to 10 groups of students having 4 members each. The groups met the instructor for briefing to carry out the assignment. From time to time the instructor also helped the groups in moving on with the project, which conveyed that the instructor was keen in the projects culminating into case material for class discussion.

(v) Conversion into Case Material

At the end of the course, the students submitted the project to the instructor. The instructor asked the ten project groups whether they were still interested in developing the case material. It was necesary to check up to ensure voluntariness and commitment to the exercise which was crucial for the slow stretching, unstructured learning process especially under situations of intense workload and competition. Two groups expressed reluctance, but the other eight assured their continued commitment.

The students had one week of examination followed by another of vacation at the end of which next term was to begin. During the examination period the instructor asked his assistant to type out as many of the handwritten reports on computer as possible since it was easy to make modifications. The students' reports contained company's background, narration of business, objective, some practices, their evaluation of organisations' strategy. It also included their own version of what the strategy should be. The narrations at places were incoherent and jumpy in logical flow and at times information provided was incomplete. It was at this stage the worth of case writing came to the fore.

The instructor rearranged the matter provided in the report more as an indicative exercise rather than doing the case writing himself. The major work done was that of separating out the analysis and recommendations from the factual data on companies, their policies and practices. The instructor also tried to put all the related information kon any issue/aspect together. The paucity of time did not permit more than four cases to be converted into this format. Looking at the information available in the cases he tried to identify important points, to describe a Strategic Management problem and draft a para to make them issue-oriented case materials.

In nutshell the instructor tried to do the skimming of the report to have the factual information presented, in the format of a case material. Added to this were the titles (company name), name of the school (WCMS), case writer's reference etc. At the end of the exercise the material looked something close to what the students had been accustomed to see, a case material.

(vi) Identification of Data Gaps, Issues and Sharpening of the Focus

The four groups of students whose project reports were typed were given a copy of the original project report, another copy with factual information (to form part of case material) separated from the analysis and recommendations (which were to be used for developing the teaching notes). They were also given a note on case writing and sample of a case, supplied to the instructor by WACRA during its 10th International Conference in July 1993 at Bratislava. They were requested to identify key strategic issues or problems the organisation was facing, the decisions involved and the information required for the purpose. The student groups were advised to think on these issues and also the ways in which the information gaps could be filled up. The other groups were promised similar versions when they returned after the vacations.

The instructor also requested the Chairman of the Master's Proramme to allow the members of each group to remain together in same section only in the next term also. The allocation of the students in sections normally changed from one to the other term, as the second year had 80 % courses as electives and a student was not necessarily kept in the same section in the following course of Strategic Management in the past. The Chairman was kind enough to ensure the same, though it created some complication for him in designing the time table. Sections of two groups were interchanged but members of every group retained together in the same section, which allowed extension of the project in organisation. In the second term the students were asked to look at the organisation from the strategy implementation point of view, *e.g.* organisation structure, resource allocation, functional policies etc.

(vii) Learning Values Involved

Once the students faced the revised draft of their own project report, it was easy for them to realise that they needed some more data at places. There were certain apprehensions about the availability of data. But the inadequacies were appreciated . It was far better way to let the students realise what they had missed rather than telling them directly. The drafting of project report was their own, just re-adjusting the information made them realise the inadequacies, especially with an invitation to identify the decision points, issues involved and hence the information required *versus* the information provided.

The opportunity to study the same organisation enabled them to appreciate the seven linkages in the organisation[9]. In the light of the existing structure, styles, systems, culture functional policies, how far the recommended strategy was appropriate? If not, what changes may be necessary and whether it was possible to effect the changes. This provided them the opporunity to realise as to how the task of managing change sets the limits to the growth aspirations of the organisation.

(viii) Increasing the Pressure for Experiential Learning

The experiment now reached the ultimate stage. The students had finished the entire Strategic Management Course (Strategy formulation and implementation) by December 1993 and thus had been imparted all the important concepts, tools and techniques of Strategic decisions making. They had been through the experience of facing unstructured situation, understanding/identifying key strategic issues with the help of above inputs. The pressure of case writing was pushing them to be more and more clear. The pressure of putting all the relevant information was making them think over and again if any significant aspects or issues were missing that had to be considered for decision-making. The pressure was building up to provide data for ETOP and SAP analysis else the case could not be discussed. This was pushing the students to bring rigour in the case material.

To re-mphasise the assimilation, the students were asked to prepare teaching note, focussing on learning points and describing how the case would be discussed/illustrated in the class. Thus the pressure for clarity was built up through both the demand for teaching note and the case writing. In teaching note the analysis and process of developing recommendations was being asked to be described so that others could also teach. The demand to provide all the information was in turn impressing upon clarity and assimilation of input without which the analysis could not be done.

The process was proving to be more time consuming with a high risk of slippage and failure like previous year. To check against such recurrence two additional actions were taken. The School was to have its annual convocation immediately after the end of third term. The students were to be enthused to commit that the cases complete in all respects would be ready before the students departed. It was, therefore, decided that cases be released for use, even by outsiders in a book form, by the chief guest of convocation. This set the dead line and quality standards to be maintained.

A second interlock was also introduced. In the process of data collection for the projects, the executives of the companies seemed to be quite impressed with the work of students. They were enquiring whether they could get a copy of the project reports. It was, therefore, decided to organise a workshop on Strategic Management in which the same cases would be discussed. That was indeed to be the trial run of the cases prepared. Efforts were then made to get two executives from each of the companies concerned. While the instructor was to give the conceptual inputs, the analyses of the cases were to be done by company executive to see the relevance of inputs and the students groups were to play the role of facilitators. The group having worked on the organisation, was expected to be able to play the role for the executive group working on the case. This role of playing facilitators was expected to increase the pressure for thoroughness and to do quality work to secure clearance of the cases from the organisations concerned.

The Results

It would be realised that the entire experiment was an evolutionary rather than a well planned one. In retrospect the whole sequence of action may sound to be a logical, planned approach, but it was not so and there were reasons for it. The experience was not a happy one last year and the instructor was very disappointed at the end. No conscious measures were thought of when the experiment started this year. It was only at a very late stage, the dream seemed to be realising. Thus it was not easy to design and use very good measures to check the efficacy of case writing as a pedagogical tool for learning process. Still some measurements have been taken to assess the value of the learning and the experiment.

The experience at the later stages was a harried one for the instructor. From January onwards when the second term SMII course ended, the instructor felt as if he was losing the control over the experiment altogether. He was wondering whether he would be able to have the case studies, teaching notes etc. completed. Whether he would be able to get the clearances of the case from the organisations concerned. Whether he would be able to organise the workshop for the trial run of the cases, which depended upon the above two factors. And last but not the least, whether he would be able to get the cases released at the time of convocation as contemplated. He himself was pre-occupied with a new course that he had launched for the first time. Two factors further compounded his worries. The students got busy with their annual event 'MANFEST', a management games-cum-cultural event that was being organised on a grand scale, as done never before. Unfortunately the students who were actively involved with the case writing also happened to be the key organisers. Immediately after the function the students got busy with their final examinations followed with the campus placement activities. It was becoming very difficult for the instructor to contact them for revising the case, teaching notes and seeking company clearances.

However, the end results were not bad. All the eight groups finished the case and teaching note writing. Five of the cases were duly cleared by the organisations concerned before the convocation. Three of the cases could not receive clearance due to non-availability of the executives. It was not easy anyway, given the fact that out of the eight organisations that were studied as many as seven were governmental ones. Even these cases were likely to receive clearance by the end of March,1994.

Invitations were extended to the five organisations, who had cleared the case studies, to participate in the Workshop on Strategic Management, requesting them to depute two top executives each. One organisation could not depute executives as it's annual planning dates coincided exactly with the dates of the Workshop. Another organisation, keen to depute could not do so since the concerned executives had to be in the office as the state assembly was in session and there could be questions to be answered by the organisation. Thus three organisations deputed the executives. The Chief Executives of four of the five organisation also visited during the Workshop.

The Chief Executives were highly appreciative of the efforts on the part of the students and their depth in understanding the organisational problems and connected issues, as brought out in the case studies.

It was a great experience for the instructor too, to conduct the sessions using the case studies for bringing out the learning points. The executives who participated in the workshop were given two cases each to analyse and make presentations. The students who had developed the cases were asked to join the executive to give clarification and add conceptual inputs wherever necessary. The executives too were highly appreciative of the cases as a vehicle to understand the key concepts in Strategic Management.

The case studies became a part of the first volume of the WCSM Case Series, released by the Chief Guest of the Convocation, Honourable Minister of Human Resources Development of the Government of India, on 5th March 1994 as envisaged. (The cases are being forwarded separately to Mr. Tim Edlund for review and inclusion in the Third Case Writers' Colloquium in the 11th International Conference of WACRA).

What did the case writers (the students) feel about the experiment? To understand this it will be necessary to go back a bit in the history of the experiment. It will be remembered that out of a batch of 98 students, 40 were given projects that had potential for case writing. Two groups *i.e.*, 8 students had regretted carrying on the project beyond the first term, bringing down the total to 32. At the end of the experiment, the students who were actively involved shared in private that not all the members of the group actively involved throughout, till the end.

On the average, they said, only two students worked on the project to see them through. This brought down the number of students, keenly involved in case writing to about 16, *i.e.*, 40 % of the students who had the opportunity to involve in case writing.

At the end of the Workshop there were hardly any students accessible as they got busy with their families who had come to attend the convocation next day, packing up for going back to home etc. Some first year's students ran around to get case collected nine responses.

The case writers were asked the following question:

> "You have been involved in the study of Strategic Management subject. The pedagogical tools used for the purpose were primarily the case discussion in the class, project work and case writing. To what extent, do you think, they have been useful and effective in enhancing the understanding and assimilation of the conceptual inputs? Use a seven point scale, 1 representing the lowest value and 7 the highest value."

The students' reponses are shown in Table 26.1 (for details *see* Annexure I)

Table 26.1—Use of Case Writing as a Learning Tool

	Enhancing understanding	*Enhancing Assimilation*	*Total*
1. Case Discussion in the class	36	33	69
2. Project Work	34	30	64
3. Case Writing	31	35	66

From the above data for the group as a whole, the case writing emerges as an important, as much as the other pedagogical tools for learning, namely the case discussions in the class and the project work. Given that the three assumed almost equally high value, it would seem that value addition is possible with case writing, almost as much as project work over the case discussion in the class. Overall, thus, the case writing emerges as an important supplementary pedagogical tool for management education even in a highly packed, highly stressful post-graduate programme. Given that as much as 40% of the students who had the oportunity to involve in the exercise voluntarily, sustained their interest to the point of successful completion, indicates that the case writing has the potential as much as that of an elective course of a programme, perhaps as an additional course, credit or non-credit one.

Implications of the Experiment

As mentioned earlier case writing has been by and large seen only as an imperative exercise to support the use of case method in management education and training. Its potential and power as a pedagogical tool for experiential learning has not been realised. The learning value of case writing, mostly done by teachers and trainers, has been considered to be purely incidental, more in the sense of undesigned case research. It's power to augment one's problem structuring capability(arising out of one grappling with the problem of identifying and understanding the problem) is perhaps not realised at all. The power potential of case writing will be well appreciated if one recalls that in most of the cases in education the focus is on second order[10] of decisions "how to do" "how to solve a problem". The aim of identifying the problems is left for one to learn on the job.

The exercise of writing teaching note is the key part of learning and assimilating the inputs drawn from existing knowledge base. Clear writing means clear thinking and that is not possible if one loses touch with existing knowledge base. The pressure of carrying out analysis that is imperative for case to be used by wider set of instructors, requiring quality, makes one clearly understand and practise the conceptual inputs given. The pressure of conducting session should further improve the clarity and assimilation process and bolster one's convictions in concepts. The success of the experiment may, thus, provide an extremely powerful pedagogical tool not frequently used today.

There is one more advantage likely. The process of learning associated with case writing transcends the boundaries of instructor supported learning. It can help the graduate to enhance the learning outside the classroom, even while discharging executive roles.

An added, although incidental but significant, contribution of the process is development of contemporary case material for teaching and training, an activity which is at such a low level in most of the management schools, in countries like India, that one has to use dated and "foreign" cases to illustrate points, much to the annoyance and reservation of the participants.

Issues for Future Research

The present experiment has evolved out of sheer concern for enhancing the internalisation of inputs in a structured learning process, especially the problem identification and structuring components that are not as much emphasised through traditional pedagogical mix. The hands-on experience is an interactive process of learning by letting one realise the gaps in the internalisation process himself, voluntarily. There were lots of "ifs and buts" throughout, *e.g.,* whether students will agree, whether critical mass will plick up, will voluntariness work in view of paucity of time with students of a highly stressed educational programme. Many actions were thought of in enterpreneurial mode by the instructor in "crossing the bridges as they came" manner. Hence the appropriate measures to evaluate improvement in internalisation of input through case writing could not be included in the experiment as a design element. Future researches may examine this properly by suitably designing the experiment.

The pedagogy seems to be as much relevant for self-learning and continuing education, even when a person is working in the executive capacity. Future researches may examine this issue of immense significance for continuing education.

This experiment has been carried out through voluntary association of students, in which the students-Instructor relationship played a very important role. What alternative arrangements may be necessary is an issue that has to be looked into if this pedagogy is to be used as an element in pedagogical mix in the management education.

Conclusions

The case writing as a pedagogical tool for enhancing internalisation in the learning process in management education is comparatively a new idea. This paper describes an experiment in this area to assess the viability and effectiveness of this pedagogical tool in a high structured management education programme (MBA). The preliminary indications are that it may prove to be a significant tool for knowledge internalisation process.

REFERENCES

1. Bhunden, Robert G., *Criticism of Business and the Case Method as a Partial Solution,* Boston (1991) WACRA pp. 211-218.
2. Jauch, Lawrence R., and Glueck, William F., *Business Policy and Strategic Management,* Singapore (1988) McGraw Hill, p. 40.
3. Smith, A.J. and Smith, I.G. *Evaluating the Case Method: A Longitudinal Approach,* Boston (1991) WACRA pp. 169-180.
4. *See* for example, Austin E. James & Kohn, Tomas O., *Strategic Management in Developing Countries: Case Studies.*
5. Chi Clemous *et al., Th Graduate Business Student Case Competition Among Public & Private Colleges/Universities in North Carolina,* Boston (1991) WACRA pp. 123-136.
6. Amelia Klein, *"Beyond Class Room Instruction : Student Learning in a Social Context,* Boston (1992) WACRA pp. 141-148.
7. De Bono, Edward, *Lateral Thinking for Management,* Englewood Cliffs (1971) Penguin.
8. Swift, Marvin H. "Clear Writing Means Clear Thinking, *Harvard Business Review"* Jan-Feb, 1973.
9. Waterman, Robert, H. Jr. *"The Seven Elements of Strategic Fit", Journal of Business Strategys,* Winter 1982.
10. Edward de Bono, *op. cit.*

Annexure-I

USE OF CASE WRITNG AS A LEARNING TOOL

	Enhancing understanding	*Enhancing Assimilation*	*Total*
1. Case Discussion in the class	3	2	5
	2	2	4
	3	4	7
	6	6	12
	5	5	10
	3	2	5
	6	4	10
	4	5	9
	4	3	7
	36	33	69
2. Project Work	6	5	11
	4	5	9
	3	4	7
	3	2	5
	2	2	4
	4	4	8
	5	3	8
	1	1	2
	6	4	10
	34	30	64
3. Case Writing	6	7	13
	2	2	4
	2	3	5
	4	5	9
	2	2	4
	2	3	5
	7	6	13
	2	3	5
	4	4	8
	31	35	66

Contributors

K.S. Narayana
Institute of Social and Economic Change
Bangalore - 560 072

Prof. Rakesh Khurana
Ex-President
All India Management Association,
Pro Vice-Chancellor
IGNOU, New Delhi

Sharat Kumar
Director,
Institute of Management Technology,
Rajnagar,
Ghaziabad (U.P.) 201 001

Dr. B.N.P. Singh
Professor of Economics,
B.R. Ambedkar Bihar University,
Muzaffarpur, Bihar

Dr. Ratan Kumar Singh
Department of Economics,
B.R. Ambedkar Bihar University,
Muzaffarpur, Bihar

L.M. Bhole
Indian Institute of Technology,
Powai, Bombay

Neeraj Prakash
The Institute of Chartered Financial Analysts of India,
Road No. 3, Banjara Hills,
Hyderabad - 500 034

M.R. Murthy
Institute for Studies in Industrial Development,
NewDelhi
K.S. Chatapati Rao
Institute for studies in Industrial Development,
New Delhi

R.P. Billimoria
Founder - President,
Foundation for Organisational Research, and Chairman,
Public Enterprises Selection Board, New Delhi

Dharni P. Sinha
Principal,
Administrative Staff College of India, Hyderabad

Dr. Francis Cherunilam
School of Management Studies,
Cochin University of Science and Technology,
Cochin - 682 022

Dr. M.L. Jha
Formerly Sr. Reader,
Lalit Narain Mishra Institute of Public Administration and Management,
Patna - 800 001

Dr. Utpal K. Banerjee
Chief Executive,
All India Management Association,
14, Institutional Area,
Lodi Raod. New Delhi - 110 003

Dr. C. Gopal Krishnan
Faculty Member,
B.K. School of Business Management,
Gujarat University, Ahamdabad

Dr. R.P. Banerjee
Fellow,
MCHV., Indian Institute of Management,
Calcutta

Dr. K. Ramakrishna Reddy
Reader,
S.K. Institute of Management
S.K. University,
Anantpur, A.P.
Dr. Mrs. Lalitha Sreenath
S.K. University,
Anantpur, A.P.

N.Sasikala Devi
PSG Institute of Management,
Peelamedu
Coimbatore - 641 004

Ranjan Banerjee
Director
Renaissance Management Consultants
Kondhwe, Pune
Maharashtra

Chandan Goswami
Department of Business Administration,
School of Management Science,
Tezpur University,
Assam

Prof.Suman Kumar Mukerjee
XLRI.
Jamshedpur, Bihar

Dr. Sanjay Kumar
Programme Executive,
Doordarshan Kendra,
Patna, Bihar

Prof. Tapan K. Panda
Regional College of Management,
Chandrasekharpur,
Bhubaneswar, Orissa

A. Shiv Kumar
T.A. Pai Management Institute,
Manipal - 576 119

Prof. P. Nariain
Ex-Director,
Indian Agricultural Statistics Research Institute,
New Delhi - 110 012

Dr. Neelmani P. Verma
Dr. R.M. Lohia Awadh University,
Faizabad (U.P.)

Dr. Atmanand
Associate Professor (Economics)
Institute of Management Technology, (IMT), Ghaziabad and Member, State Finance Commission,
Govt. of Bihar, Patna

Prof. Krishna Kumar
Professor in Strategic Management
IIM, Lucknow (U.P.)

Shipra
3657
24-2-97

32